PEAK DISTRICT PUBS

PEAK DISTRICT PUBS

A pint-sized social history

ANDREW McCLOY

GRITSTONE
PUBLISHING

First published by Halsgrove, 2005 as
Peakland Pubs: A pint-sized history

Second edition Gritstone Publishing, 2020

Copyright text and photographs © 2020 Andrew McCloy

British Library Cataloguing-in-Publication data
A catalogue record for this book is available from the British Library

ISBN 978-0-9955609-9-4

Designed and typeset by
Carnegie Scotforth Book Production

Printed and bound by Cambrian Printers

Gritstone Publishing Co-operative,
Birchcliffe Centre,
Hebden Bridge HX7 8DG

Gritstone Publishing Co-operative is jointly owned by its
members, some of Britain's best-regarded authors writing about the
countryside and the outdoors. Look out for our other titles:
https://gritstonecoop.co.uk

Contents

This book is dedicated to Bob Steel, author of CAMRA's Peak District Pub Walks guidebook and a friend since the days he taught me geography at school, who passed away in 2020.

Preface to the second edition

Inevitably there have been some significant changes in the Peak District pub landscape since the first edition of this book appeared in 2005. Fifteen years might not seem a very long time when measured against the history of some centuries-old pubs, but even in a popular national park with its thriving visitor economy the number of establishments that have recently closed or fundamentally altered is a cause for concern. Accordingly, I have updated the list in Chapter 8 (Lost to History) to reflect those pubs consigned to the great brewery wagon in the sky; and I have amended references to these pubs elsewhere in the text, but because this is fundamentally a book about the social history of Peak District pubs rather than a pub goers' directory I have left them in to record their contribution to the heritage of the region's inns, alehouses and taverns. They are still there, of course, usually as private residences or some other form of holiday accommodation, but they are no longer public houses. And as for those that remain – 'use them or lose them' is the phrase that should be in all of our minds.

And then, just as the second edition of this book was about to be printed, the Covid-19 pandemic broke out and all UK pubs were forced to close for 15 weeks.

As I write, the Peak District is out of lockdown and its pubs have, a little warily perhaps, opened their doors once more. There are obvious changes to reflect social distancing and a heightened awareness over cleanliness, but at least most are open again. However, whether through lost income, new regulations or simply the personal pressure and general fatigue faced by those running them, it's uncertain whether some of the more marginal establishments will survive as going concerns. It's why this book can do no more than capture moments in time in the unfolding story of the pubs of the Peak District.

Acknowledgments

For the first edition I am grateful to Jim McIntosh, from the Campaign for Real Ale (Chesterfield and District branch), for his advice and information, especially regarding the Derby Tup. I'm also indebted to the Dore Village Society for permission to reproduce details about the Old Horse, and to a number of other local heritage groups who have produced some fascinating and valuable research. These include the Hathersage Millennium Group, Elton Local History Group, Bakewell & District Historical Society, Winster Local History Group, Bonsall History Project and Eyam Village Society. Also, grateful thanks to Nicky Crewe, Julie Bunting and the (former) Peakland Heritage Project run by Derbyshire County Council's Libraries and Heritage Department.

For the second edition I would like to thank my fellow authors at Gritstone Publishing, the UK's first publishing co-operative run by authors for authors, for their all-round encouragement and support: Andrew Bibby, Chiz Dakin, Chris Goddard, Laurence Rose and Colin Speakman. I am also grateful to a number of local historians for allowing me to draw on their knowledge and research, especially in the sometimes tortuous process of identifying long gone pubs. These include Steve Lewis on New Mills and Hayfield, Rosemary Lockie on Stoney Middleton, Gavin Repton on Wirksworth, plus the Glossop Victorian Architectural Heritage website and Tim Boddington's Happy Valley Bollington website. Thanks also to Karl Webster and the hardy men and women of Matlock Athletic Club for sharing the pain and pleasure (but mostly pain) of completing the Great Kinder Beer Barrel Challenge. Finally, thank you to all those publicans, regulars and all-round barflies with whom I spent many happy and fruitful hours discussing the life and times of their much-loved 'local'. This has been a truly wonderful book to produce. After all, who else can genuinely say that they're just popping down the pub for "a spot of research"?

CHAPTER ONE

Introduction: Mine's a Pint

"Nay, I am for the country liquor, Derbyshire ale, if you please; for a man should not, methinks, come up from London to drink wine in the Peak." So said Dr Samuel Johnson, the 18th-century essayist and raconteur, and a man who visited plenty of inns and taverns on his travels.

If he were alive today, it would be fascinating to hear his opinions on how the pubs of the Peak District have changed; but some of them we can probably guess at. I imagine he would be uneasy at how hard-nosed commercialism can subsume local distinctiveness, dampen originality and turn some pubs into characterless restaurants. He might not be too keen at how relentless piped music tends to subdue what, for Dr Johnson, was a key ingredient of the public house – good conversation. And I suspect he wouldn't be too keen on cold gassy lager and perhaps rather bewildered by alcopops and diet coke, although it must be said that there were some decidedly odd concoctions served up in his day.

However, there are still plenty of pubs and inns dotted around the Peak District where he almost certainly would feel at home, and where I can picture him ensconced at the end of the bar or sitting by the fireside and holding forth on the issues of the day. Once he had got over paying up to four pounds for a pint of best bitter, I can see him settling down and entertaining the assembled audience with one anecdote after another, and creating that timeless bonhomie that comes with a relaxed, social drink and a damn good chat.

Mind you, just like the alehouses, town taverns and coaching inns of Dr Johnson's time, the present-day pubs of the Peak District are a mixed bag, and reflect what is a diverse and fascinating region. In this book I'm treating the Peak District in the widest sense – from the Staffordshire Moorlands to the South Yorkshire Pennines; from Derbyshire's Derwent valley in the east to the rolling Cheshire hills out to the west; and certainly beyond the administrative boundary of the Peak District National Park.

A loaded carriage (photo courtesy of Julie Bunting)

The pubs range from isolated moorland cottages to bustling town centre taverns, former coaching inns to historic hotels; although for a region that is overwhelmingly rural in nature, the traditional village inn and roadside hostelry remain the cornerstone of this study. We look back at over three centuries of social upheaval through the eyes of the public house: farming, mining, transport, tourism – all of these are reflected in the fortunes of the Peak District 'local'. There are haunted pubs, themed pubs, estate pubs, grand pubs and frankly some quite odd and unusual pubs, as well as one or two pubs which are not what they seem at all. And despite the best efforts of some of the large breweries and the so-called 'pubcos' (profit-hungry pub companies running chains of establishments) there are still enough well-run pubs of character and individuality that make these places worth searching out.

And what stories some of them can tell! I am reasonably sure that most of the tales related in the following pages are true, or at least started off rooted in fact. However, some of them were probably a little iffy to begin with and were no doubt embroidered through repeated telling;

and a small number were almost certainly rubbish from the outset, but are so entertaining that I have relayed them anyway (with a clear health warning).

It should also be acknowledged that when it comes to the spelling of their names many pubs in the Peak District (indeed countrywide) have a relaxed attitude to punctuation. In other words, they don't use any. Although I find this deeply regrettable, I suspect that these days most publicans have more pressing concerns than the correct use of possessive apostrophes. Where a particular pub uses an apostrophe in its name (for instance, the Bull's Head) I have gladly gone with it, but there are inevitably grammatical inconsistencies aplenty throughout this book.

The Great British pub

As with many other aspects of everyday life that we now take for granted, the origin of the Great British Pub can be traced back to the Romans. Whether it was their thirsty footsloggers who needed regular refreshment stops, or simply travellers needing somewhere to stay, the roadside *taberna* was the precursor of our modern taverns. As the saying goes, fermentation and civilisation went hand in hand.

By medieval times, drinking establishments had become permanent fixtures in settlements across the land at a time when ale seemed almost as plentiful as water (and usually safer to drink) and home-brewing was commonplace. But foreshadowing more recent concerns about the effects of so-called binge drinking, the authorities made attempts to curb the number of alehouses in any one community, as well as the amount that an individual could drink. As far back as AD 970 pegs were introduced to the inside of wooden drinking cups to indicate the maximum amount that each person could drink before handing it on to someone else – hence the common expression 'taking a person down a peg or two'.

Early inns provided accommodation for weary travellers, be they pilgrims, soldiers or merchants; and as transport and communications developed so did the range and number of licensed premises that offered hospitality, as well as a place of refuge from the toil and hardships of everyday life.

Pubs have played a central role in our society ever since, and whether your fascination is with names and signboards, architecture and design, or simply the enjoyment of a tasty and distinctive pint of beer, there is nearly always something of interest to be found in an authentic and well-run public house.

The enduring bonhomie of the public house.

Beer today, gone tomorrow

There's a uniqueness about the British pub and the notion that you can, in essence, simply walk into what is often someone else's home and ask for a drink. In his entertaining but thoughtful book *Man Walks into a Pub*, Pete Brown describes the pub as being "a curious combination of the security of the home and the excitement and freedom of being out". This familiarity and basic hospitality harks back to the early days of the alehouse when beer was dispensed from a jug to paying customers from the kitchen or parlour of a domestic property.

However, as much as people might view their traditional local as their own private and cosy little world, pubs are inevitably businesses, and I've been surprised and a little dismayed at how many pubs I've visited over the last few years with 'For Sale' or 'Pub to Let' signs. It's inevitable that some establishments will go under and you only have to look at the long list of ex-pubs in Chapter 8 to see what has gone before. Despite evidence that the alarming rate of pub closures is levelling off, it's clear that the pubs in small communities and rural areas, in particular, remain vulnerable. And that was before the Covid-19 pandemic came along. In Chapter 9 and new to this second edition, I reflect on what the future holds for our traditional pubs and the changes that are taking place in the pub landscape as a result, from diversifying and extending the conventional business model through to the recent emergence of micropubs. As I write, although the immediate aftermath of lockdown is now behind us, publicans and pub-goers alike are still coming to terms with the changes; and the long term impacts on the local pub scene remain unclear.

Despite the ongoing pressures, there are also cheering stories of pubs that have been rebuilt and re-launched. However, it's no coincidence that the more resourceful and often most distinctive pubs continue to be freehouses (not owned or controlled by a brewery chain or pubco); and that the Peak District now has its first community-owned and run pub.

I hope that this book will encourage you to seek out some of the more unusual and interesting pubs and inns of the Peak District, and by doing so I hope it will help these places survive and even prosper. They certainly deserve to, for bound up in these wonderful places is a heritage that is as rich and potent as the stuff that comes foaming out of the pumps at the bar.

It certainly appealed to Dr Johnson, whose words even today ring true: "No, Sir, there is nothing which has yet been contrived by man, by which so much happiness is produced as by a good tavern or inn." I'll drink to that!

CHAPTER TWO

A Traditional Way of Life

The age of the alehouse

It may come as something of a surprise to learn that the quaint image of the traditional village pub or country inn is relatively new, with most dating from the 1700s onwards. Of course, there are a number of pubs that proudly display notices declaring that their particular establishment dates back much further – oh, till medieval times, at least. Perhaps part of the actual building does; or maybe the present pub replaced a much older dwelling. The Bull i' th' Thorn, on the A515 near Pomeroy, south east of Buxton, claims to date from 1472, although the original farmstead was older still. Sadly, by the time the second edition of this book appeared, the Bull i' th' Thorn was no longer a public house.

Likewise, the Old Bulls Head at Little Hucklow, near Bradwell, has been serving customers for many years and is reputed to date from the 12th century, although I've seen no evidence for this bold claim. Latterly this establishment, too, had fallen on hard times and for almost 20 years was closed and becoming derelict. Happily, the pub has now reopened, albeit under its new name of the Blind Bull (see Chapter 9 for more on this).

In early medieval times, households tended to brew their own alcohol and communal brewing was also common. The surplus would often be sold on to neighbours or anyone else that happened to be passing, and so, with few restrictions on its sale, simple alehouses proliferated. In particular, they were a common sight along roadsides where walking was the main form of transport and weary travellers needed refreshing. It was quite normal for any reasonably large dwelling to incorporate a so-called brewhouse, and since women often used to undertake the work they were known as alewives. Alehouses were usually denoted by a pole or stake outside displaying some sort of evergreen foliage, which had its origins in Roman times when the sign for a tavern was a bush, since ivy and vine leaves were associated with Bacchus, the God of Wine. This was the precursor to today's pub sign, of course.

Over time there was a gradual separation between the private house, where ale was dispensed directly out of the dwelling, and what were more commercially-minded premises which expressly catered for those who wanted to stop for a drink and perhaps a bed for the night. These new establishments began to identify and promote themselves with signs, but since the majority of people couldn't read or write these tended to be simple pictorial affairs.

Ultimately it was changing demand and shifts in social behaviour, as well as tighter regulations, that led to the demise of the alehouse.

A typical example is the White Peak village of Winster, which once had over 20 alehouses and inns, and where the village stores was even known as the Old Brewhouse. Today just two pubs remain. Eyam, another ex-mining village, is said to have sported as many as 23 alehouses (as well as 11 inns) in the early 19th century. In 2020 just the one pub remains.

Back then, ale and beer were different drinks. Ale was originally brewed from water, malt barley and yeast, and was a popular, everyday drink. It was sweet, often flavoured with spices and herbs, and not as strong as most beers today, and was probably often safer than local water, since it was effectively sterilised in the brewing process as the water was boiled. In 1820, a doctor at Great Longstone, correctly guessing that infected water was responsible for a local epidemic, actually prescribed new beer for the villagers to drink.

Until the 1500s ale was the staple drink throughout Britain, but by the 1550s the introduction of hops into the brewing process was increasingly commonplace and 'beer' as we know it today took over in terms of popularity, since when the two terms have become interchangeable. However, ale and beer ale were such common drinks that they were consumed throughout the day, and bearing in mind this was a time largely pre-dating morning tea and coffee, there was even a weak brew drunk at breakfast that was less than 2% alcoholic strength and known as 'small beer' (hence the saying: 'only small beer').

Love it or loathe it, there is no doubting the central role that ale or beer has played in our social development over the centuries. Even the Church embraced brewing, and many religious establishments had brewhouses attached to their premises.

What were known as Church Ales and Whitsun Ales were an annual fixture in the calendar for many communities in the Peak District. It was basically seen as a means for the church to raise extra revenue (as well as an excuse for people to eat and drink to excess) and involved churchwardens collecting malt from all the parishioners in order to brew beer for the whole village. The special brew was presented at a ceremony officiated by a chosen 'lord and lady of the ale', and from all accounts was an excuse for much merry-making. In addition, there were so-called Bid Ales or Help Ales, when villagers got together over a communal brew to raise funds for someone or something specific.

Hospitality for visitors

Pubs, inns and taverns have, from the earliest days, provided hospitality for those visiting or passing through. From monks and merchants through to soldiers and salesmen, the roadside inn has offered refreshment and accommodation for many centuries. Some of the first travellers were pilgrims and religious types, who journeyed between ecclesiastical houses, or from abbeys to outlying granges (farms owned and run by monasteries, sometimes a long distance away).

From Norman times, monasteries themselves provided basic hospitality for any passing traveller, including pilgrims en route to the shrines of various saints at home and abroad. Indeed, the term 'hospital' or 'hospice' originated from the Latin *hospitalis* which meant shelter or guesthouse, rather than caring for someone that's ill as we tend to understand it today. Monasteries often brewed their own beer and ale, which would then be dispensed to weary travellers. Indeed, it was accepted that monasteries and religious houses had a duty to offer overnight accommodation to anyone that asked for it; and in some ways, early alehouses did much the same.

As we will also see in the later chapter on the origin of pub names, religion and pubs are (perhaps surprisingly) closely connected. Should you venture a little outside our patch, to Nottingham, make sure to visit Ye Olde Trip to Jerusalem, an historic inn located next to the city's castle. The back bar has even been carved out of the sandstone bedrock underpinning the fortification. The inn claims to be the oldest pub in England, supposedly established around AD 1189 by a group of soldiers preparing for Richard the Lionheart's Crusade to the Holy Lands. However, there is no firm evidence that this is the case, and it is more likely that it was simply a brewhouse established in the 1600-1700s to serve the castle.

Even as late as the 18th century, soldiers were lodged in pubs and inns,

The themed Knights' Table at the Travellers Rest, Flash Bar.

since barracks were in fact quite rare until Victorian times. But following on from the early pilgrims and religious crusaders, it was mainly traders and itinerant salesmen who trod the paths and roads and who required board and lodging, and the names of some Peak District pubs still bear testimony to this early role.

There are two pubs called the Traveller's Rest, one located in the Hope Valley at the Bradwell turning, and the other on a bend of the Buxton-Leek road (A53) at Quarnford Flash Bar, high up on the wild and exposed western moors near the source of the River Manifold. It's one of those places where the fire can be lit even in the summer and you can imagine why early travellers struggling across the moors were grateful for such places. The pub was originally called the Brown Cow, but a mix-up over new pub signs saw it become the Travellers Rest by mistake, and the name evidently stuck. It was owned for a long time by the Harpur-Crewe family and was gradually extended and adapted over the years. Its recent heyday was surely the 1970s when the pub held the Guinness World Record for having an astonishing 76 separate beer pumps on the bar. For a short but colourful period the pub was hugely popular, no doubt helped by the choice of 42 different brews – and the fact that there were said to be five particularly attractive barmaids. According to someone who was a regular at the time, it was not unusual to have to queue to get in.

Since that time the pub has had a chequered history, and was even closed completely following a tragedy in the early 1990s when a car full of joy-riders failed to negotiate the tight bend outside the pub and ploughed into the main bar. The pub was subsequently sold and the new owners renovated the interior, reopening for business in 1997. In recent years it has been re-branded as The Knights' Table and now has a medieval theme running throughout, relating to the legend of Sir Gawain and the Green Knight that comes from a medieval poem supposedly set nearby. There's armour hanging up, pewter tankards aplenty, toilets labelled 'Knights' and 'Damsels' – you get the idea.

The open road

A pub in Hathersage remembers a specific type of traveller through its name. The Scotsman's Pack, on School Lane, takes its name from the packmen or travelling drapers as they were sometimes known, who used to visit from Scotland in the 1500s–1600s with their tweeds and woollens, and who went from village to village and farm to farm selling their wares. Sited on the old road to Sheffield, the original building dates from around 1650.

At the rear of the inn there was an area of common land that was often frequented by gypsies, squatters and sheep thieves. The pub was initially called the Scotchman's Pack, but the name and building changed in 1913 when new landlord William Simpson added the mock Tudor façade, which was a popular architectural feature at the time.

The Scotsman's Pack would almost certainly have also hosted the familiar packhorse trains which wound their way over the Peak District

moors. Lines of the hardy beasts sometimes 40 or 50 strong would regularly criss-cross the hills with their various cargoes of coal, wool, salt, corn, malt, and so on. What a sight they must have been!

The packhorse trains were led by men known as jaggers, whose name possibly originates from the tough

The name of this Hathersage pub remembers travelling drapers from several centuries ago.

10

The Cheshire Cheese Inn at Hope, where it's said that some packhorse men paid for their overnight lodgings in cheese.

German ponies called jaegers that were often used. They followed ancient routes through the valleys and hills, and crossed rivers and streams by the familiar narrow bridges which walkers still use today. In terms of pubs, they are remembered by an Old Packhorse Inn at Chapel en le Frith, and Packhorse Inns at Crowdecote, Hayfield, New Mills and Little Longstone, near Bakewell (see Chapter 6).

There are former packhorse routes all over the Peak District, some of them walled green lanes and others simply overgrown paths, and although a few are now metalled roads, there are plenty of reminders of their past use if you look closely at local maps. For instance, on the eastern fringe of the Peak District a packhorse route led from the Kelstedge Inn across the moors to Two Dales, following a route that is still called Jaggers Lane.

The Packhorse Inn at Hayfield was on the old packhorse route between Edale and Holmfirth and no doubt provided sustenance for man and beast alike. Packhorse trains are also associated with the Cheshire Cheese Inn at Hope, plus there are others of this name at Castleton, Buxton and Longnor.

Hope's Cheshire Cheese was originally a farmstead built by the Hall family in 1662 as two cottages. When it became a pub in the mid 1700s it was originally called the Wagon and Horses. Later, two annual fairs were held here, when cattle and horses, as well as cheese and cloth, were sold. Original cheese hooks can still be seen in the lower room, and the pub's website explains that payment for lodging at inn was sometimes made in cheese.

Cheese and salt would be carried eastwards from Cheshire, while bales of wool would travel in the opposite direction from Yorkshire. Malt and wood came north from Derby. However, the packhorse ways were often an extension of far more ancient routes. These included the Portway across the central limestone plateau, used since before Roman times; and the network of saltways emanating from key salt-producing locations such as Northwich in Cheshire and which had been in use since Saxon times. There were also so-called corpse or coffin roads, such as the well-established track from the Edale valley over Hollins Cross to Castleton, used to carry the dead for burial at St Edmund's in Castleton before Edale church was consecrated in 1633.

Up until the mid 1600s travel was slow and arduous, with few decent roads and long journey times, but with the coming of the turnpikes everything changed. Stagecoaches dramatically cut travelling times and coaching inns began to appear on the main routes, where horses would need changing and passengers refreshing.

However, some of the travellers and men of the road who frequented the local inns had ulterior motives, and this is borne out by the name of a former pub on the road between Macclesfield and Whaley Bridge at Rainow. The Highwayman is a handsome, whitewashed stone building that dates from around 1600 (when it was known as Patch House), and consists of four small and atmospheric rooms. Until 1949 it was called the Blacksmiths Arms, but its renaming is a reminder of one notorious regular from the past. The highwayman in question was Charles Pym, after whom Pym Chair above Errwood Reservoir is named (there was once a chair-shaped rock here, bearing the carved initials 'PC'). He is said to have used the pub as his hideout as he went about his business of robbing travellers on the surrounding highways. Unfortunately in recent years the pub fell on hard times and in 2013 was converted into a private residence.

A place in the country

For centuries, the village pubs and alehouses of the Peak District have played an important role in community life, in particular in lead mining (see next chapter), farming and animal husbandry. The name of the (now closed) Drovers Arms in Glossop is a throwback to a time when large herds of animals would be driven sometimes long distances across country to market, with the drovers often staying at inns along the route.

The village pub or moorland inn was where farmers and shepherds met, and nowhere is this more evident over the years than at the Fox House Inn, high on the moors between Hathersage and Sheffield. It began life in the 1770s as a two-roomed shepherd's cottage, and is not actually named after the animal as many suspect but almost certainly after George Fox of Callow Farm, near Hathersage, who built the place.

Records show that it was originally named the Travellers Rest, most likely when it was first licensed in 1816. Like the Cat and Fiddle, the moorland inn is such a prominent and well-known feature, sitting 1,132ft (345ft) above sea level, that it's given its name to the location. It stood at a key junction of two important turnpikes (Dronfield to Chapel en le Frith, and Sheffield to Buxton), but during the 19th century it was also used by the Duke of Rutland to house his shooting guests when nearby Longshaw Lodge became full. Incidentally,

Over the years the Fox House Inn has offered shelter to shepherds and even their sheep.

his visitors to Longshaw included King George V and the Duke of Wellington.

The Fox House Inn has long been a popular tourist destination and there are some fascinating stories from a time when horse-drawn carts and coaches (and flocks of sheep) rather than cars and motorbikes filled the yard outside. Because of its situation off the Burbage valley amid the rough grazing and heather moors, the inn once housed local shepherds – indeed according to one source it was briefly called the Shepherd's Rest. In especially rough winter weather it was not uncommon for straw to be strewn on the floor of the tap room so that the sheep could take overnight shelter as well as the shepherds!

During the 1890s the Duke of Rutland is said to have provided free refreshments for farmers and shepherds attending the annual sheep gatherings; but regardless of this, sheep were important business on the moors around Longshaw and Fox House. Before the animals were turned out for winter pasturing they had to be branded with the Duke's letter 'R', and since he took as many as 9,000 sheep each winter, there was a lot of work to do.

One story from 1880 describes how local shepherd Peter Priestley spent all day branding hundreds of sheep, and with the pitch still wet on his breeches called in at the Fox House for a pint or two on the way home. Tired out, he fell fast asleep in front of the fire with his legs crossed, only to wake some time later with his legs stuck together.

Below the shooting lodge at Longshaw is Longshaw Meadow where, every year since 1898, reputedly the oldest sheep dog trials in England are held. Although there are different accounts of how it started, one describes an argument in the Fox House Inn between farmers and shepherds over who owned the best sheepdog. Early on they played for stakes of quarts of beer, but before long it became serious business and a matter of professional pride.

Much further west, one of the oldest pubs in Whaley Bridge is the Shepherds Arms on Old Road. It was formerly a farmhouse, when the town was probably no more than a modest village, and the attractive whitewashed pub almost certainly predates most of the other buildings around it. Situated on a slope, there are two outside terraces where you can sit and enjoy a pint, but for many the highlight is indoors where the traditional tap room features original stone flags and simple furnishings. Another unusual feature is the small, square entrance room to the pub, known locally as the 'lift shaft' – primarily, it seems, because of its wooden-clad box shape. In fact, contrary to its name, the Shepherds Arms was the favourite of local miners who worked on the Cheshire coalfield in the 1800s, since there were small mines on the coalfield's eastern fringe around Whaley Bridge.

Shepherds are also remembered at the Packhorse Inn at Hayfield. Here it was customary for a 'shepherd's dinner' to be held on the first Saturday in July, before which there would be an auction in the car park of all the unclaimed stray sheep recently rounded up in the vicinity – then the proceeds would be spent in the pub.

Some pub names allude to various past times, practices and 'sports' now long consigned to history. The Bear at Alderwasley, an out-of-the-way hamlet located between Wirksworth and Whatstandwell, might possibly take its name from bear-baiting, since this was a common practice in some pub yards. The pub was originally recorded as the Olde Brown Bear Inn, then simply the Bear Inn after 1735, but as we will see in Chapter 7, animals in pub names can also have a religious or royal signif-icance. A bear, for instance, was the crest of the Earls of Warwick and Leicester, although some of the pubs commemorating these esteemed families went by the full title of the Bear and Ragged Staff.

At Ashover, bear baiting is said to have regularly taken place in a hollow above the Black Swan as recently as 1810. In his 1924 book *The Saint and Sinners of Ashover*, C. E. Lugard reports that a John Smith was sent to prison as a vagabond for being in charge of a bear. Travelling bear keepers, sometimes known as bearwards, usually stayed the night at the pub. At Matlock they lodged at the old Crown Hotel, and its cellars were used as pens for the bears.

A number of hostelries in the Peak District are known to have had purpose-built cockpits where the equally unsavoury spectacle of cock-fighting once took place. Like bull and bear baiting, cock fighting was all about gambling, and it was popular with all classes of society.

Although there is no evidence that it ever took place at Sheldon, Whaley Bridge and Disley, the bird is still celebrated at the three locations by pubs called the Cock and Pullet, the Cock and the Dandy Cock respectively. (The Dandy Cock is a localised name for a bantam fowl – also known as a Dandy-hen – and regarded as a spirited fighter.) What is certain, though, is that there was certainly a pit behind the Hanging Gate pub on the edge of Chapel-en-le-Frith, although the building did not actually open as a public house until 1836, and Ordnance Survey maps still refer to this area as Cockyard.

Not every pub bearing the name or picture of a cock bird denoted cock-fighting, however. In the 17th century something known as cock ale could sometimes be found for sale, which was ale mixed with the jelly of minced meat of a boiled cock. Thankfully, pub fare has improved considerably since those days. Although cockfighting has long been illegal, its legacy lingers on. Not only are there pubs still bearing the name, but the brewers Courage still have a cockerel as their symbol. Cock fighting was finally banned in Britain in 1849.

Getting together

Public houses, as their name suggests, have always been important as venues for local people to come together on neutral territory to enjoy some social interaction and discuss the issues of the day. As the American journalist and writer Martha Gellhorn once said, "In the end, in England, if you want to find out how people are feeling, you always go to the pubs."

Whether it was lead miners, farmhands or mill workers unwinding after a hard day's work, a drink and a chat in 'the local' has always been an important part of everyday life.

Like now, many local groups and institutions met at pubs. In the time before most small towns had purpose-built venues, the local magistrates court would sometimes meet in a function room of the leading inn. Examples include the Green Man and Black's Head Royal Hotel in Ashbourne, and the Royal Oak (The Royal) at Chapel-en-le-Frith. Indeed, the latter housed the town's magistrates court until 1851 when a purpose-built town hall was finally erected.

Pubs were also the meeting places of friendly societies, which began to appear at the end of the 1700s in an effort to help the less well-off and supplement the Poor Laws. These groups, sometimes known as Benefit Clubs, often had grandiose and occasionally bizarre names, but their intentions were honourable, and they played an important part in making the lives of the needy a little more bearable and providing financial support to ordinary people in times of need. The White Hart at Whaley Bridge used to be where the Ancient Order of Foresters, a co-operative organisation, used to meet. Meanwhile, a pub originally called the Princes Arms at Whitehough, north west of Chapel-en-le-Frith, was the meeting place of the Whitehough Victoria Lodge of Oddfellows, formed in 1830. They continued to meet up until 1970 in the handsome, 18th-century pub that for many years was called the

The Foresters Friendly Society parading past the Ordnance Arms Hotel in Hathersage, probably in the early 1900s, as part of their annual pilgrimage to Little John's Grave at the parish church.

Oddfellows Arms; but following extensive refurbishment it reopened in 2012 under its old name of the Paper Mill Inn.

The Temple Inn at Padfield, near Glossop, was actually built by the Padfield Order of Oddfellows (in 1845) and within a few years the Temple Perpetual Money Society also held their meetings there. However, according to David Field's research into the history of pubs in the Glossop area (see Bibliography), the Padfield Oddfellows then reputedly fell out with another lodge who had lent them money to build the pub, and as a result they changed its name to the Peels Arms after Sir Robert Peel, Prime Minister of the day.

The Duke of York at Elton also hosted the Oddfellows, and here the Lodge was known as the Loyal Faithful Shepherd (there was even a junior branch for boys under 16 called the Loyal Lamb Lodge). The Elton Local History Group has published a fascinating booklet all about this Lodge, which was established in 1842, and it includes extracts from original documents and a wonderful photo of Lodge members with their banner and staffs lined up outside the pub in 1895.

The Duke of York was not unusual, since many pubs had club rooms where local societies met, and at a time well before the National Health

Service these voluntary groups were sometimes known as 'sick clubs'. One of the most impressively-named orders was the Humane Friendly Indefatigable Union Society, which had branches in Tideswell and elsewhere. The Independent Friendly Society at Crich met 'for the benefit of sick and infirm members' and their venue early on was the Black Swan public house.

The Women's Conversational Club came together in a Bakewell alehouse, while the Masons and Foresters convened elsewhere in the town. Then there was the Loyal Lily of the Valley Lodge at Hope, the Inkerman at Great Longstone, Wensley Jubilee Friendly Society and the Loyal Welcome Traveller of the Peak Lodge at Bradwell.

Although many of these mutual benefit societies have now disappeared, or live on in name only, some still meet and organise fund-raising events for local charities, including the Royal Antediluvian Order of Buffaloes (commonly known as 'the Buffs') who have met occasionally at the Farmyard Inn at Youlgrave and the Duke William at Matlock.

Although the village pub has been the natural meeting place for all sorts of community groups, not all of them dispensed charity. In the 1700s, as industrialisation began to take hold across the country and profound social change began to affect even the rural way of life, a rise in crime and unrest led to the formation of Associations for the Prosecutions of Felons in towns and villages. These were basically groups of local men who paid subscriptions into a central fund that was used to bring criminals to justice, either through a reward or the cost of catching a felon, or even as compensation for victims of crime. Associations were established in places like Bakewell, Baslow, Brassington and Wirksworth; and while most disappeared when Derbyshire Constabulary was formed in 1857, a few kept going, including in Eyam and Stoney Middleton where the Prosecution of Felons committee met in both the Miner's Arms and the Moon Inn.

Dance and be merry

However, pubs are about more than just a chat over a pint. Many are well known for their music and dance, while others are established live entertainment venues, like the Fishpond at Matlock Bath (see Chapter 9) which has regular gigs at its upstairs ballroom.

The Winking Man takes advantage of its isolated position high on the Staffordshire moorlands near Upper Hulme to stage regular rock nights and other (presumably quite loud) music events, claiming that it has "the distinction of being the highest function room in England (1,500ft above sea level)." Meanwhile, the Nelson Arms at Middleton-by-Wirksworth also hosts the village's popular Mid-Folk Festival each autumn; and live music has proved so popular at the Globe Inn at Glossop that in 2000 enthusiastic regulars formed The Lift Global Music Club and have subsequently put on musicians from every continent except Antarctica!

Rural pubs have often played an important role in keeping alive traditional song and dance, including some very local and almost unique performances like the Derby Tup (see Chapter 5) and the more familiar Morris dancers. Travel writers, essayists and diarists have found rich pickings in the humble wayside inn – from Celia Fiennes, Samuel Johnson and William Cobbett and through to J.B. Priestley, H.V. Morton and Bill Bryson – and through them we can piece together pieces of our great cultural jigsaw.

As an example, in John Hutchinson's account of his Peak District wanderings (published in 1809 as *Hutchinson's Tour through the High Peak of Derbyshire*) it's believed he stayed at the George Hotel at Hayfield. This was the day of the fair and clearly a lively occasion which, he observed, had "enticed the country lads and lasses, though nearly up to the knees in dirt." He retired to a room in the pub and watched various singing and dancing, but was particularly struck by one song which he wrote down and reproduced in his book. This was the traditional folk tune 'Come Lasses and Lads' which has become a popular and well-known ballad:

Come, lasses and lads,
Take leave of your dads,
And away to the fair let's hie;
For every lad has gotten his lass,
And a fiddler standing by;
For Jenny has gotten her Jack,
And Nancy has gotten her Joe;
With Dolly and Tommy, good luck,
How they jig it, to and fro'.

Hunting, shooting and fishing

With its vast expanses of heather moorland and its well-stocked streams and rivers, the Peak District has long been renowned for hunting, shooting and fishing. Since Norman times much of the Peak was a royal hunting ground and the names of many Peak District pubs, as well as some of their histories, reflect this age-old pursuit.

The Sportsman Inn at Lodge Moor, on Sheffield's western fringe near Redmires, may be near the moors and so suggests a link to grouse-shooting, but it's also next to a large recreation field that has been used for various sports, even including a horse racing track, according to a recent book on the history of Redmires Ridge by Keith Baker.

The second Sportsman is at Hayfield, on the road from the village to Kinder Reservoir, and close to Bowden Bridge quarry where many of the protesters on the celebrated Kinder Scout Mass Trespass of 1932 met before setting off. Their actions were an attempt to gain public access to the huge swathes of private moorland which stretched across the highest and wildest part of the Peak District, and which at that time were managed solely for shooting. It may seem incredible to today's generation of walkers and climbers that back then virtually the whole of the Dark Peak uplands were out of bounds save for a few paths.

There are plenty of other pub names which continue the theme of hunting and shooting. There is a Poachers Inn at Bollington, although it used to be called the Masonic (and also Mason's) Arms, and until recently another one at Hope. You can also find a Grouse Inn at Darley Dale and Longshaw, as well as two more that have closed recently at Birch Vale and Chunal Moor (south of Glossop). You can sup at the Cock and Pheasant at Bollington, or go elsewhere in this large and pub-rich Cheshire village for the Dog and Partridge. This name also appears in the south of the Peak District at Swinscoe, west of Ashbourne; and formerly at nearby Thorpe (it's now the Old Dog). There's another beside the A628 on the high South Yorkshire moorland near Flouch where it was first licensed in 1740 as the Border Hill House. The Hare and Hounds at New Mills was once a police station and the cells used for prisoners now house beer barrels.

Hunting has a close association with country pubs, of course (brewers Tetley chose a red-coated huntsman for their logo) and just look at the number of thematic prints and replica hunting horns which still adorn the walls of rural inns. Many hunts met at village pubs, including the Duke of York at Elton where huge joints of meat were roasted to feed the hungry participants.

In terms of names, there's the Roebuck Inn at Chapel en le Frith, the town's traditional and handsome market pub. Three Stags Heads can be found at both Wardlow Mires and at Darley Bridge, by the River Derwent north of Matlock. The latter is a tastefully maintained, 18th-century building, with the letters 'GOQ' carved above the main

The last indigenous wild boar in England was supposedly killed in the Peak District.

door. Apparently they stand for 'Go out quietly', and if you do you may be treated to the sight of deer feeding at the far end of the beer garden, since a small herd roam wild among the wooded hills towards Winster and Bonsall.

A few years ago (until it changed ownership) the Crag Inn at Wildboarclough, off the Buxton-Congleton road, was notable for a large and slightly alarming collection of stuffed wild animals. The building began life as a 17th-century farmhouse originally called Bottom o'th' Bank, until it became an inn in the 1830s. For a while there was a flourishing local textile industry, as Clough Brook was harnessed and a 30ft water wheel used to power a small calico-printing unit. This was short-lived; but latterly local spring water is helping to revive the fortunes of this out-of-the-way pub (see Chapter 9).

The name of Wildboarclough also relates to another pub called the Wild Boar Inn further along the A54. It refers to England's indigenous and now extinct wild pig, the last one of which was supposedly killed around here in the 15th century. The head, tusks and hides of actual wild boars (though hopefully not that one!) adorn the walls of the bar.

At that time, this area would have formed part of Macclesfield Forest, kept solely as the hunting preserve of the nobility. The Steward of Macclesfield Forest imposed strict Forest Laws that were harsh and unforgiving. You could lose an arm if caught poaching and there were also penalties for collecting firewood or letting your animals stray into the forest.

Fishing is also represented in the names of the Angler's Rest at Bamford and Miller's Dale, the Lazy Trout at Meerbrook, near Tittesworth Reservoir and the Grouse and Claret at Rowsley. This last refers to a type of artificial 'wet fly' used by fly fishermen in the likes of the Rivers Wye and Derwent, which meet at Rowsley. Apparently it was a favourite of the local water baliff and its distinctive winged pattern is meant to imitate caddis pupae, as well as mayflies and stoneflies. Until they disappeared a few years ago there were glass cases mounted inside the pub with other examples of these expertly-created, look-alike flies.

They will almost certainly be used by the some of the guests at the historic Peacock Hotel, on the other side of the river from the Grouse and Claret, and which, like the Square and Compass at Darley Bridge, is one of several pubs in the Peak District to boast its own fishing rights. In the case of the Peacock it includes a long stretch of the River Wye upstream to Bakewell through Haddon Estate, and is popular with fly fishermen seeking trout (rainbow and brown) and grayling. In fact, the Derbyshire Wye is famous for its strain of breeding rainbow trout, and the Peacock Hotel hires rods and sells flies and other equipment for visiting anglers.

Overlooking the admittedly artificial Ladybower Reservoir is the Ladybower Inn (see Chapter 6), which was once the meeting place for the One O'clock Thursday Club of local fishermen. They may not sup here any more, but the menu always features fresh trout that are caught daily in the reservoir and delivered straight to the pub.

Traditional pub games

Despite change and modernisation, a number of Peak District pubs retain traditional pub games, which have been enjoyed in various forms for many years. Many pubs continue to run darts and pool teams, and there are still local pub quiz leagues. Some pubs have their own football and cricket teams, and the Bull's Head at Monyash even once has its own netball side.

The French game of boules has established itself at a number of pubs, and most take part in competitive leagues. The Derbyshire Dales Boules League includes pubs such as the Rising Sun and Nelson Arms (both Middleton by Wirksworth), Cliff Inn (Crich), Miners Arms (Carsington), Derwentwater Arms (Calver) and Plough Inn (Two Dales). There's a floodlit boules pitch across the road from the Malt Shovel Inn on Wirksworth Moor, while the car park adjoining was once a lawn tennis court. The Duke William at Matlock even has separate boules pitches behind and in front of the pub.

It's hard to imagine many pubs having their own tennis court these days, but the Ram's Head at Disley does own two crown bowling greens behind the pub. The Bowling Green pub at Ashbourne is named after the green that could once be found next door; the Old Bowling Green at

Winster remembers a green tucked away behind the Old Market House; and Ye Olde Bowling Green at Bradwell shares a similar story.

The Fox and Goose at Wigley, high on the eastern edge of the Peak District at the top of the long climb out of Chesterfield, has been a pub for several hundred years, but in fact the building's history dates back to 1392 when Richard II presented it to the monks of Beauchief Abbey. The pub's name is derived from an ancient Viking board game (Fox and Geese) which apparently the monks used to play at the time. Today you can play a specially adapted modern version of this board game at the pub. It's described as an ancient European strategy game for two players, one player having 18 geese and the other a single fox. The object is for the geese to try and trap the fox before they are captured; and the fox must try and capture as many geese as possible to stop being trapped first. The geese cannot capture the fox, instead they have to completely surround the fox and make any movement impossible, and this is usually done by crowding the fox into a corner. The fox has to capture enough geese to make this impossible. It's a game of cunning and apparently quite addictive, so what better than to settle back in the corner of the namesake pub with a drink for a spot of mental exercise?

The genteel indoors pursuit of bar billiards, which is thought to have originated from the popular 19th-century pub game bagatelle, is still quite popular in southern England and in the Peak District one of the last tables could be found, until a couple of years ago, at the Cheshire Cheese in Buxton, but sadly it was removed to make more space for diners.

Another traditional English pub game which has also virtually died out in the Peak District is skittles, or nine pins, the forerunner of ten-pin bowling, where wooden balls are rolled down a lane to knock over skittles. It used to take place at the Royal Oak at Tansley (before it ceased to be a pub) and at the Red Lion at Kniveton. At the Duke William at Matlock punters still play skittles outside the pub, where there's a metal bar across the edge of the car park that the skittles are placed upon.

Games of dominoes still continue in a few of the more traditional Peak District pubs and it hasn't changed that much since the Chinese first played it in the 14th century. It arrived in Britain in the late 18th century from France, possibly via French prisoners of war, and the word domino is French for the black and white hood worn by priests in winter.

It might be imagined that old-fashioned pub games are remembered in the name of the Board Inn in Whaley Bridge (now renamed the Drum and Monkey), although it may also refer to the general hospitality for visiting stagecoach passengers (board of fare). There again, in the mid 19th century there was a surge of beerhouses calling themselves The Board after new legislation made it easier to turn domestic properties into beerhouses for a fee, provided they erected a sign outside with their own name. Apparently many became known simply as 'The Board', although before long they began assuming more personalised names.

Golf is not necessarily a game that you associate with pubs, nor are there many golf courses in the Peak District. Normally you would expect to retire to the clubhouse bar after a morning's round, but rather unusually the Robin Hood Inn near Baslow created its own six-hole course on ground to the rear of the pub. Although the course is no longer in use there are trophies, prints, old clubs and other golfing memorabilia still on show in the function room at the rear of the pub.

Meanwhile, Buxton and High Peak Golf Club claims to be the oldest in Derbyshire and its 18-hole course was designed as far back as 1887. Next to the fairway is the splendidly-named 19th Hole pub, which until the 1950s was a private house, until Marstons switched their licence from a town centre pub that was due to close. The pub sign depicts a golfer teeing off from inside the bar, with one door open in front of him (I hope his aim is good!).

Moving with the times – or not?

Luckily for pub-goers, the wide variety of Peak District inns cater for just about everyone – from the busy family dining pubs and trendy town centre bars to the unassuming village local. But despite the Peak District's rural character, it's hard to imagine that there are many pubs that have not been touched in some way by the forces of 21st century consumerism, especially given the role and impact of the tourist sector in one of Britain's most popular and accessible national parks.

Despite this, there are still a handful of pubs which have refused to yield to the demands of the modern pub industry, and remain as beacons from the past, traditional and unspoilt in appearance and attitude.

The Duke of York is the village pub of Elton, a former lead mining community near Winster. Although the shops, cafe and youth hostel have all closed, Elton retains its village school and the community spirit is such that it is even a past winner of the Derbyshire Village of the Year competition. It's a peaceful place and popular with visiting walkers and cyclists.

The Duke of York Elton at Elton is listed by CAMRA in its National Inventory of Historic Pub Interiors.

You would think that the situation would be ripe for an enterprising village pub offering bed and breakfast and evening meals, possibly with some self-catering rooms at the back. Not a bit of it. The Duke of York has waved it all away and remains a true locals' pub where people go to have a drink and socialise. It's certainly not an unfriendly or unwelcoming place, although rumour has it that once upon a time Friday nights in the pub were locally understood to be for the men of the village only. Rather, it has refused to yield to the modern pub culture that sees tables laid and numbered for diners before they cross the threshold.

The Duke of York is demonstrably unshowy. The exterior simply has the name of the pub – not a swinging sign, just a board – attached to the front wall. There are no picnic tables and parasols, nor any overflowing hanging baskets. This is a basic and unspoilt village local which doesn't dress itself up (inside or out) for the tourist market, and as such is described by CAMRA as having an "historic pub interior of national importance".

It's a relatively plain, 200-year-old stone building, with sparsely-furnished front rooms and a cosier tap room at the back where the bar is situated. This small and attractive room features wooden panelling and fitted seats, a quarry-tile floor and a huge stone fireplace. There's a serving hatch from the bar into the corridor, probably designed for off-sales but useful for when things get a little crowded; while above the bar is a glazed screen behind which the glasses are stacked. Steps at the far end of the corridor lead to a door into the yard through which, until fairly recently, you had to venture to find the toilets on the far side.

That the pub has stayed virtually unaltered is mostly due to the fact that it has remained in the same family ownership since 1968. Long-time landlady Mary Elliott, 90, has now passed on the day to day running of the pub to her nephew, though she still likes to pop in once a week to check how everything's going.

Although there's some confectionery on sale behind the bar, the pub does not serve food. So-called 'wet-led' pubs like this that focus on selling drinks rather than food are rare in the Peak District. Because there's no need to cater for diners, the pub doesn't actually open until 8.30pm in the evening.

Another Peak District pub widely praised for its unspoilt interior is the Barley Mow at Kirk Ireton. The last surviving pub in the village, which is located south of Wirksworth, the Barley Mow is a three-storey, Grade II* listed stone building which is believed to have been built as a farmhouse. Mostly Jacobean, there's an old sundial under the centre eaves which bears the date 1683.

Inside, the three simply furnished rooms sport tiled or parquet floors, are heated by open fires or stoves, and the basic furniture includes slate tables made from the four quarters of a former billiards table. There's a piano in the small front room known as the parlour, but otherwise there's no piped music and certainly not a fruit machine in sight.

The previous landlady was Lilian Ford, who spent her entire life – all 90 years of it – at the Barley Mow. She was the daughter of the previous licensee and, since 1884, there have been just four licensees. Lilian was very much from the old school, and was adamant that traditions would be maintained and no truck would be given to these silly modern ideas. In 1971 she resisted decimalisation and up until she died five years later insisted that customers pay in 'old' money. Her cash till was an old biscuit tin.

Mary Short, whose husband bought the pub for £26,500 in 1976, ran

Until recently barrels used to be racked up behind the bar of the Barley Mow in the traditional manner.

it for the next four decades and simply carried on in Lillian's wake, preserving the timeless character of this lovely village pub. She opened up two rooms which had previously been private and made cold rolls and cobs to order, but there was no busy kitchen and the beer was still served from racked barrels behind the bar in the traditional manner. Mary, in turn, has now handed the day to day running on to her daughters who have introduced a few revolutionary ideas, such as serving hot food and hosting occasional small-scale social events like the pub's first beer festival. The barrels are now kept in the cellar as the beer was getting too warm upstairs, but it's still brought up from the cellar in glasses or jugs as required. They are carefully helping this historic public house, whose dark and crafted interior still oozes character, make a gentle and measured transition to the present day.

Whereas the Barley Mow has the air of a well-to-do village farmhouse, the Three Stags' Heads at Wardlow Mires is an altogether different proposition, and probably reflects its remote and exposed location. The 300-year-old cottage, plain yet robust, has also served as a farm, and with its stone-flagged floor and handsome, black-leaded range it remains largely unblemished; indeed, there was not even a proper counter until the present one was installed in the 1950s.

The doorway is straight off the busy A623, almost opposite the Ashford turning, and just crossing the main road to the pub can be hazardous enough. You enter straight into the small, simple bar, which doesn't take many to get crowded, and here the place comes into its own. The room on the right is a relatively new addition, but both are kept very basic and no frills, with wooden benches and settles, and a scattering of stools gathered around three scrubbed wooden tables.

The pub is determinedly authentic and has refused to bow to modern trends, as demonstrated on a number of counts. Whereas many pubs now ban dogs outright, the Three Stags' Heads has no such qualms, and a small pack of dogs (previously lurchers and now whippets) belonging to Geoff Fuller, the long-serving licensee, are nearly always to be found pattering around the floor or curled up on the seats.

The approach to serving beer and lager is straightforward, with basically plenty of the former and none of the latter. Aside from Guinness, there are usually four real ales on offer, supplied by Abbeydale brewery

Three Stags' Heads, Wardlow Mires – don't ask for a pint of lager.

of Sheffield. The house beer is, most appropriately, called Black Lurcher, a dark and malty ale brewed specially for the pub in honour of its dogs, and at an ABV of a whopping 7-8%, it is not for the faint hearted. As it says on the pump badge: 'Its bite is worse than its bark'.

Although there's wine and spirits behind the bar, as you would expect, there is no lager tap in sight, and a notice at the side of the bar spells out the establishment's position in no uncertain terms: 'PLEASE don't ask the landlord for DRAUGHT LAGER as a smack in the gob may cause offence'. Don't say you haven't been warned.

However, if all this gives the impression that the Three Stags' Heads is a hostile and unwelcoming place, then you would be mistaken. It's a pub that is exactly what it sets out to be: traditional, simple and without pretension. In general, it's open from Friday evening to Sunday only, although it has been known to open midweek; but freshly-prepared hot food dishes are available, usually featuring locally-caught game including pheasant and rabbit and served on crockery made in the barn-turned-pottery out the back. On Sunday afternoon folk musicians often gather in the second room for an impromptu session, and with the fire roaring and the conversation buzzing it can be a lively place.

Two other pubs fall into this broad category, perhaps best summed up as 'timeless'; although since the first edition of this book appeared one has succumbed and is now permanently closed. The Red Lion at Wensley, between Winster and Darley Dale, has been in the hands of the Bellfield family since 1949. George Bellfield and his sister Barbara ran the pub for many years, and I remember George vividly recounting to me how he helped his father manage the adjoining farm while his mother and sister ran the pub.

The pub remained largely unaltered over the decades, with Formica tables and pub memorabilia from a time when Guinness was good for you and Double Diamond worked wonders. There was no draught beer or lager, only bottles; and the pub was renowned for its home-made milkshakes, including the 'Milliguin' made out of half a pint of milk (fresh from the farm's cows) and half a pint of Guinness. It was a decidedly eccentric place. Smoking was banned as early as 1968, but not, it seems, so much because of health issues, but rather in protest against the increased tax on cigarettes. You were not allowed to swear in the pub, and local author Richard Bradley (in his book *Secret Matlock*) reports how a couple were once thrown out for holding hands! He also recalls the time that the irascible landlord George

Bellfield stood for the parish council and received one vote – his own. The Red Lion closed in 2010.

The Royal Cottage is a pub that has given its name to the location, on a junction of the A53 high up on the Staffordshire Moorlands above Leek. It was once described by an old guidebook I came across as "uninviting", but I suspect that colourful hanging baskets and even picnic tables wouldn't last long in this windswept environment.

It's a solid old building, dark and sombre as the gritstone moors which surround it, and in appearance like a small and not particularly profitable farmstead. Most people whizzing past in their cars on the busy Leek-Buxton road probably don't even register the plain building, since it's one of several huddled by the roadside. In fact, you have to look quite closely in order to work out that it is actually a public house, for the only indication is a modest sign above the door – there's nothing in the windows or on the door, nor even a traditional swinging board.

The pub's name refers to the advance to Derby (and ignominious retreat to Scotland) of Bonnie Prince Charlie's army in 1745. The Young Pretender is supposed to have slept in the pub (on a settee under the back window to be precise, according to Clifford the landlord); and

if he or his followers stepped into the Royal Cottage today they probably wouldn't be too unfamiliar with the surroundings.

It's one of those places where, as you walk in, you have the uncanny feeling of entering someone's private room. Sure, there is a small bar, but there are also armchairs and a settee covered by old throws, plus an open fire. There's a side room, which can be handy for

There are no frills at the Royal Cottage.

30

when folk musicians occasionally turn up for an impromptu session. The décor, it has to be said, is basic and no-frills, with fake brick wallpaper above the fireplace that must surely be several decades old.

Even more curiously, it must be one of the very few pubs anywhere in Britain that is actually owned by a National Park Authority. When wealthy landowner Charles Harpur-Crewe died in the early 1980s his family were unable to pay the considerable death duties, so the Government accepted much of his vast estate in lieu of payment. The family home of Calke Abbey in south Derbyshire went to the National Trust, but the Warslow Moors estate in Staffordshire was given over to the Peak District National Park Authority. Not only did it cover a sizeable area of rough upland moor, but it also included 13 farm holdings and cottages, numerous field barns, a church and schoolroom at Reaps Moor – and the Royal Cottage pub.

It's a pub which won't appeal to large numbers of people, not least because it generally only opens on Friday and Saturday evenings, although they say that the landlord may open at other times if you knock on the door politely.

Meanwhile, a few miles away at Reaps Moor, just along the road from the aforementioned church and schoolroom, is Ye Olde Butchers Arms. An out-of-the-way roadside building dating from the 1700s, traditional and unshowy, you enter via a simple room sparsely but not unattractively furnished, save for a splendid range and old leather sofas.

There's a similar experience at the Quiet Woman at Earl Sterndale (see Chapter 7 for more on its unusual name). A plain-looking, almost drab rendered building from the outside, the main room inside is low and quite dark, with a small fire in the grate and a few tables dotted along the tiled floor. It's unobtrusively decorated and homely in a rather changeless way. Ken Mellors, the landlord of 30 years, has never bothered with meals and hot food because he never wanted to. Instead, this is a traditional village local of drinking and conversation, where you can find light snacks at the bar (pork pies, flapjack, crisps, etc); free range eggs from the pub's own hens are on sale; and once a week the village post office sets up shop in the pool room (see Chapter 9). Straightforward, uncomplicated and authentic.

The Duke of York, Royal Cottage, Butchers Arms and Quiet Woman are reminders that not every pub has to go down the route of chef's specials and wine lists, fruit machines and piped music; and that there is still (and must be) a place for traditional public houses, even amid the full-on tourism of the Peak District. 'Traditional' doesn't have to

The Quiet Woman at Earl Sterndale.

mean scruffy, unwelcoming or second-rate, either. In this consumer-led digital age where pubs are almost expected to have their own website and offer free wi-fi, or lure you with the promise of ample parking or kids-eat-free deals, it's important to allow for all-comers and accept that some long-established public houses (almost always freehouses) are simply continuing a centuries-old tradition of providing a place where people can come together to drink, relax, talk and socialise. It's not so much old fashioned, as holding on to the true origins of the public house; but how long these sort of places will survive unchanged into the 21st century – or survive at all – is the big question.

CHAPTER THREE

All in a Day's Work

The Peak District remains overwhelmingly rural, characterised by scattered farmsteads, hamlets and villages, with a few towns like Buxton, Bakewell, Matlock and Chapel-en-le-Frith. It's fringed by larger settlements, such as Ashbourne and Glossop; and then ringed by the cities of Sheffield, Derby, Stoke and Manchester.

The region's pubs reflect this, with a mixture of village inns and town taverns, and the names and histories of these establishments can tell us a lot about the everyday lives of the men and women who have lived and worked the Peak District for generations.

Although tourism has usurped agriculture as the major local employer, farming is still a strong historical theme when it comes to pub names. The Wheatsheaf is common, found in Bakewell, Baslow, Old Glossop and Wirksworth, and you might not be too surprised to discover that three golden wheatsheaves appear on the coat of arms belonging to the Worshipful Company of Bakers (as it has done since 1486). It also has a heraldic reference to the Earls of Exeter.

The rural theme continues with the Barley Mow, the name given to a rick of barley from which ale used to be brewed (apparently the 'mow' should rhyme with 'cow'). Such a sign was sometimes used simply to indicate that beer was sold from the building. There are fine pubs of this name at Bonsall and Kirk Ireton, both of which are featured in more detail in other chapters.

Although today the name of the Farmyard Inn at Youlgrave, near Bakewell, may seem out of place among the cottages and houses, 300 years ago it was indeed a farm building, which was converted into a pub in 1829. The low-slung ceiling, dark beams and grand open fireplace at the far end of the bar still give it an authentic feel with plenty of atmosphere, and on the walls are some fine old sepia-tinted photographs showing regulars lining up outside the pub across the previous two centuries.

The Plough is another familiar pub name, found at Two Dales near Matlock and Hathersage. 'Plough Monday' was the first Monday

Regulars mark Coronation Day in 1953 with a group photo outside the Farmyard Inn at Youlgrave.

after the twelve days of Christian celebration at Christmas, and represented the beginning of the new agricultural year. Ploughs would be decorated and hauled through the village to raise 'plough money' for what was known as an ale frolic. In his book on Matlock, Richard Bradley reproduces an extract from *The Derbyshire Courier* of 13th January 1849 which describes how "50 plough bullock, followed by an excellent plough, and preceded by the Matlock Brass Band, started from the Horse & Jockey, Matlock Bank, and proceeded to Matlock Bath, Cromford and Starkholmes, and returned to the Bank, where a good supper awaited them". The 'plough bullock' were farm labourers attired in gaudy costumes, who in addition to pulling the plough would perform "rough music" and guising plays in order to elicit money from the spectators along the route.

Moving logically on to matters equine, the Monsal Head Hotel, although historically catering for the tourists who once alighted from the train in the valley below (see later in this chapter), does have next to it a cosy bar situated in the former stable block. The appropriately-named

Stables Bar once housed the animals that pulled the coaches and carts full of passengers and their luggage, and now the open, stone-flagged building contains seated areas grouped around the individual stalls, each of which are named after horses: Samson, Blossom, Captain and Betty. The bar is decorated by horse brasses and saddles, and in front of the warming stove is an original wooden pig bench (once used, as you might have guessed, for chopping up pig carcasses).

Sheep-farming is still widespread in the Peak District, especially on the uplands, and the Fleece Inn at Holme, in West Yorkshire, and the Ram's Head at Disley in Cheshire, are a reminder that for three centuries, wool was the mainstay of the English economy.

But surely the most common pub name we immediately associate with farming and the rural way of life is the Bull's Head. There are pubs of this name at Ashford in the Water, Buxton, Castleton, Foolow, Old Glossop, Hayfield, Monyash, Tintwistle and Youlgrave, making it one of the most popular pub names in this region. There was formerly an Old Bull's Head at Little Hucklow that has now reopened as the Blind Bull (see Chapter 9); and in Chapter 8 we will discover a whole lot more Bull's Heads that are no longer pubs. So it's no wonder that as little as a century ago there were reported to be between twenty to thirty Bull's Heads in the Peak District.

Predictably enough, nearly all of them depict the picture of a huge great beast, and indeed many may simply have been named after the animal or have something to do with a market place or bull baiting. On the village green at Foolow, for instance, close to the Bull's Head pub is a surviving example of an original bull ring attached to a boulder; and the base of Eyam's former bull ring can be seen on the Square near the Miner's Arms. Bull baiting also took place by the 17th-century village cross in the centre of Bonsall, outside the King's Head, although the bull ring itself is now kept in the local church. The reason that it resides in the church is that in 1834 the vicar, in a fit of compassion, paid a guinea to buy the bull so that it would be saved from baiting during the Wakes.

There are two other possible reasons why the Bull's Head was such a popular pub name. In the days before the Reformation it had a religious significance, referring not to the farmyard animal but to the Papal bull, since the seal of a monastery or collegiate body was known as La Boule (from the Latin *bulla*). A further explanation, not entirely unrelated, suggests that the Bull's Head moniker was a sort of code, denoting that the establishment had royalist sympathies.

Among the various Bulls Heads dotted about the Peak District are some particularly attractive and interesting pubs. The one in the centre of Youlgrave has a striking carved stone relief of a snorting bull's head above the handsome coaching arch; and a similar, decorative relief can be found above the main doorway of the Monsal Head Hotel, which began life as a simple pub called the Bulls Head. There's another surviving example on the outside of the former Bulls Head Inn at Chapel-en-le-Frith, near the entrance to the church, which is now a private house.

The Bulls Head at Ashford in the Water is set back from the main street near the church and originally opened as an alehouse in 1701 under the name of the Turk's Head. Back then it stood at the edge of the village and was predominantly a farm. Meanwhile, the Bulls Head in Castleton was a popular stopping-off point for travellers in the Hope Valley, including Daniel Defoe who visited Castleton in 1726.

Indeed, it was quite common in those days for the rural pub to be part of a wider family business, such as a farm. The husband may well have been running the farm or shoeing horses, while the wife looked after the selling of drink.

The national census of 1851 found that of 22,082 farmers, over 1,500 were innkeepers and a further 1,898 beershop keepers. There are numerous examples of publicans holding down other occupations. In

The head of a bull is depicted in these fine stone reliefs at the Bulls Head in Youlgrave (bottom) and above the main door of the Monsal Head Hotel (which was originally called the Bulls Head).

Peter Fellows's absorbing book *Bonsall at Work* (part of the Bonsall History Project) we learn that James Briddon was the landlord of the Via Gellia Inn, which later became the Pig o' Lead Inn. In addition to the pub, he also ran a thriving blacksmith's business in the cottage across the road. At the nearby Barley Mow, landlord Jesse Bunting was also a spar miner; and at the King's Head, Isaac Doxey was a joiner for almost 40 years. In 1860, George Statham is recorded as 'a butcher and innkeeper' at the Miner's Standard, which once stood on Bonsall High Street, but by the 1920s this pub, like several others in the village, had closed.

The Gate Inn at Tansley was also run as a farm, and stayed in the same family for two centuries until 1900. The Anchor Inn at Tideswell was originally a farmstead, as was the original building on the site now occupied by the Waterloo Inn at Taddington; and the Bluebell Inn at Tissington was a working farm until as recently as the 1940s, when landowner Sir Henry Fitzherbert of nearby Tissington Hall converted it into a pub.

Records from the 1860s show that the George Hotel at Hathersage contained a hay loft and cowhouse, in addition to the coach house and stabling for eight horses. The landlord at the Star Inn at Taddington (now closed) used to be a saddle and harness maker; while the name of the Square and Compass inn at Darley Bridge alludes to the tools of the stonemasons who worked in places like the nearby Stancliffe quarries (as well having a connection with the freemasons). In the 1880s the innkeeper of the Jug and Glass Inn, on the A515 near Hartington, was recorded as being both a landlord and a land merchant; and Ye Olde Bowling Green at Smalldale in Bradwell – an alehouse since the 1500s – also doubled up as a local slaughterhouse.

There was once an abattoir at the back of the Nelson Arms at Middleton by Wirksworth. Like other pubs with reasonably-sized meeting rooms, it also held public auctions; and later there were petrol pumps in the car park that served as the village's filling station.

The Bear Inn at Alderwasley (see Chapter 2) has been both a farmhouse and alehouse in its long and chequered existence, and often at the same time. In 1851 the tenant was recorded as a Mr William Clarke, 'victualler and farmer of 16 acres'. In July 1920 the Alderwasley estate was sold off by the Hurt family, the local landowners, and that included the Bear Inn. A copy of the auction notice is framed on the wall of the present pub, with Lot 38 including the house and four acres, a well of water, range of piggeries, calf pen, cowhouses, hay store and cart shed.

As was the case in Bonsall, some publicans were also blacksmiths, at a time when virtually every village had its own smithy. Smith's Tavern on St John Street in Ashbourne would seem to celebrate this activity, although it seems that the pub was actually named after the Smith family who owned it for many years. Squeezed between modern shops, the building dates from the 1680s, and as unlikely as it sounds, originally had a monastic purpose as lodgings for religious visitors. The back room even has the original bishop's chair, along with a few other splendid period furnishings.

While some of the pubs in the centre of Ashbourne have lost a little of their original character thanks to over-vigorous refurbishment, it's probably true to say that the interior of Smith's Tavern remains authentic and largely untarnished. But despite the picture of a blacksmith at work on the sign outside, there's not an anvil in sight.

However, one pub which can certainly lay its credentials on the bar with pride is the Leather's Smithy by Ridgegate Reservoir in Langley, south east of Macclesfield. This 18th-century building was formerly a blacksmiths and is named after William Leather, a local farrier who was the licensee in 1821, although for a while it was known as the New Inn.

The former smithy at the Rose and Crown at Allgreave, on the A54 in Cheshire, is now the pub's restaurant. According to local historian Antony Borrow, in an informative and entertaining article on the pub's website, the pub was built as a roadhouse to serve the Congleton to Buxton Turnpike Road and was first licensed in 1802. A toll house stood on the site of what is now the pub's car park, although various innkeepers appeared to collect tolls; but in addition to this, the smithy must have been kept busy shoeing the extra horses required for the long pull up on to the moors.

The New Inn at Langley around 1903, today called the Leather's Smithy (photo courtesy of Bollington Civic Society collection).

Other pub names refer not so much to the blacksmith as his four-footed charge, but their fate is a sad reflection of not just changing modes of transport but also changing times for pubs generally. The Horseshoe Inn at Longnor (which dates back to 1609), the Horseshoe on Lime Tree Road, Matlock, the Three Horseshoes at Spitewinter on the Matlock-Chesterfield road, and the Horseshoe Inn at Matlock Green, have all closed in recent years. On the south western edge of the Peak, the name of the Three Horseshoes, on the A53 outside Leek, must also relate back to the time when most of its guests arrived on horseback or by some horse-drawn transport. Now the self-styled Country Inn and Spa has parking for over 100 vehicles.

The miner's lot

Along with farming, the other traditional industry of the Peak District has been mining. Although there are still quite a few active quarries and mines, lead extraction has been replaced by limestone (mostly aggregate for roads) and gritstone for decorative building work, plus some fluorspar is removed for the chemicals industry.

However, it is lead that made the Peak District famous, and its legacy stretches back two millennia when the Romans laid one of their characteristically straight roads (now the A515) in order to link their settlement of *Aquae Arnemetiae* (Buxton) with the centre of their lead mining industry at the still-to-be conclusively identified place called *Lutudarum*.

Derbyshire is the only lead mining county recorded in the Domesday Book, although the heyday of lead mining was not until the 18th century, when as many as 10,000 miners were employed. But the lead veins were often difficult to work, and the mines prone to flooding, and by 1901 less than 300 lead miners were left working in Derbyshire.

Today lead mining has been consigned to the history books, but if you look carefully as you tour the White Peak you can still see tell-tale signs from the past. The odd bumps and grassed-over hollows spread around the fields are often the remains of old excavations and spoil tips, while here and there you will spot occasional chimneys and ruined mine buildings, such as Magpie Mine, near Sheldon.

Not far away is Lathkill Dale, today a tranquil limestone dale much loved by walkers and naturalists, but once it echoed to the sounds of lead mining, with steam engines, a 50ft-high water wheel and mile-long drainage tunnels known as soughs constructed in an effort to drain the water and make the mines more viable. At the head of the dale lies the village of Monyash, and it was in the Bulls Head overlooking the green that – drinking aside – much of the important mining business was conducted.

The Bulls Head is the sole survivor of what were once five pubs in Monyash. It's a spacious and solid, 17th-century stone building, part of which is three-storey. Two centuries or so ago the Bulls Head would have been particularly well frequented, since it was the venue for a special miners' meeting known as the Barmote (or Barmoot) Court. It met twice a year and adjudicated on disputes and contentious claims, settling disagreements over who had the right to work a specific vein.

Indeed, the freeing, giving and selling of mines was an integral function of the Barmote Court, presided over by the Barmaster. If a mine was considered idle and unworked, the Barmaster would cut a nick in the wooden winding gear (the stowe) at the top of the shaft once a week. If, after three weeks, nothing had changed, the mine could then be 'freed' by another miner – hence the origin of the word 'nicked'.

In addition to the Bulls Head in Monyash, Barmote Courts met at other pubs in the Peak District, including the appropriately named

The historic Barmote Court once met at the Bulls Head in Monyash to adjudicate on mining matters.

Miner's Arms found in Eyam, Milltown near Ashover, Carsington and Brassington. In the mid 1800s, the landlord at the last was Thomas Slack, and he must have been quite a powerful man. Not only was he a publican but also the Barmaster of the Brassington Liberty (a 'liberty' was the district in which the miners searched for lead ore, and there were up to 50 in Derbyshire); and he sat with a jury of 24 men to rule on mining matters.

According to research by local historian Ron Slack, a detailed accounts book from this time still survives and shows just how central the pub was to community life. As the relatively wealthy landlord, Thomas Slack gave long credit and loans for various goods and services to the miners, and that of course included ale.

There is no doubt that after many long and demanding hours spent underground in fairly awful conditions, it would be quite normal to want to slake your thirst at the local pub or alehouse. But the Peak District miners' considerable need for liquids was also based on the fact that they believed ale protected them against lead poisoning. Whether the local landlord shared their belief is not known, but a man as astute as Thomas Slack would certainly have not tried to dissuade them.

As his namesake Ron Slack notes: "The characteristic entry in almost all the accounts held by miners is 'ale to mine' and he seems to have sold his ale whenever he carried out his official duties – 'ale at measuring' is a frequent entry, as is 'ale at gift' or 'ale at giving a mine'. This Barmaster prospered."

As landlord and Barmaster, he covered the fees for prospecting miners who hoped to go on and strike it lucky; but inevitably some ended up deep in debt, and these were often forced to help out at the landlord's bidding, doing odd jobs and helping at harvest time.

Once there were 10,000 miners at work in Derbyshire's lead mining industry.

Indeed, the records show that many of the miners practiced a dual economy and also farmed, and there are details of transactions involving animals and fodder.

Today only the Wirksworth Barmote Court still meets; but although it is technically still a court of law with judicial powers its role is mostly ceremonial. In simple administrative terms, your average Peak District ore field was split between major landowners such as the Duke of Devonshire and Duke of Rutland, but the Crown also had a stake as well. Via the Duchy of Lancaster, it owned what's called the King's or Queen's Field – a term that was kept alive in the name of the Kingsfield pub in Wirksworth until its closure a few years ago.

The legacy of lead mining is ingrained in the heritage of many White Peak villages. Until it closed in the mid 1990s, there was a hostelry in Via Gellia at the Bonsall turning called the Pig o'Lead. A few miles away is the attractive village of Winster where the Barmote Court once met at the Angel Inn, opposite the Market Hall. The pub is now a private house, but the lovely arched hall, which dates from the 1600s, has been preserved by the National Trust and is open to the public at certain times. Once the farmers used to trade their wares upstairs, while the miners would weigh their lead below.

At the head of Banktop, above the village, is the Miner's Standard pub, and like others of this name which used to exist in Bolehill (near Wirksworth) and Bonsall, they were named after the so-called standard dish once used by the lead miners to measure their ore. It was usually a rectangular vessel which held around 15 pints, nine dishes making one load. The Winster pub dates from 1653, when it was originally built as a farmhouse. A century later it became an inn, thanks in no small measure to the increasing trade from the turnpike road from Grangemill.

However, a contrary view to the origin of its name is that it refers to the royal standard or flag of Charles II, raised at Nottingham marking the start of the Civil War against Parliament. Derbyshire's lead miners rallied to the King's cause after he promised to cut the tithes payable on lead ore. Incidentally, there are a set of initials carved into the stone above the front door to the pub: EP EP FP. It's believed to refer to the original owners, who are either Edward, Elizabeth and son Francis, or Edith, Ella and their son Frank – depending on who you talk to. However, an alternative and far more entertaining version is that the initials stand for: 'Every person entering pays for a pint'.

Another long-gone Winster pub is the Crown, which was located almost opposite Winster Hall and is now a private house. It was so cramped that they say that even sitting down you could still touch the ceiling! According to one story, miners used to meet at the pub in the evening to have a drink and compare samples of their best finds. Bits that dropped off were swept up and thrown into the fire when the landlord cleared the tables, causing the flames to leap up in bright and colourful patterns.

One night a young man mischievously put a live firing cap on the table, and the publican not noticing what it was went to throw it into the fire with everything else. As he did so, other miners realised what it was and within seconds the pub emptied as people scrambled for the door. After the loud explosion, they all crept back in to find the landlord and his bar covered with a layer of soot. Apparently the landlord's wife was livid and refused to clear up the mess, forbidding her husband to come to bed until the pub was clean.

The overall decline of the lead mining industry in the Peak District was reflected in a change of name for a number of local pubs. The George Hotel at Youlgrave was formerly called the Pig of Lead (as well as the Church Hotel), while the ubiquitous Miner's Arms was often ditched for something more current or universal. Local examples include the Lathkil Hotel at Over Haddon and the Queen's Arms at Taddington – and see Chapter 7 for what happened at the latter when a new landlord suggested changing the name back again.

Food and drink

Side by side with liquid refreshment, pubs have always offered the weary traveller a bite to eat. In the past this might have been a hunk of bread and a lump of cheese, or a bowl of warming broth. The more sophisticated roadside inns, town taverns and hotels would no doubt have had some meat roasting, as the hungry and fatigued passengers alighting from the coaches stumbled towards the door.

Catering continues to be an important factor in the economic viability of most pubs today. Indeed, it has got to the stage where it is now uncommon to find a pub in the Peak District that doesn't serve food; and some places are more or less restaurants in all but name.

The Flouch Inn, which once stood near Langsett on the edge of the moors north west of Sheffield, turned from a roadhouse pub to a split Cantonese/Italian/Balti restaurant in an effort to re-invent itself and attract more custom. It didn't work and in 2013 was demolished to make way for new housing.

A sign outside a former pub in Birch Vale.

Elsewhere, a few local pubs have also undergone sometimes short-lived transformations. The Beehive Inn at New Mills is unusual to start with, as the town's only triangular-shaped pub with two bars on two floors. The building was originally a toll house, hence the unusual design, but after the railway was built it was moved – lock, stock and all its barrels – to the present site on the junction of Albion Road. A few years ago, following a change of ownership, the pub became the Taste of Bengal and the downstairs bar a holding area for the Indian restaurant upstairs, but now it has reverted to a straightforward (and very welcoming) pub again.

A similar thing happened with the Board Inn at Whaley Bridge a few years ago, which the new owner more or less turned into a Chinese restaurant. It subsequently changed back to a pub, was later closed and then sold, and has subsequently reopened under the new name of the Drum and Monkey. Likewise the Bull's Head on Fairfield Road in at Buxton and its namesake at Old Glossop were both run for a time as half-pub, half-Indian restaurant/take-away. The Old Glossop Bull's Head, in particular, is a large and historic 18th-century inn that (legend has it) was once linked by a secret tunnel to the church opposite, allowing the monks to flee in times of difficulty. (Escaping to a pub might seem a good option to many people.)

Some pubs, however, have been given over entirely to diners. The Grouse and Claret at Rowsley lost its small tap room in 2004, when owners Wolverhampton and Dudley knocked it through to create a vast, open-plan dining area. This was despite protests from the parish council who wanted it kept as a place where local people could chat over a drink

The distinctive shape of the Beehive Inn, New Mills.

(without having to eat), since apart from the upmarket hotels there are no other pubs left in the village.

Rather inevitably, some prominent Peak District pubs have been given the full treatment by national pub chains. For instance, the Highwayman at Eastmoor, on the A619 Baslow-Chesterfield road, is a perfectly friendly and well-run Beefeater pub, but if Dick Turpin turned up today he would no doubt be a little puzzled by the concept of unlimited breakfasts and kids activity packs, not to mention Loaded Nachos and Halloumi Fries.

Food and drink is not surprisingly celebrated in the names of pubs in our region, although they are quite diverse. Until just a few years ago there used to be both a Pineapple Inn on the High Street in New Mills and Bakers Arms on West Street in Buxton. The Cheshire Cheese, just round the corner on the old High Street, is one of four such named pubs in the Peak District (see Chapter 2). You can get a Shoulder of Mutton at Bradwell and Chapel-en-le-Frith, and flavour it with a trip to Ye Olde Mustard Pot at Midhopestones, between Langsett and Stocksbridge.

Ye Olde Mustard Pot is first recorded as a licensed pub in 1780 and was then called the Barrel Inn. It served coaches and wagons on the turnpike between Penistone and Grindleford, but was also an end-of-the-day destination for hunting parties from the surrounding moors.

In addition to New Mills, there's a Beehive pub on Hague Street in Glossop; and another of the same name in the village of Combs, two miles west of Chapel-en-le-Frith, which replaced an earlier pub. It was rebuilt in the 1860s and financed mainly through spending at the original pub by navvies who had been working on the new railway line and new road to Chapel-en-le-Frith.

As you would expect there are various references in pub names to the brewing trade itself. The Malt Shovel Inn at Wirksworth Moor, the Barrel Inn at Bretton (see Chapter 4) and the Jug and Glass near Hartington turning are all good examples; and Ashbourne (and formerly Wirksworth) boasts a pub called the Vaults. At Marsden, in West Yorkshire, you can also find the Riverhead Brewery Tap, which as its name suggests brews its own beer. There are more details on this worthy establishment in Chapter 9.

The changing face of industry

Throughout the late 18th and 19th centuries as the Industrial Revolution took hold, new pubs were built to serve the growing workforce. Even in what we consider the relatively rural Peak District, there are plenty of public houses which date from this industrial period.

The Derwent valley south of Matlock is often described as the cradle of the Industrial Revolution, and it's been internationally recognised with its designation as a World Heritage Site. It was here, in 1771, that Richard Arkwright built the world's first water-powered cotton spinning mill, and paved the way for mass production techniques that would usher in the modern factory system.

The small community of Cromford was largely established to house Arkwright's new workforce, and that included the provision of pubs, of course. The Greyhound Hotel, originally called the Black Greyhound (and known to locals as the Black Dog Inn), occupies a central position on the Market Place and was built in the late 1700s for the mill bosses and visiting businessmen. The hotel was also a stopover on the Ashbourne to Chesterfield turnpike and for the regular coach to Manchester.

It's a grand and statesmanlike building, from its imposing Georgian entrance complete with pillars, through to the ornate clock at the top of the building, and was obviously built to impress. According to the local tale, the mill workers were not allowed inside the Greyhound, and instead were confined to one of the other pubs in Cromford, except on the two occasions a year when Arkwright used the hotel to host balls for his workmen and their families (where the so-called 'distinguishing dresses' he awarded as prizes to his best workers were presumably shown off).

Chapter 8 details some of Cromford's pubs that have now closed, including the Bull's Head, George and Dragon and Crown Inn, but one that has survived is the Boat Inn (out of sight around the corner from the Greyhound) that was almost certainly a watering hole for the masses. It was built in the 1770s as a flour merchant's business, and later became a beerhouse known as the New Inn. The first landlord, a Mr Anthony Boden, was also a butcher, and the pub was described at a later auction as a brewhouse and slaughterhouse. At some point it changed its name to the Hit and Miss – a reference to the varying quality of the beer, perhaps? In 1835 it was owned by William Allen, who was a boatman on the Cromford Canal, and it was he who changed its name to the present-day Boat Inn. (See the colour plates for photos of both the Boat and Greyhound.)

Many of the older houses which line Cromford Hill, on the road up to Wirksworth, were also built by Arkwright to house his workforce, and in particular the well-preserved terraced rows on North Street, off the Hill. On opposite corners of this junction stood the Cock Inn and Bell Inn. The former is now a private residence, but the Bell Inn, once known as the Blue Bell, remains open and is a fine example of a period public house (probably early 19th century), even retaining a traditional snug bar in the corner.

Another ostensibly rural location was also a focus of industrial activity. Bollington, on the north western side of the Peak District near Macclesfield, once boasted 13 cotton mills, but although production later switched to synthetic fibres, all the mills eventually closed. A couple have been preserved – Clarence (1841) and Adelphi (1856) – which now function as private apartments and offices.

With such a sizeable workforce, it was not surprising that the large village needed plenty of places for refreshment. The Happy Valley Bollington website has a fascinating feature on old pubs and breweries, and it quotes from a book by George Longden and the Bollington Civic Society History Group which states that by 1900 Bollington had 27 licensed premises – one for every 194 inhabitants! Exactly a century later there were still as many as 24 licences, including the two hotels, but not counting local restaurants.

Even today there are 16 pubs and clubs dotted around the place. The name of the Spinners Arms, on Palmerston Street, is a reminder of times past; and the Poachers Inn on Ingersley Road was converted about a century ago from several end-of-terrace millworkers cottages. There is also now a flourishing Bollington Brewery, whose output can be enjoyed locally at The Vale Inn.

The Printers Arms at Thornsett, between Birch Vale and New Mills, remembers the period during the 1800s when beaching, dyeing and calico printing took place locally, perhaps most notably at Garrison Printworks.

Turnpikes and coaching inns

As we've seen in the previous chapter, the development of many of the early pubs in the Peak District was due to the needs of passing travellers and merchants, who used what were sometimes rough, arduous and dangerous routes.

The advent of turnpikes in the mid 1700s improved some journeys, but travel beyond your own patch was still a long and often difficult affair. The Waggon and Horses at Langsett, and formerly at Bollington, and the Coach and Horses (Ashbourne and Fenny Bentley), were among many roadside pubs and inns which offered stabling, and in some cases that could mean provision for dozens of horses.

Many of the larger pubs and inns that we use today were previously busy coaching inns. The Red Lion at Wirksworth is a handsome, 18th-century coaching and posting inn (as they were known) located on the

The Red Lion Hotel at Wirksworth.

48

The stables of the Old Sun Inn at Buxton probably don't see many horses these days.

Ashbourne turnpike. Its full title used to be the Red Lion Commercial Hotel and it offered generous stabling at the rear, as well as its own bowling green, and you can imagine a horse-drawn coach clip-clopping across the cobbles to emerge from under the handsome archway. Most if not all of those original stables from that era are now gone, with pubs converting them into the likes of garages and shops, or sometimes into attractive accommodation, such as at the former Crewe and Harpur Arms at Longnor and the Castle Inn at Castleton. The latter, together with the Nags Head, was a regular stop-off for stage coaches on the Manchester to Sheffield route.

Road conditions were still generally very poor, but turnpikes offered an improvement and so cut travelling times, which was important for the stagecoaches (and in particular mail coaches) which demanded ever-speedier journeys. Passengers had to be fed immediately and horses changed at the double. For mail coaches the turn-round time was as little as a minute or so, which required the main coaching inns to have considerable resources.

One example of a fine old coaching inn that continues to be a popular modern pub is the Ram's Head at Disley. Look out, in particular, for its surviving mounting steps out the front. Although in existence before the Manchester to Buxton turnpike came along in 1724 (the first turnpike in Derbyshire), it was in a fortunate position at the junction of several local routes. As late as 1860 the Manchester to Buxton Turnpike Trust was granted an Act of Parliament to sort out its financial affairs, but by then the viability of turnpikes was almost at an end.

Further along the route, at Buxton, two well established coaching inns were said to have worked out a mutually beneficial system, with traffic on the Manchester to London route shared by the town's main coaching inns. On the southbound journey passengers breakfasted at the White

The Ram's Head at Disley, c1910 (photo courtesy of the Bollington Civic Society collection).

Hart, while on the return journey they enjoyed evening dinner at the Eagle and Child.

The Chequers Inn was a regular refreshment and refuelling stop on the steep road up from the Derwent Valley via Froggatt Edge. The pub was originally a row of terraced cottages and in 1735 its first landlord is recorded as Thomas Marples. (Curiously, the same list shows that Mr Denzal William Horbury was in charge between 1936-1941 and 1945-1954, and in between Mrs Annie Elizabeth Horbury was the landlady. Presumably this was because Mr Horbury went off to fight in the Second World War and came back unscathed to resume his business?) There's a splendid period photo in the main bar of a stagecoach and team of horses in front of the pub; and a mounting block can still be seen by the roadside.

Another coaching inn which benefited from the coaching trade was the Newhaven House Hotel, built in 1795 by the 5th Duke of Devonshire at the meeting point of important new turnpikes from Derby and Nottingham on what is now the A515. It was originally called the Devonshire Arms until, it seems, the land became part of the Duke of Rutland's estate in the 19th century.

Writing in 1905, J. B. Firth described his impressions: "Such an inn was badly needed, for previously there had been only a few mean little houses of call between Ashbourne and Buxton, and travellers were grateful to the Duke of Devonshire for this roadside palace which he built for their comfort. It now looks ghostly and deserted... but it used to have every bedroom occupied every night, and was as gay and fashionable as a London hotel."

Today Newhaven still remains little more than a hamlet, as isolated and remote as it was a century ago, and for most car drivers just a blur as they journey between Ashbourne and Buxton, or emerge on the A5012 from Cromford. But once this was a meeting point for travellers, farmers and merchants from Nottinghamshire, Derbyshire, Staffordshire and Cheshire, and until the early 20th century it was the venue for an annual fair held at the end of October that attracted huge numbers of people buying and selling all manner of goods, including sheep and cattle.

It its heyday, the Newhaven House Hotel was described by one visitor as "a large handsome and commodious inn, where travellers meet with every requisite accommodation, including stabling for 100 horses." A story connected with the inn, almost certainly apocryphal, is that George IV once stayed there while on his royal travels, and so delighted

The Newhaven House Hotel on the Ashbourne-Buxton road was once a popular coaching inn.

was he with the hospitality he received that he granted the inn a free and perpetual licence.

Regardless of this, the hotel closed a number of years ago, since when it has remained in a semi-derelict state on the verge, you hope, of making a comeback. Mind you, it's not the only pub on this stretch of road to have struggled against adversity. A mile to the north the Jug and Glass Inn is said to have acted as the alehouse to the hotel at Newhaven, although records show that long before that it offered refreshment to packhorse trains bringing copper up from Ecton mine. According to the pub's website, the earliest known licensee was a John Webster in 1753. More recently it has gone through several different owners and in the 1990s the building was completely gutted by fire, but fortunately it was restored and the pub continues to serve travellers on this busy Peak District route. Perhaps its best claim to fame in modern times is that Rod Stewart and his friends sought overnight accommodation at the pub one particularly snowy night.

Other imposing coaching inns include the George Hotel at Tideswell, the Ashford Arms at Ashford in the Water, the Wheatsheaf at Baslow and the George Hotel at Hathersage. The last is today a comfortable hotel catering for the upper end of the car-driving market, but in its time was a popular stopping place for passengers en route from Castleton to Sheffield – a journey which now takes under an hour but 250 years ago took eight times as long.

Chapel en le Frith was evidently a key location for travellers venturing east across the moors of the Peak District, with stagecoaches and wagons regularly setting off from its busy market place. Dotted around this hive of activity were a number of pubs, including the Royal Oak. As well as being a Magistrates Court (see Chapter 2), the Royal Oak was also the departure point for two stagecoaches, called Peak Ranger and the Celerity, that left for Stockport and Manchester. According to the official town trail, the Kings Arms was also a stopping place on the Buxton-Manchester Turnpike. It was once known as Town Head and consisted of two farm houses called Old House Farm and New House Farm.

Canals and railways

The days of turnpikes and universal coach travel were cut short by the advent of industrialisation, which ushered in a transport revolution in the form of canals and then railways. The topography of the Peak District didn't necessarily suit either, but that didn't stop the engineers from trying. The Cromford Canal linked the Derwent Valley with the national canal network to the south, while the Peak Forest Canal did the same in the north west at Whaley Bridge. The wharf, at the northern end of the town, is still popular with narrow boats, and is a busy and colourful place. Pubs like the former Navigation Inn, on nearby Johnson Street, flourished with the labour-intensive construction of the canals.

This was also the case at another local pub called the Dog and Partridge, a little further down Buxton Road, and which has also recently closed. Located within a few yards of the canal, it was built to satisfy the considerable thirst of the navvies, although as at Cromford, this smart and attractive pub tended to be for the managers, while the rank and file headed for the beer house which was once located through the archway a few properties away.

The Dog and Partridge sat beside the short, Whaley Bridge arm of the canal, which after it connects to the main waterway goes on to join the Macclesfield Canal. However, the Peak Forest Canal continues another mile or so eastwards to Buxworth, where the old canal basin remains Britain's only canal and tramway interchange.

Quarried limestone from Dove Holes was brought down a gravity-fed tramway 6½ miles long and loaded on to the waiting boats at Buxworth Basin. Teams of five horses then pulled the empty wagons back up the incline plane. On the downward journey a boy called a nipper was employed to brake the leading wagon by thrusting a wooden rod into the wheel spokes.

Throughout most of the 1800s the canal and tramway provided an important source of employment and commercial activity, with local paper and cotton mills also benefiting from the new access. Such was the level of business that Buxworth was at one time described as "a thriving inland canal port", but by the early 20th century its fortunes had declined and both canal and tramway fell into disuse. However, recently a dedicated Heritage Trust has been restoring the historic canal basin, a scheduled ancient monument, in order to make Buxworth navigable once more.

Next to the basin, where the horses from the Peak Forest Tramway would be marshalled and the stone prepared for loading, is (another) Navigation Inn. This long and handsome brick-built building was constructed over 200 years ago and served a shop and office for the canal company, with considerable stabling added on to cater for the horses that towed the boats. Today, rather inevitably, the pub is decked out in all manner of canal memorabilia, and there are some interesting old photos of the basin in its industrial heyday. Another claim to fame is that it was once owned by Pat Phoenix, Coronation Street's Elsie Tanner.

One other interesting story connected with this intriguing location concerns its name. You might notice that some local interpretation boards refer to Bugsworth Basin, but the road signs spell the name Buxworth. In 1929, the local headmaster and vicar jointly led a successful campaign to gentrify the name from the traditional Bugsworth to the apparently more respectable Buxworth.

The name originally came from the Buggesworth family, who moved here from Nottinghamshire in the Middle Ages, and in Old English it literally means Bugge's enclosure. Since the change in 1929, there have been a number of attempts to switch it back, and in 1949 someone rather cheekily suggested changing it altogether to 'Mugsworth' since they had been foolish to alter such an historic name in the first place. The latest attempt to restore Bugsworth was defeated by three to two in a local vote in 1999.

Much further to the north another former canal pub is located on the Huddersfield Narrow Canal near Marsden in West Yorkshire. Now called the Watersedge café rather than a fully fledged pub, it stands by the entrance to Standedge Tunnel, which was re-opened in 2001. The nearest authentic pub used to be the Tunnel End Inn (formerly the Junction Inn) on nearby Waters Road, but despite being rescued from near dereliction in 2002 this has now recently closed.

Thomas Telford's 3½-mile tunnel below the Pennines was hewn out of solid rock at the turn of the 18th century and today is the longest (3¾ miles), deepest (638ft/194m underground) and also the highest (645ft/196m above sea level) navigable canal tunnel in Britain. Organised trips explore the subterranean waterway during the summer, and it's a fascinating, if rather chilly, experience.

The tunnel emerges on the western side of the Pennines at Diggle, where the Diggle Hotel at the hamlet of Digglea served as an alehouse and stores for the navvies employed to dig the tunnel. Before that it was a weaver's cottage, with the mill and looms on the top floor. Some of the spoil from the navvies' backbreaking work was dumped on the bare moorland above, including piles that can still be seen near the former Great Western pub on the A62 high above Marsden.

Other pubs from this time reflect the changing face of transport, and as is often the case you can tell a lot about local life through their actual names. In general, most coaching inns didn't specifically take a related name (such as the Coach and Horses), since the pubs themselves were refreshment points or overnight stops and so were integral to travel by stagecoach.

But when the railways came along in the mid 1800s, publicans realised that their establishments were no longer involved in the actual running of this new form of mass transport – there were separate stations, of course. So when a new railway line was built it was common for pubs which considered themselves in the vicinity to change their name in an attempt to attract new customers. Hence the rash of Railway Hotels or Station Taverns, even though some of them weren't always particularly close to a line.

The Midland railway company forged an ambitious new route through the centre of the Peak District, via Matlock and Bakewell, and although it was not without its problems and setbacks, it inevitably provided new opportunities for pubs and inns. The names of two pubs by the road bridge at Matlock Bath – the County and Station (now closed) and the Midland – remember this early period; and further up the line the origin of the former Railway Inn (also currently closed) at Matlock is self-explanatory. In its heyday the County and Station was originally two pubs. The County was a little grander and tended to be where the gentry took their refreshment, while the commoners wetted their whistle in the Station immediate next door. Eventually the two were knocked into one.

A few miles north along the Derwent valley at Rowsley, what is now the Grouse and Claret used to be called the Station Hotel. Nearby was a large marshalling yard complete with engine shed, while Rowsley Station was often busy with visitors alighting for Chatsworth House (the original station building designed by Sir Joseph Paxton is now marooned in the middle of the modern Peak Shopping Village development). The railway didn't continue up the Derwent to Chatsworth because the Duke of Devonshire refused to let the line through his grounds; so instead the railway veered sharply west along the edge of the Wye valley and via a tunnel beneath Haddon Hall (a hard-won compromise with the Duke of Rutland) to Bakewell.

The railway brought new custom to the market town on the River Wye, even though the station was not exactly in the centre, and unsurprisingly a Station Hotel soon appeared; but further up the line the Monsal Head Hotel profited considerably from the new trade.

This was originally a two-storey, traditional whitewashed stone pub which, as we've already learned, was called the Bull's Head. However, when the modern tourist industry came knocking the pub was completely rebuilt some time around the 1880s and renamed the Station Hotel.

Guests were met at the halt in the dale bottom below and brought up to the hotel by horse and carriage. Today's rather ostentatious, three-storey building bears little resemblance to what went before – nor, with its almost Alpine wooden frontage, does it have much in common with any other local building. That said, it's a popular destination, with stunning views down to the famous railway viaduct in Monsal Dale which now carries the well-used Monsal Trail walking and cycling route.

Beyond Monsal Head, the line negotiated more tunnels, viaducts and cuttings before arriving at Miller's Dale, where apart from the limestone quarries there was a connection for a branch line service to Buxton. The station, which had three platforms, was also unusual in having its own post office. Nearby was the Railway Hotel, which later changed its name to the Dale Hotel. With the closure of the line and station in 1967, the hotel soon followed suit, and now forms two private dwellings.

In Buxton, which still has both a passenger line (to Manchester) and separate quarry lines, the Railway remains a fine old pub located at the

The Monsal Head Hotel reinvented itself to cater for new customers arriving by train.

foot of a huge railway viaduct on Bridge Street. Rather appropriately, the pub is owned by brewers Joseph Holt of Manchester, which was founded amidst Manchester's mid 19th-century industrial boom.

Much further to the north, trade at the former Stanhope Arms at Dunford Bridge, South Yorkshire, was given a boost with the construction of the railway across the Pennines. This was the famous route up the Longdendale valley via Crowden and Woodhead, and until the first tunnel was built, passengers transferred to coaches for the journey across the bleak central moorland section.

Over 1,000 thirsty navvies were employed to dig the tunnels and lay the route, living in temporary accommodation at the head of Longdendale. Two pubs high on the moors by the turning off the A628 to Dunford Bridge did particularly well out of the huge influx of itinerant workers. The Plough and Harrow was located at the actual summit, a place sometimes known as Fiddlers Green, while its rival was the Miller Arms, which could be found just across the bleak moorland at the now long-vanished community at Saltersbrook. However, once the tunnels had been dug, and the dams for the new reservoirs constructed, the inns and alehouses soon died away – see Chapter 8 on the lost pubs of Crowden and Woodhead.

Today's visitors to the Royal Oak at Hurdlow often turn up by bike.

There's also a Railway Inn at Whaley Bridge, near the station as you would expect; and further along the line, at Furness Vale, a pub called the Crossings is appropriately next to the level crossing by Furness Vale station. Across the valley, at New Mills, the North Western was handily-placed for Newtown Station, with its sign depicting a steam train in full flight, but sadly the pub closed a few years ago.

The Railway Hotel near Hurdlow, a hamlet off the A515 north of Hartington, was originally a farmstead, but took advantage of the opportunities presented by the new Cromford and High Peak line built between 1825-30 across the high limestone uplands; and then later the Ashbourne-Buxton line which joined the former at Parsley Hay.

Both lines were closed by 1967, but thanks to the Peak District National Park Authority and Derbyshire County Council, reopened a few years later as traffic-free recreational routes for walkers, cyclists and horseriders called the Tissington Trail and High Peak Trail. Since then, the Railway Hotel has been renamed the Royal Oak and the pub is now busy with walkers and cyclists.

The southern terminus of the Tissington Trail is in the centre of Ashbourne, where the name of the former Station Hotel is a reminder of days gone by.

Inevitably, with a growing volume of traffic on the roads of the Peak District, instead of providing for wagons and horse-drawn coaches modern pubs have wide strips of tarmac for lines of cars, caravans and motorbikes; and some, like the Bluebell Inn on the A515 near Tissington marked out designated bays for coach parking. A few decades ago some so-called roadhouse pubs even offered their car-driving customers a complete service.

The Red Lion at Wirksworth, previously cited as an example of a coaching inn, also offered a motor garage; and in my own village of Youlgrave, people remember the sight of petrol pumps outside the Bull's Head and Farmyard Inn. The famous gallows sign belonging to the Green Man and Black's Head Royal Hotel in Ashbourne, which stretches across the street, used to have boards either side of the central picture reading 'garage' and 'petrol'. And now, of course, pubs are starting to provide charging points for electric vehicles. Plus ça change.

CHAPTER FOUR

People and Places

Lords and Ladies

The most common pub names nationally are connected with the church and monarchy (see Chapter 7), but locally they also reflect an allegiance to or ownership by the Lord of the Manor.

In the case of the Peak District one of the names which regularly crops up is the Devonshire Arms, named after the Cavendish family of Chatsworth. It's hardly surprising that the name is so popular, given that the Duke of Devonshire owns large tracts of the surrounding land, including pubs.

Inevitably most of the Devonshire Arms are to be found in the centre of the Peak District in and around the main estate. Baslow, Beeley, Pilsley and Sheldon all have or have had Devonshire Arms, and there is another at Hartington.

Until only a few years ago, the Ashford Arms at Ashford in the Water also used to be called the Devonshire Arms (and before that the Stags Head); while the Devonshire Arms at Peak Forest is also named after the family, but along with much else in the village was sold by auction in 1954 to pay the 10th Duke's death duties.

However, the connections with the Cavendish family are not severed quite that easily in Peak Forest. Opposite the pub is the parish church, which unusually is dedicated to 'Charles, King and Martyr'. The original church was built in 1657 by the Countess of Devonshire, an ardent Royalist, after her favourite son was killed by Parliamentarians while fighting for Charles I fourteen years earlier. The present church dates from 1877 and was built by the 7th Duke of Devonshire. Previous ministers included an enterprising chap who granted on-the-spot marriage licenses to eloping couples, and for a while Peak Forest had the reputation as the Gretna Green of the Peak.

A little further west along the A623, at Sparrowpit, another Devonshire

The Devonshire Arms, Pilsley.

Arms changed its name to the Wanted Inn in the 1950s; while one of the Duke's most famous racehorses, the Flying Childers, is commemorated in the name of the village pub at Stanton in Peak (turn to Chapter 7 for the full story of these two unusually-named pubs).

The family is also identified with the Cavendish Hotel at Baslow, which paradoxically was originally owned by the Duke of Rutland and called the Peacock. The hotel was bought by the Duke of Devonshire in 1830, and rebuilt in the early 1970s. The sign for the Cavendish Hotel depicts a snake, which is part of the family's coat of arms. This, in turn, explains the name of one of the Peak District's most famous roads, and with it another pub.

The Snake Pass Inn stands beside the A57, about four miles from the western end of Ladybower Reservoir, and was built in 1821 following the opening of the major east-west road over the high and inhospitable moorland of Bleaklow. The new route across the Dark Peak, plotted by Thomas Telford, links Sheffield to Glossop and Manchester. It rises to 1,680ft (512m) at its summit, where the Pennine Way National Trail crosses on its way from Kinder Scout to Bleaklow, and today the road is still regularly cut off in bad weather each winter.

The inn sits amid some fine walking country and naturally has served ramblers and other outdoor types for many years. In fact, the first outing of the Clarion walking club in 1900 called into the Snake Pass Inn for refreshment, according to an account in one of its famous little handbooks. Unfortunately the landlord announced that the kitchen didn't have enough bread for 14 unexpected guests. "But good hotelier that he was, he forthwith ordered that some should be baked, and in no time at all the party were able to assuage their moorland tramping hunger with freshly baked oven bottom bread cakes and slices of excellent home cured ham."

The Snake Pass Inn, which was originally called Lady Clough House after the clough or valley above which it stands, is not named after the tortuous and looping course of the road as many suspect, but after the snake which features on the Duke of Devonshire's crest as displayed at the Baslow hotel. It was he that petitioned for the route and engaged the services of Telford. The pub closed in 2019 and now offers self catering accommodation only.

There are plenty of other, well-known local families rooted in the Peak District. The Manners of Haddon Hall are still important ducal landowners, with the Duke of Rutland once remembered by a pub bearing his name at Baslow (it closed a few years ago and is now a convenience store). The pub was originally called the Green Man, according to a former landlord, who also repeated the well-known story of the secret tunnel that supposedly runs from the pub to Chatsworth. Why the two should be connected is anyone's guess.

The well-known Rutland Arms Hotel dominates Rutland Square in the centre of Bakewell (see Chapter 6), and further down Haddon Road you can also find the Manners Hotel. The Duke's crest features a peacock, which is why there are Peacock Hotels at Bakewell and Rowsley, as well as others on the edge of the Peak at Cutthorpe and Owler Bar.

The Peacock Hotel at Rowsley is particularly interesting, since it was built in 1652 as the private residence for John Stevenson, agent to the Manners family, and was originally called Rowsley Manor. After briefly becoming the dower house and later a farm, it was converted into a hotel in the 1820s, at the same time as the closure of Rowsley's two coaching and posting inns on the Square (the Nag's Head and Red Lion).

The elegant, ivy-clad building has had its fair share of distinguished and unusual guests, including the poet Henry Wadsworth Longfellow, and Maximillian, the 19th-century Emperor of Mexico. Today the stylish dining room and atmospheric Peacock Bar, with its beamed ceiling and

The elegant and historic Peacock Hotel at Rowsley.

ornately carved wooden bar, still exude elegance, and it remains one of the relatively few pubs/hotels in the Peak which is licensed to hold weddings.

Of course, landowners like the Dukes of Devonshire and Rutland owned other pubs in the Peak District whose name bore no obvious connection with their families. We have already seen how the Duke of Rutland once used the Fox House Inn as overspill accommodation for his shooting parties, while further down the road towards Froggatt, he also owned the Chequers Inn. The Duke used this 18th-century coaching inn to collect rent from his local tenants, but it was said that after he had gathered it up he would treat them all to food and ale at the pub.

Another powerful local family were the Eyres, most closely associated with Hassop, Calver and Hathersage. The sign for the Old Eyre Arms at Hassop shows the family coat of Arms, the centrepiece of which is a solitary leg.

The story behind this curious design apparently goes all the way back to an incident involving William the Conqueror at the Battle of Hastings in 1066. Knocked from his horse during the fighting, the King was helped by a soldier who loosened the King's helmet. William asked the fellow for his name (it was, rather improbably, Truelove) to which the King said: "I shall call you Air, for you have given me air to breathe."

Later in the same battle the King discovered that Truelove (or Air) had been injured, and had to have a leg amputated (hence the unusual family crest). William told him that when he was sufficiently recovered he would give him some land – to which the grateful soldier replied: "I shall call it Hope, for you have given me hope to live."

Despite the rather fanciful tale, the Eyres went on to own a considerable amount of land and a number of properties, such as Nether Hall in the Hope Valley and North Lees Hall above Hathersage, although the ancestral home until the 1850s was Hassop Hall.

The 17th-century Old Eyre Arms is located a short distance away. It's a handsome, creeper-covered building with a walled garden to the side. The traditional interior has been well-maintained and remains full of character, especially when the open fires are roaring on a chilly winter's night. Apart from the resident ghost (see Chapter 5), the most eye-catching feature is the massive coat of arms on the wall of the lounge bar, which belongs to Rowland Eyre, a Royalist officer in the Civil War. The Eyres were fervent Roman Catholics and diehard supporters of the King, and Rowland Eyre raised a regiment in Derbyshire and fought for the Crown at the Battle of Marston Moor in 1644.

Another pub with connections to the Eyre family is the Derwentwater Arms at nearby Calver. It used to be called the Newburgh Arms, since the Earldom of Newburgh was one of the Eyre family titles. In fact, the Old Eyre Arms at Hassop was also called the Newburgh Arms until 1902. There was also once another Newburgh Arms in Bradwell, but it is now a private house. And just to really confuse things there is also a pub by the crossroads at Calver Sough, just a couple of miles from the Old Eyre Arms, called the Eyre Arms.

The Duke of Norfolk (the Howards) also owned considerable

The Norfolk Arms in Glossop is associated with the powerful Howard family.

tracts of land around the fringes of the Peak District, especially in the vicinity of Sheffield and Glossop, and as late as 1924 the Howards still retained the title of Lords of the Manor of Glossop. Indeed, the Duke was instrumental in the development of the modern mill town, which was originally known as Howardstown, and it's no surprise that there's an old coaching inn and posting office called the Norfolk Arms on Norfolk Square in the centre of Glossop. It dates from 1823 and was where Royal Mail horses were rested on their long journey between Manchester and Sheffield across the high moors of the Peak District. There's another pub of the same name on the moors above Sheffield at Ringinglow, as well as others in the city.

The Earldom of Surrey was another title that belonged to the Howards, which explains why there was once a Surrey Arms off the A57 towards Moscar Top west of Sheffield, as well as two more in Glossop: the one on Victoria Street was known by locals as 'Top Surrey' and the other on High Street West was called 'Bottom Surrey'. The family's coat of arms features a white lion, which of course has itself become a recognisable pub name these days.

Meanwhile, the Earls of Derby are remembered by the Stanley Arms, located deep in a remote valley off the Buxton to Macclesfield road at a location known as Bottom-of-the-Oven. The unusual name is thought to come from a large oven or spit roast that was once a feature of nearby Oven Lane, and which fed the men of Lord Stanley of Crag Hall (at nearby Wildboarclough, and still the family's summer home).

Former pubs at Gradbach and Buxton, both called the Eagle and Child, referred to the Stanley's family coat of arms. Their main seat is at Knowsley, near Liverpool, where their family crest is known as the "bird and babby". The story behind the unusual design – according, once more, to popular tradition – dates back to the 1300s when, unbeknown to his wife, the Earl of Derby had an illegitimate son. He hid the baby in an eagle's nest on his land, and then when out with his wife they 'discovered' the child, which he claimed must have been taken by an eagle. They subsequently adopted the child, hence the family's unusual coat of arms. You can still see the simple drawing and inscription above the door of the former roadside pub near Gradbach, which was open between 1738 and 1919.

Another unique family name is celebrated by the Woodroffe Arms in the village of Hope, near Castleton. The Woodroffes (or Woodroofes) were the official King's Foresters of the Peak, acting as forest officers to supervise the royal hunting ground which once spread across much

The sign above the door of the former Eagle and Child pub near Gradbach.

of the High Peak. According to a fascinating booklet by the Hope Historical Society, the Woodroffes pre-eminence dates back to the mid 1400s, when they distinguished themselves fighting for Edward IV and were granted the right to bear Arms. The family motto reads: *Quod transtuli restuli*, or 'That which I took out I brought back'. In the past, family members have been innkeepers at the pub; and the position of Hope Parish Clerk was, until 1855, passed down from father to son for over 200 consecutive years.

The Maynard Arms at Grindleford was built in 1908, and its imposing countenance, as well as its roadside location just to the north of the village near the turning for the station, reflects the importance which the railway played in bringing visitors into the area. Totley Tunnel, which begins just after Grindleford station and takes the Sheffield-bound trains deep under the moors, was dug in the 1890s and at 6,230 yards (5,694m) is one of the longest railway tunnels in Britain.

The Maynards, incidentally, have an impressive family pedigree, although their connection with the Peak District only goes back to the 1800s when Anthony Maynard acquired land, including the Manor of Nether Padley. Sir Richard Maynard fought for King Henry V at

Agincourt in 1415; then a century later Thomas Maynard helped defeat the Scots at Flodden Field.

Meanwhile, much further south along the Derwent valley at Ambergate, the Hurt Arms is named after a notable Derbyshire family whose seat has traditionally been at nearby Alderwasley. It was built in 1874 on the site of an earlier pub called the Thatched House Tavern and Posting House that was demolished by the Midland railway company to make room for their new tracks. After the pub was refurbished in the mid 1990s the owners decided to change its name, but such was local resistance to the plan (residents even staged a protest meeting) that the idea was quickly dropped and the Hurt Arms it remains.

The Okeover Arms at Mappleton on the River Dove north of Ashbourne remembers the local Okeover family, who have lived at the hall since Norman times. Both the hall and church were plundered by the Jacobites of Bonnie Prince Charlie's army as they swept through here in 1745.

Another noteworthy Peak District family is remembered in the name of the Jodrell Arms Hotel by the railway station at Whaley Bridge. It's named in honour of the Jodrells who were major landowners in these parts from the 13th century, and whose fortunes took a sharp upward turn after William Jodrell distinguished himself as an archer at the Battle of Crecy in 1346. He established the family home at Yeardsley Hall, and the estate grew to include Shallcross Hall near Taxal.

The present Jodrell Arms at Whaley Bridge replaced an earlier building thought to date from the 16th or 17th century and it was outside here that cattle and sheep were traditionally bought and sold, as well as being the venue for community events and celebrations. Among the major alterations in the late 19th century was an elaborate Tuscan porch on its west side, constructed so that the building would face west and so tempt passengers alighting at the new station of the London and North-western Railway. The *High Peak News* of 1896 reported how the new manager of the premises anticipated that the new bar, billiard room and lavatory would cater for the "tourists, cyclists and picnic parties" that they expected would come into Whaley Bridge.

During the 1980s the landlord of the Jodrell Arms was Jack Bond, former Captain of Lancashire County Cricket Club; but for the last decade the pub has stood empty as plans to redevelop the premises seem to have fallen through. At the time of writing the pub remains closed and the fate of this Grade II listed building remains uncertain (see Chapter 8). The Jodrell family is also remembered by the rather more modern Jodrell Bank radio telescope on the Cheshire Plain.

Peak personalities

There are plenty of interesting and distinguished people who have associations with the pubs, inns and hotels of the Peak District, and one of the best known of the historical figures is Mary, Queen of Scots.

During her captivity she was held at Chatsworth, from where she was taken on four occasions to Buxton in the hope that the health-giving spa water would improve her poor health. Her custodian at Chatsworth was the 6th Earl of Shrewsbury, fourth husband of the famous Bess of Hardwick, and it was at his hotel in Buxton that the doomed Scottish queen stayed.

Her confinement at the Old Hall Hotel was carefully ordered, and followed the strict instructions of Queen Elizabeth. Mary was required to give one hour's notice if she wanted to leave her rooms, and she was not allowed any guests after 9pm. Strangers to the town were quizzed or even prevented from entering when Mary was resident at the hotel.

Mary, Queen of Scots, stayed at the Old Hall Hotel in Buxton.

There was also a rumour – and only a rumour – that Elizabeth intended to journey north and visit the hotel in disguise to see for herself her troublesome young cousin Mary.

Despite the curbs on her freedom, Mary apparently enjoyed her visits, and looked forward to her trips to the spa town. It is said that on her last visit to the hotel, in 1584, Mary scratched a message on the window of her bedroom with her diamond ring: "Buxton whose warm waters have made thy name famous, perchance, I shall visit thee no more, farewell!"

The Earl of Shrewsbury's hotel, built in the 1570s, is thought to have replaced an older inn on the same site with the same name but spelled 'Auld Hall'. The present building mostly dates from the time of the Duke of Devonshire's renovations in 1670, and it was always believed that most of the original building had been demolished. However, careful investigation has shown that the original structure is still in place behind the newer façade.

The building is located opposite the Pavilion Gardens at the end of the newly-restored Crescent. The hotel includes a tiny bar popular with visitors to performances at the Opera House across the road, offering pre- and post-theatre evening supper, and a special side door opens for just that purpose. The elegant Opera House (designed by Frank Matcham and opened in 1905) has undergone fairly recent and extensive renovation and is once more resplendent with its interior furnishings of gold leaf and velvet. It holds a variety of performances throughout the year, including the annual Buxton International Festival.

And, as a final footnote to this story, the Dog Inn on Market Street at Chapel-en-le-Frith was once known as the Talbot, remembering a type of hound that featured on the Earl of Shrewsbury's coat of arms. It's now changed its name to The Cobbles.

Royal and military figures, many of whom have given their name to a pub, are covered in Chapter 7, but on top of this there are other notable characters and personalities who are remembered by the names of Peak District inns.

Charles Cotton and Izaak Walton are perhaps two of the most well-known literary figures, famous as the 17th-century authors of *The Compleat Angler*. This reflective treatise on fly fishing in the Peak District has been reprinted innumerable times, and although the authors praise a number of rivers the one that is most closely associated with the two philosophical anglers is the River Dove. The Izaak Walton Hotel at Ilam and the Charles Cotton Hotel at Hartington celebrate this pair, although the latter was originally built as a coaching inn and called the Bull's Head. It was then acquired by the local Sleigh family and re-named the Sleigh Arms; becoming the Charles Cotton Hotel in 1905.

However, all is not so clear-cut when it comes to identities at Grindleford, where there is some measure of confusion after who the Sir William Hotel is named. On the face of it the public house (which was originally called the Bluebell, and then the Commercial Inn) appears to take its name from the well-known Sir William Hill Road. This runs directly westwards up the hillside from Grindleford towards the 1,407ft (427m) Sir William Hill summit, and then on to Eyam and Hucklow Edge and the Barrel Inn at Bretton. However, the Sir William Hill Road proved to be so testing for horse-drawn traffic that an easier route was created via Eyam – the B6521, also called New Road – but recent landslips have in turn caused problems with this route.

So much for the name, but *who* does it actually refer to? There are, rather confusingly, a large number of candidates. An early suggestion, put forward by guidebook writer M. Baddeley in 1899, is that the hill might have been named after Sir William Peveril, illegitimate son of William the Conqueror. He was certainly a big cheese in this area in

But who is the real Sir William?

Norman times, and of course left us Peveril Castle in nearby Castleton, but it's not clear if he was ever knighted.

Then, moving on a few centuries through local history, there's Sir William Cavendish of the Chatsworth line – all four of them, in fact. They kicked off with Sir William Cavendish, Bess of Hardwick's second husband (1505-1557), who was followed by their son Sir William (1st Earl of Devonshire) and so on.

As influential as the Cavendish family have been and to some extent still are in the Peak District, these Sir Williams are probably not front runners when it comes to having a pub in Grindleford named after them. A far better proposition is Sir William Saville, who was the 2nd Marquis of Halifax and Lord of the Manor of Eyam, and whose family had been given the Derbyshire parish by his relative Mary, Countess of Pembroke, in 1616. Sir William commanded Royalist forces during the Civil War, occupying Leeds and Wakefield, but being denied Bradford by the Roundheads under Fairfax. He became Governor of Sheffield and was killed in Yorkshire in 1644.

Over a century later came another strong contender for the pub title in the shape of Sir William Bagshawe, local landowner and country gentleman. He inherited his Derbyshire estate at the age of 30, and in a long and productive life raised 23 children (of whom 19 survived), was a respected physician and patron of the arts, and ultimately was appointed High Sheriff of Derbyshire. Sir William held land at Oakes Park at Norton near Sheffield, Goosehill Hall at Castleton, and Wormhill Hall near Miller's Dale, and it is he who is *supposed* to have constructed the eponymous road across the hill in order to link his estates.

Perhaps bearing in mind this, plus the hill, then the last Sir William would seem the most likely candidate in terms of also having the pub named after him; but if you ask behind the bar they tend to favour Sir William Saville. To bolster their case they reproduce this sad entry from the Eyam Parish Register of 4th February 1692: "Elizabeth, wife of John Trout, she dyed upon the moor near unto Sir William a place so called, coming from Tideswell market in the snow." On this basis, Sir William Bagshaw, who wasn't born until 1771, came along 80 years too late.

I turned to the local Women's Institute, that bastion of common sense, for some help, but in their otherwise excellent booklet guide to the village, they sit firmly on the fence when it comes to the origin of the pub name. Mind you, they do confirm that the Sir William Hotel used to be called the Commercial Inn, as it still is by some older residents, and only gained its present name in 1925. Perhaps those wise locals are steering the best course?

A local character we do know more about was John Charles Watts Russell. His name lives on at the Watts Russell Arms at Hopedale, a hamlet tucked away in a narrow valley south of Alstonefield. He was the son of wealthy, 19th-century industrial magnate Jesse Watts Russell, who lived at nearby Ilam Hall, and was responsible for redesigning the estate village as well as the hall and church. The angular peaks of Dove Dale were said to remind him of the Alps, so he had the new buildings follow a mock-Gothic, Alpine theme. What's left of the hall is now a youth hostel, and the estate is managed by the National Trust. John Charles Watts Russell was a Conservative MP and wealthy landowner who, after marriage, emigrated to New Zealand, where he went on to become a notable politician and sheep farmer.

Someone else who was active in industry was Joseph Whitworth (1803-87), who although born in Stockport, spent the last 15 years of his life at Stancliffe Hall in the Derwent Valley north of Matlock. He was a gifted mechanical engineer and inventor of the standard screw thread, but he also made a name for himself in armaments and is remembered by the Whitworth rifle. Like other Victorian industrialists, Whitworth also had a strong philanthropic streak, and founded a complex of public buildings centred on the Joseph Whitworth Institute which still stands in Darley Dale by the side of the A6. Adjoining the main centre is Barringtons, a recently renovated hotel (Grade II listed) that dates from the same period.

I don't suppose Florence Nightingale was ever much of a pub-goer, but she spent much of her early life in Derbyshire, centred on the village of Lea above the Derwent valley, south of Matlock. The family home was Lea Hurst, which for a while was used as a nursing home. The 'Lady with the Lamp' made her name tending wounded soldiers in the Crimea, of course, but later on she returned to Derbyshire in an attempt to shun the publicity that had enveloped her.

The pleasant village pub at Lea, the Jug and Glass, is closely associated with her family, if not Florence herself. It was part of a row of weavers' cottages built in 1782 by landowner Peter Nightingale (Florence's uncle) for use as a health centre or makeshift hospital for his estate workers. Following its conversion to a pub, the building was used for annual rent collection on so-called 'Nightingale Rent Days'. After collecting all the money and receiving the usual comments and complaints, the day would traditionally end with the landlord serving everyone a complimentary meal.

Folk heroes

Although Nottinghamshire lies outside the edge of the Peak District, the legendary outlaw Robin Hood is remembered in the names of several pubs on our patch. The first used to stand on the London Road in Buxton, but was demolished in 2014 to make way for a Premier Inn. The second can still be found in the Cheshire village of Rainow. According to information compiled by Rainow Women's Institute (see Bibliography), records from 1825 show that Joshua Ainsworth was the licensee of a Rainow pub called the Robin Hood and Little John; and up until around 1930 the pub had a sign outside which read:

> *My ale is fine my Spirits good*
> *So stop and drink with Robin Hood*
> *If Robin Hood is not at home*
> *Stop and drink with Little John*

The third Robin Hood pub is on the Baslow-Chesterfield road (A619) east of Baslow and has given its name to the location. Apart from nearby Robin Hood Farm, there's not much else there apart from the pub. It's thought that an inn of some sort has stood either here or near here since the late 1600s, as it's on one of the main eastbound routes out of the

The Robin Hood at Rainow (photo courtesy of Bollington Civic Society collection).

central Peak District. The Duke of Rutland once owned the buildings and surrounding land, but in 1920 it was sold to the Chesterfield Brewery, who in turn were taken over by Mansfield Brewery in 1935.

In the last few decades the pub has become an increasingly popular destination for weekend walkers and climbers, so much so that in 1974 the landlord opened an uncarpeted bar called the Hiker's Den, where muddy boots and dogs were made welcome. The main attraction for outdoor types is the gritstone outcrop of Birchen Edge, which rises amid the bracken and heather behind the pub, towards the far end of which is Nelson's Monument. This commemorates the Battle of Trafalgar and three prominent tors on top of the edge are known as the Three Ships and inscribed with the names of ships from Nelson's fleet: Victory, Reliance and Soverin (sic).

But back to Robin Hood once more, for there are more and intriguing connections with the outlaw further up the Derwent valley. At Hathersage you can toast another of the Merrie Men at the Little John Hotel. The corner pub was originally called the Butchers Arms, and also the Drum and Monkey, then with the arrival of the railways it changed its name to the Station Hotel. But in the late 1940s it was renamed in honour of Robin Hood's oversized companion, for according to local legend Little

John is supposedly buried in the village churchyard, where there is indeed a grave fully 10ft long. When the grave was opened in the 1700s it is said that a human thighbone 32 inches long was unearthed. Near Hathersage you will also find Robin Hood's Stoop; above Bradwell is Robin Hood's Cross; and among the gritstone rocks of Stanage Edge there is also Robin Hood's Cave.

There's another larger-than-life character from folk

The Station Hotel at Hathersage is now known as the Little John Hotel or LJ's.

73

lore who also has a connection with the pubs of our region. However, this one didn't exactly rob from the rich to give to the poor – he just robbed.

We start at the Bull's Head in Tintwistle, at the western end of Longdendale, which still boasts that it once entertained the notorious highwayman Dick Turpin. He supposedly dined here on his way back to his Yorkshire home after attending the Manchester Races, and on one occasion they say he even had his horse re-shod at the village smithy. Mind you, such are the stories that have grown up around this inevitably shadowy figure that they all must be taken with a large pinch of salt.

Interestingly, Dick Turpin (real name John Palmer) was born at a pub – the Bell in the village of Hempstead, Essex, where his father John was landlord (although the Crown, at Hampstead in north London, also claims this title). Fittingly, it was also a visit to a pub 34 years later that spelled Turpin's ultimate downfall. After a liquid lunch at the George and Dragon in the village of Welton, by the River Humber west of Kingston upon Hull, he went outside into the road and fired off his pistol at a crowing cockerel. Turpin was subsequently arrested and when his true identity was established, the gallows at Tyburn beckoned, and today his bones rest in a grave in the city of York.

The tales surrounding Dick Turpin – even in the Peak District, where he never lived – are legendary. For instance, it is said that apart from visiting Tintwistle, he also called in at the Bull i' th' Thorn near Pomeroy; but of course there is no record of his having ridden the Ashbourne to Buxton road. One local highwayman who certainly did was William Buxton, born at Elton, near Winster, and who for a short while terrorised travellers on this popular route. After robbing a stage coach in 1780 he was pursued to Ashbourne, where he was finally arrested outside the Anchor Inn. He was hanged in Derby shortly afterwards.

Although Turpin may not have used this particular route, it is more likely is that he travelled the Chesterfield to Derby road, since Derby in the 18th century was already a prosperous market town and not too far from his Yorkshire base. In fact, this historic coach road has numerous associations with the infamous highwayman. There's a Turpin's Road near Makeney, where the Coach and Horses pub was said to have once kept Turpin's pistols; he's supposed to have had family connections at Horsley; and Heage Common was notorious as the hide-out of a particularly ruthless gang of highwaymen. For further information on this subject make sure to read Peter Elliott's book *Dick Turpin in Derbyshire?*

An inn with a view

Although by no means a mountainous region, the Peak District boasts a number of well-sited country pubs from where you can enjoy tremendous views, often stretching over several counties. However, some of the most remote have struggled to attract enough customers, let alone staff to work there. On the Peak District's western moors alone the Mermaid, Hanging Gate and Cat and Fiddle inns have all closed (for more on each see Chapters 5, 6 and 7 respectively).

The Lathkil Hotel has also been alluded to in the previous chapter. This charming establishment in the village of Over Haddon, near Bakewell, today thrives on the tourist trade, but it was once frequented by hardworking lead miners. In the mid 1800s, James Bateman was the Agent and Mineral Surveyor for both the Alport and Mandale Mining companies, active in Lathkill Dale, and he made the astute decision that since he was paying the miners for their ore he would open a local alehouse so that they could effectively give their money back to him.

In the early days the pub at Over Haddon was called the Miner's Arms, but when the mining declined at the end of the 1800s the name was changed to the Lathkill View, and later the Lathkill Dale Hotel, as successive publicans tried to tap in to the growing visitor market and entice visitors up the hill from Bakewell. (Incidentally, the Grigor-Taylor family who have now run it for many years spell the hotel's name with just one 'l'.)

Certainly few other local pubs can boast such a wonderful situation high on the rim of a deep, lush valley with views out across the gentle hills of the White Peak. Indeed, there are few better bars in the Peak District in which to loiter and admire the panorama, with huge, south-facing windows in both the main bar and dining room.

Other pubs that enjoy wide-ranging views include the Thorn Tree Inn, where the whole of Matlock is spread out at your feet; the Millstone Inn overlooking the Derwent Valley above Hathersage; and the Old Horns Inn at High Bradfield, South Yorkshire. The last sits in the 'higher' part of the village with views out across the reservoirs that dot the small valley. Indeed, the pub was formerly a farmhouse that switched to a beerhouse in order to provide refreshments to the workers building the new reservoirs in the mid to late 1800s.

However, keeping your eyes peeled is clearly nothing new to the good folk of Bradfield. Nearby is the Church of St Nicholas, which apart from having the largest parish in England also sports a curious

The Strines Inn sits high on the edge of moorland, west of Bradfield.

18th-century watch house by the entrance to the churchyard. It was built to keep a lookout for nocturnal body-snatchers! The pub probably takes its name from the annual Bradfield fair, since the patron saint of the fair was St Luke, and his symbol was an ox. Presumably the ceremony therefore involved a pair of horns?

A few miles westwards along the lane you come to another well-placed pub, this time virtually on its own above Strines Reservoir at the head of the valley. Strines Inn sits at 1,015ft (309m) above sea level, and according to information provided by the pub dates all the way back to 1275 when a manor house was built on the site for yeoman farmers the Worrall family.

It's located on Mortimer Road, a former packhorse route that in 1771 became a turnpike between Grindleford and Penistone, but not a very successful one, by all accounts, and the present inn dates from that time. 'Strines' is believed to be an Old English word meaning the meeting of water; although another explanation is that it derives from the 'strides' of stepping stones once used to cross the stream below the inn, but there is little evidence to support this.

The pub was once called the Tailors Arms, possibly after some of the regular tradesmen who came this way, and it retains its authentic, period feel, with a series of dark and rambling rooms complete with stuffed animals and birds, interesting prints and other curios.

While the Strines Inn enjoys a pleasant setting, the Barrel Inn at Bretton is surely the most spectacular in terms of views, and at 1,250ft (381m) it is also the highest pub in Derbyshire. (The Cat and Fiddle is the highest in Cheshire and the New Inn at Flash is the highest in Staffordshire – more on both in Chapter 7.)

The Barrel Inn is around 400 years old and was originally a farmhouse; and according to an artist it had a heather or thatched roof (see the mounted sketch in the bar). It stands on a pronounced ridge known as Eyam Edge, and overlooks a high and bare limestone plateau criss-crossed by drystone walls and dotted with small villages.

The road that runs along the top of this panoramic edge was once a well-used trading route from Cheshire to Sheffield, as well as a turnpike authorised by the Road Act of 1757. It's also been known as Bretton racecourse and apparently it was not unusual for horses to be raced up and down this long, straight stretch, and wagers to be taken (then probably spent in the Barrel Inn afterwards). With the comparatively flat surface and intense clear air, it's said that some horses were trained here for other race meetings.

At the far western end of the ridge gliders from the Derbyshire and Lancashire Gliding Club regularly take to the skies and the sense of space and airiness is overwhelming. However, an exposed location such as this also has its downsides. In January 1947 the Peak District experienced one of its most severe snowstorms on record, with temperatures plunging to -18 deg.C in Buxton, and drifts as high as 20 feet.

Perhaps not surprisingly the position of the Barrel Inn meant that the awful weather hit it particularly hard. For a long period the pub was *completely* cut off (it varies from 12 days to three weeks depending on whom you ask), but for certain snow was piled up around the pub in enormous drifts so that it covered every window. When help eventually arrived a tunnel had to be dug from the outside to locate the front door and rescue publican Stanley Drewett and his wife. A man from Eyam who managed to struggle up to the pub said it looked like a "huge igloo". Such was the severity of the weather during that winter that blizzards continued on and off until March, and the Barrel was effectively out of reach for over five weeks.

Elsewhere in the Peak District conditions were equally bad. Earl Sterndale was cut off for almost seven weeks, and the people of Longnor were so desperate for food that an RAF airplane dropped supplies by parachute, with the pilot guided by a bonfire and a large black cross marked out in the snow with soot. Villages and hamlets ran out of supplies, farm animals perished, and a funeral party from Foolow had to be led by a snowplough.

Less than seven decades later and wintry weather was still making it

The Barrel Inn glimpsed through snowdrifts on the first day of Spring, 1979 (photo by Jack Bricklebank, courtesy of the Derwent Gallery, Grindleford).

difficult for Peak District publicans. Heavy snows in Easter 2013 caused havoc across the region and especially for Mick Coleman, who at the time was landlord of the Bull i' th' Thorn near Pomeroy and for five days was completely trapped inside the pub. He told BBC News: "It was frightening. It was totally black downstairs because the snow covered the front of the building. I had to dig myself out with a little coal shovel because my spade was in an outhouse. Thankfully, because it's a pub, there were plenty of supplies and the power stayed on. It's every man's dream being trapped in a pub."

The natural world

Ever since King Charles II escaped his captors by hiding in an oak tree (see Chapter 7), pubs have been named after this most English of trees. But in fact naming the pub or inn after something identifiable that grew outside was nothing new, and long before Charles hid in the Boscobel Oak, clumps of evergreen were being stuck above beerhouse doors to denote their purpose.

Apart from the ubiquitous Royal Oak, such as at New Mills, Hurdlow

The Shady Oak at Fernilee, near Chapel-en-le-Frith.

and Wetton, there's a Shady Oak at Fernilee, south of Whaley Bridge; a Thorn Tree and Sycamore Inn at Matlock; two more Sycamores at Birch Vale and Parwich; and a Yew Tree Inn at Holloway (currently closed). The yew was especially significant, since its wood was used to make bows for archers. An Act of Parliament was passed during the reign of Henry V to protect the tree, and it was subsequently planted in churchyards to act as an evergreen symbol of immortality.

As always, it's tempting to assume that the many Yew Tree inns date from this time, but in reality many were probably named much more recently. If any of our pubs should be called the after this tree it should be the Church Inn at Darley Dale. Just across from the pub, on the other side of the railway line, is the 12th-century St Helen's Church, outside which is believed to be one of the oldest yew trees in Britain. Its 33ft girth is astounding, and estimates of its age vary from 600 to 2,000 years.

Particular places and geographical features like rivers are inevitably commemorated by pubs and inns, including the Goyt Inn at Whaley Bridge and the Manifold Inn at Hulme End. The latter is a handsome, 200-year-old coaching inn by the road bridge over the River Manifold. It stands opposite the old toll house and in previous years has gone through something of an identity crisis, being at one time or other called the Jolly Carter, Wagon and Horses, and the Manifold Valley Hotel. I have even read that it was once named the Light Railway Inn, since the nearby hamlet was the northern terminus of a curious little narrow gauge line called the Leek and Manifold Light Railway which ran between 1904-34.

The Crag Inn at Wildboarclough (see Chapter 2) puts me in mind of rocky slopes and awkward summits, as does Rock Tavern at New Mills and Ye Olde Rock Inn at Upper Hulme, which sits below Hen Cloud at the southern end of the Roaches. A mile or so away is the Winking Man, a pub which takes its name from a nearby rocky outcrop called Ramshaw Rocks. When viewed from a particular angle as you drive up the A53 towards the pub, a 10ft rocky protuberance bears an uncanny resemblance to the profile of a man's face, complete with a hole like a winking eye.

You can stay up for the Star (Inn) at both Tideswell and Glossop, dance over the Moon at Stoney Middleton; and if you've got any energy left (or if the pub goes in for 24-hour opening) witness the Rising Sun at Middleton-by-Wirksworth.

Another pub named after a specific local feature is the Lantern Pike Inn at Little Hayfield. It takes its name from the shapely, National Trust-owned hill nearby, since a 'pike' is local dialect for peak or pointed hill, and for some years Lantern Pike was crowned by a beacon that was lit to signal momentous events. The pub is a converted 18th-century farmhouse originally called the New Inn on the former Buxton-Old Glossop turnpike, and today it's a friendly place that welcomes all-comers. It's also stuffed full of curiosities, including a signed letter from *Coronation Street's* original scriptwriter and former local Tony Warren, who supposedly based some of the show's early characters on the pub's regulars.

At nearby Hayfield, the Kinder Lodge, which began life as a weaver's cottage, used to be called the Railway, but changed its name when the line was scrapped. Not too far away is New Mills, where the Torrs was once a former coaching inn in the town centre named after the dramatic Torrs gorge, but is now a cafe and events venue. Here, below the shops and houses, the award-winning Millennium Walkway provides an exciting aerial route above the River Goyt, while the Heritage Centre at the back of the bus station provides more details about the pub heritage of the town.

CHAPTER FIVE

Ghostly Tales, Dastardly Deeds and Unusual Goings-on

Spirits in the bar?

It should come as no surprise to learn that many of the Peak District's pubs are reputed to be haunted, but differentiating fact from fiction – especially after the witnesses have had a drink or two – isn't always easy. It's not hard to imagine ghostly goings-on in the long-established public houses, with their chequered histories and array of guests, not to mention the dark corners and creaking passageways. As we shall see, a resident ghost can be very good for business, although perhaps not always appreciated at the time by those who experience first-hand a ghoulish apparition or strange phenomenon.

There are some pubs that really do lend themselves to ghost stories, but at the Olde Gate Inne at Brassington the tales are more real than most. Situated in this quiet and attractive former lead mining village near Wirksworth, the Grade II listed building dates from 1616 and was substantially altered in 1874. It's said that some of the beams came from ships from the Spanish Armada. On the opposite side of the road from the pub there used to be a tollhouse, so it is likely that the pub took its name from the gate across the road. Apparently there was a small window specially constructed in the side of the pub where passing coachmen would be served a drink.

Almost four centuries on, and a cursory glance inside would lead you to suspect that little has changed. There's a traditional range at the far end of the main room, with scrubbed wooden tables along each side and a stone-flagged floor. Together with the low ceiling and exposed beams, the pub exudes atmosphere, and nowhere more so than downstairs in the old dining room with its wall-to-wall oak panels and open fireplace.

In 2004 the then landlord, Paul Burlinson, told me about the

The main room of the Olde Gate Inne at Brassington.

experiences of some of his guests. "Not so long ago there were two lads who took their drinks into the old dining room," said Paul. "Suddenly they rushed out ashen-faced, saying that they'd seen a mysterious old woman sitting by the fireside in turn-of-the-century dress. They were that scared they left the pub immediately and didn't even finish their drinks – and it was only their first!"

The building has witnessed centuries of comings and goings, reaching as far back as the Civil War when it was used as a temporary hospital after a nearby skirmish. Some of Bonnie Prince Charlie's soldiers were supposedly billeted here during their ill-fated march to London. You can't help feeling that if ever there was a pub custom-made for ghosts then surely it's the Olde Gate Inne?

Perhaps not surprisingly, therefore, a number of customers have reported mysterious sightings and odd feelings while visiting the pub, so much so that a previous landlady invited an exorcist to rid the building of ghosts (apparently unsuccessfully); and in 1998 a team of paranormal experts spent a night in the pub to record the goings-on using digital cameras and EMF (electro-magnetic field) equipment. They concluded that there was without doubt unusual and unexplained activity, and they noted the heavy atmosphere and sudden drops in temperature, rushes of cold air and the way their candles would oddly flare and flicker. One complained of piercing headaches, another that he felt he was being hit on the head with a heavy weapon, while a third was convinced that she kept on hearing the nearby sound of stabled horses. It's not recorded how much they had to drink.

A similar exercise in the paranormal was conducted at the Hollybush Inn at Grangemill, near Winster, where the landlord told me that members of the visiting group were equally convinced of the presence of 'unnatural' goings-on. Apparently there are frequent sightings around the pub of a woman called Alice, dressed in period clothing, and who can be seen in a very old photo on the wall by the front door standing behind a former landlady. The current landlord also mentioned three highwayman who have supposedly been seen plotting over their tankards in the back room.

The three-storeyed building has been both a working farm and inn for much of its life – which, depending on who you believe, might stretch back all the way to the 16th century. Located at a prominent crossroads at the top of Via Gellia and without much of a resident local community, it's likely that the Hollybush has always relied on passing trade and travellers to get by. But this may well have included some who were compelled to stay their against their will, as it's believed that the pub served as an overnight lock-up or holding prison for inmates being transferred between Derby and Manchester gaols. The evidence for this, which you can see for yourself, are the holes in the stone mullions of the main windows, which suggest they were once heavily barred. (Are spirits of any ex-prisoners still present, I wonder?)

Haunted houses

There are many ghosts and hauntings recorded at pubs across the Peak District, but one or two establishments seem to go a little overboard. An article in the *Derbyshire Times* of October 1995 suggested that the Crispin at Ashover is haunted by as many as 17 separate spirits, including monks, cavaliers, children and former landlords. However, in 2004 when the pub was being renovated workmen reported a number of unnerving experiences and the strange sensations of being pushed from behind. This persisted when customers subsequently began feeling cold draughts and sudden drops in temperature, which are apparently known as psychic breezes.

Although many pubs claim to have ghosts, some of these non-alcoholic spirits are a little more friendly than others. One of the upstairs bedrooms at the Wheatsheaf Hotel at Baslow is haunted by an ostler (a man employed to look after the horses at a coaching inn) who occasionally makes the journey across from the courtyard stables to the main building – except that the bridge that he uses that once connected the former stables disappeared many years ago. Apparently he has been seen more than once passing through the outside wall and moving across the bedroom.

Meanwhile, the Old Eyre Arms at Hassop is home to the ghost of a Cavalier who supposedly hid in an upstairs priest's hole to avoid being captured, since the Eyre family's seat at Hassop Hall was a Royalist stronghold during the Civil War. This malevolent, ill-tempered apparition still descends the stairs (now long-gone) which run down behind the bar, then goes out into the road.

There he is sometimes joined by a coach and horses, and according to a local tale, a passing motorist was once killed trying to swerve to avoid them. Before he expired he managed to explain that the horse-drawn carriage appeared to be coming straight towards him, and then afterwards vanished into thin air. On another occasion, one dark evening in the 1980s, a distraught stranger rushed into the pub saying that he had just run someone over with his car. Of course, everyone immediately went outside to help, but as hard as they looked, no-one was ever found.

Incidentally, the Eyre family is also associated with Highlow Hall, south west of Hathersage, once described by local author Roy Christian

The Old Eyre Arms at Hassop is reputedly haunted by a phantom Cavalier.

as "reputedly the most haunted house in Derbyshire". It's supposedly troubled by all manner of ghostly forms, including a murdered servant and the White Lady who came to a brutal and untimely end long ago in a bedroom.

The Old Nag's Head at Edale has been spooked by more recent events, if you believe certain people. Over the last 75 years a large number of aircraft have crashed on the high and treacherous moors of Kinder Scout and Bleaklow, and especially during the Second World War. Many were Allied planes returning from bombing missions, and due to bad weather and unfamiliar terrain they came to grief on the 2,000ft-high hills. After one such crash, the bodies of the RAF bomber crew were retrieved and carried down to the Old Nag's Head. Since then, several customers have reported seeing ghostly figures in airmen's uniform, and there have been unidentifiable sounds and voices around the pub.

A ghoulish woman dressed all in black is supposed to haunt the Travellers Rest pub in the Hope Valley, located opposite the turning to Bradwell. They say she died after falling down a spiral staircase while trying to escape the clutches of a drunken labourer on Christmas Eve many years ago, and can be witnessed each year on that same night, gliding along the upstairs corridor holding a bunch of keys.

The Duke of York at Pomeroy is haunted by the ghost of William Pomeroy, a local man who was killed in a horse-riding accident on the roadway outside several centuries ago. Apparently he is responsible for switching the kettle on when there's no-one around, hiding car keys, and everyday things like that.

Ghostly girls also feature at the Miner's Arms at Eyam, which despite the village's reputation surrounding the visitation of the Plague, seems to be doing well enough with unrelated ghouls and phantoms. The two little sisters are called Sarah and Emily, and they died when fire consumed the run-down shack which stood on the site of what later became the pub. One of the girls died in the fire, started accidentally when they were playing with a candle, and the other fell down a hidden mineshaft while trying to escape.

Former landlady Michele Hunt said that guests staying in Room 6 have reported hearing a girl shouting out the name "Emily!", while others speak about strange noises, especially footsteps, and unexplained cold spots. "People come here specifically to stay in the haunted room," she says, "while others learn of the stories once they get here and are too scared to go back to their room. You have to be a believer, of course, but we've never heard or seen anything ourselves, because we live in the cottage next door and not on the premises."

A previous landlord said he heard a clock being wound up in the early hours, and his daughter's record player began playing in an empty room. He also reported that the air on the landing was always cold, despite his repeated efforts to heat it, and that his family all heard the mysterious sound of heavy footsteps and rustling of a skirt in the corridor outside – even though it was thickly-covered by deep-pile carpet. Only later did it come to light that over 200 years ago an earlier landlord murdered his wife by forcing her along the landing and pushing her downstairs.

This may also be the apparition encountered by a former chairman of the parish council, who reported seeing an elderly woman dressed in a bonnet and old-fashioned clothes enter the building not long after it had been refurbished. Apparently she wandered about in a confused state for some time before vanishing into thin air.

At the Thorn Tree Inn in Matlock an old wall clock in the lounge bar is said to be haunted, based on the fact that it goes forwards then backwards apparently at a whim and without any human intervention. On my last visit it seemed to have decided to wind back time and the seconds hand was spinning round anti clockwise, which if nothing else must be handy when 'last orders' approaches.

A ghost dressed in Victorian clothes and known as Old Sarah is purported to roam the George Hotel in Tideswell late at night in search of her long-lost husband, and on one occasion in the 1930s scared away an entire party of guests.

A young girl supposedly haunts the Rising Sun at Middleton-by-Wirksworth, and it is said that in the 1950s when the landlord was undertaking some rebuilding work he came across a secret, boarded-up bedroom. Meanwhile, the Strines Inn in South Yorkshire is said to be haunted by a Grey Lady who can be seen wandering along the former driveway in a melancholy fashion.

A large, framed print of the Laughing Cavalier by Frans Hals gazes down from the oak-panelled wall of the reception room at the Norfolk Arms at Ringinglow, but when staff once tried to move it all sorts of unexplained and eerie things started happening throughout the pub – so the picture was swiftly moved back and, of course, they all stopped.

The Derwentwater Arms at Calver is another pub which is supposed to be haunted, but the ghost in question is actually a previous landlord. Apparently he was fond of practical jokes, and one day pretended to be dead by lying motionless under a sheet in the bar. However, his just desserts came the next day. He was travelling back from Bakewell market when he fell from his horse and was killed, and his ghostly presence is supposed to remain in the building.

A long-departed landlord is supposed to still frequent the Queen Anne at Great Hucklow, where he apparently died in the cellar; while in Bakewell the Peacock Hotel is prone to mischievous pranks of a former landlord's daughter from the 1840s. The girl, called Harriet, is often blamed for turning off the beer pumps and switching lights on or off.

According to Nicky Crewe, who for many years led regular 'ghost walks' in the town, another of Bakewell's haunted pubs is the Wheatsheaf, on Bridge Street. She said that here the supernatural presence is through smell, with customers reporting the sharp and unpleasant smell of rough pipe tobacco in otherwise empty rooms. Apparently it's the same brand used by a pipe-smoking former regular, long since departed for the great public house in the sky.

"Old pubs and inns are a common place to find ghosts and unexplained happenings," said Nicky, who completed an M.A. in folklore and cultural traditions at Sheffield University. "They are a great example of what are known as 'liminal' places, which means that they represent a threshold or a crossing-point of different forces. With their cellars, attics, stairs and corridors, not to mention all the people who pass through them over the years, they provide an interface between two worlds."

People have also spoken of ghostly goings-on at the Miners Standard, in Winster. They take the form of unexplained noises, such as footsteps in empty rooms and doors creaking. Others report hearing a girl (apparently called Mary) singing 'Three Blind Mice', although I have found another source which claims it is sung in the weak and shaky voice of an old woman. Either way, there is a framed parchment on the wall with more background to these mysterious happenings.

Mind you, pub-goers in Winster might be relieved that they no longer have to set foot in the Angel Inn, which once occupied the three-storeyed building opposite the old Market House. According to local stories, the pub was haunted by a headless bride in a wedding dress. One woman spied her in a mirror while putting on make-up, and such was the shock that she fainted with fright.

Spooky nuptials also concern nearby Winster Hall, for a while a pub in the 1980s and early '90s. Apparently it is haunted by two young lovers, the well-to-do daughter of the house and the lowly coachman, whose relationship was frowned upon and the union strictly forbidden. Instead, marriage to another man was hastily arranged, but the night before the wedding the two sweethearts flung themselves off the balustrade to their death. Inevitably their ghosts remain, and the Hall is sometimes referred to as Lover's Leap. Other stories tell of long-locked doors suddenly found open, and strange noises in the night. A soldier who was billeted at the Hall during the Second World War was so alarmed by a nocturnal apparition that he fired off his revolver at it.

If you stay at the Red Lion at Wirksworth be prepared to bump into a headless coachman dressed in a dark green cloak and striding along the corridor or wandering about the yard. This unfortunate man met his end a couple of centuries back, when the pub was a busy coaching inn. The story goes that he was approaching the pub, as usual sitting high up on his box, when for some reason the horses bolted forwards under the archway and the coachman didn't duck in time.

However, in terms of the sheer number of sightings the most haunted pub in the Peak District is probably the Castle Hotel at Castleton, which is rumoured to have as many as four separate confirmed ghosts. A bustling and popular place in the daytime and early evening, this former 17th-century coaching inn has some more unusual guests at other times – if you believe the stories.

The pub has variously been a beerhouse, post office, court house and mortuary, which may go a little way to explaining its rather complicated haunting arrangements. First up is a small, elderly woman called Agnes, about five foot four and who wears her hair in a bun. She is supposed to be have been a former housekeeper, and walks around the pub in a black uniform and white apron. Another story relates to a soldier and a nurse who have been seen in the cellar; while two former licensees reports witnessing a 50-year-old man in a blue pin-striped suit near the (now closed) side entrance. He was a local man called Mr Cooper, who

lived on nearby Castle Street and regularly popped into the pub for a drink in the early 1900s. However, because his wife didn't

The Castle Inn at Castleton – stay in Room 4 if you dare!

approve, he tried to be discreet and always used the side entrance. The story goes on to relate how, by trade, he was a tin miner, but on Sunday he would dress up in his best outfit to enjoy a leisurely drink at the pub. He died, of course, on a Sunday, wearing the pin striped suit.

In both instances, witnesses describe how the apparitions of Agnes and Mr Cooper simply vanished into thin air.

There is also a newspaper report from 1962 recounting how the Castle's new landlord and a friend both saw a hazy figure of a woman appearing to wade waist-deep and without any difficulty through the floorboards of the corridor. A later inspection of the building revealed that the corridor had been raised during earlier structural work, and that the ghostly figure was probably walking along the level of the original floor.

However, if you want the full-on experience and have already survived Room 6 of the Miner's Arms at Eyam, then book yourself into Room 4 of the Castle. It's located upstairs on the front corner of the building, overlooking the road, and is reportedly haunted by a Grey Lady called Rose.

One explanation is that she was a chambermaid at the hotel who tended its gardens and sold flowers to the guests; but the more common version is of her as a jilted bride. She supposedly walks along the corridor to the dining room to have her wedding breakfast, which of course was abandoned when the ceremony was called off. One servant who saw her gliding along the corridor in a white gown and a veil fled the building screaming, while staff say that many guests have reported feeling something creepy and unsettling in and around the room. What is remarkable is that these encounters have continued right up to modern times, so much so that there was a séance held in Room 4 in May 1999, when spiritualists believed they made contact with the unfortunate Rose.

Mermaids and murders

There are other pubs that while not haunted themselves, are associated with strange or dastardly tales. The (former) Mermaid Inn sits high and isolated on a moorland ridge in the Staffordshire corner of the Peak District. On a clear day the views are superb, and they say you can even see the mountains of North Wales; but when the biting wind rattles in or the mist is swirling off the desolate moorland it feels distinctly unwelcoming.

The pub was originally known as Blakemere House, after a nearby moorland pool called Blake Mere, and it is here in the dark and supposedly bottomless waters that the tragic and grisly tales emanate. According to legend, a man called Joshua Linnet drowned a beautiful young woman in the pool, believing her to be a witch. As she disappeared beneath the waters it is said that she had a look of the Devil, screaming vengeance on Linnet. Three days later he was found dead, drowned in Blake Mere, his face seared as if by talons. Ever since then the siren has haunted the pool, appearing at midnight to haul the unsuspecting into the depths. The saying goes:

> *She calls on you to greet her*
> *combing her dripping crown*
> *and if you go to greet her,*
> *She ups and drags you down.*

(Incidentally, if you're a convinced sceptic and consider this is a load of 'cock and bull', you might be interested to know that the expression comes from a pub setting. The Cock and the Bull were rival pubs at Stony Stratford in Buckinghamshire, but such was the competition that news and gossip picked up at one was quickly exchanged with customers from the other. Of course, things got exaggerated in the telling, so that

In one particularly harsh winter customers at the former Mermaid Inn turned up on skis (photo courtesy of the Peak District National Park Authority).

the more preposterous sounding tales became known as a 'Cock and Bull story'.)

A more credible tale dates from 1679 and concerns Andrew Simpson, an ostler at the Red Lion at Leek, but who had an ulterior motive for getting to know the inn's wealthier customers, for he was also a robber on the side. One of his luckless victims was a woman pedlar from Bakewell who had come to Leek market to sell thread and cloth. Aware that she had made some money before returning home, Simpson ambushed her on the moors above Leek near Blake Mere, then strangled the poor woman before weighing her body down and throwing her in the pool. But he made the mistake of giving away some of the stolen linen and lace to a maidservant at the Mermaid Inn, and after this was traced and the pool dragged for her body, Simpson was arrested and hanged for murder.

Other pubs have also been associated with grisly goings on. A Scottish pedlar (they were often called 'Scottish' because they sold cheap Scottish linen) met an untimely end at the Moon Inn at Stoney Middleton, when two rival pedlars – jealous of his success at the Eyam Wakes – dragged him outside and, it is believed, did away with him. Two decades later his body was eventually discovered in a nearby cave and identified by his distinctive buckled shoes. The man's bones were removed to Eyam Church where they were later buried, while his shoes were taken away and worn by a local bellringer.

Another gruesome event was the so-called Winnats Murder, when a young couple running away to get married at the church at Peak Forest met their untimely end in the spectacular limestone gorge of Winnats Pass near Castleton in 1758.

Allan and Clara were first documented stopping at the Royal Oak Inn at Stoney Middleton to feed their horses, but it was while they dining at an inn at Castleton that they were sized up by a group of drunken miners who had noticed the well-off strangers whom they suspected of carrying money and valuables. They laid in wait for the couple further up the valley by Odin Mine, and dragging them into a barn proceeded to rob and murder them.

The bodies were eventually thrown down the mineshaft and discovered a decade later; but according to the well-known story, although the five miners were never made accountable for their crimes, they all lived out sad and desperate lives after the double murder. One was later killed by a falling stone near the scene of the crime, another broke his neck in an accident, a third committed suicide, the fourth went insane and the last made a death-bed confession. It is said that on stormy nights you can still hear the ghosts of Allan and Clara wailing in the Winnats Pass, and what purports to be Clara's red leather saddle is on show in Speedwell Cavern museum shop at the foot of the Pass (it was kept at the former Royal Oak in Stoney Middleton for many years).

Another place that can sometimes feel bleak and evoke an eerie atmosphere is Wardlow Mires. It's a bare limestone plateau between Tideswell and Eyam and home to the renowned Three Stags Heads, described in Chapter 2. The name of the location is hardly redolent of sunny dales and tinkling streams, so no wonder that it was once the haunt of highwaymen who used to prey on travellers using the Chesterfield to Manchester route.

Perhaps the most notorious outlaw was Black Harry, a local highwayman who frequented the former Bull's Head in the nearby village of Wardlow. He stood and delivered for the last time around 1700, and after being apprehended he was hanged and gibbeted, with the gibbet post erected opposite the Three Stags Heads.

The same fate awaited 21-year-old Anthony Lingard from Tideswell who, in 1815, was in fact the last person to be gibbeted in Derbyshire. He had been convicted of the brutal murder of Hannah Oliver, the tollkeeper of the Wardlow Mires turnpike. Her body was discovered by the landlady of the Three Stags Heads, and it is said that a few days later Lingard actually watched the funeral procession pass by from the doorway of a pub. Unfortunately for him he was arrested after a pair of new red shoes he had taken from Mrs Oliver for his girlfriend were found at his home (a shoemaker from Stoney Middleton identified them as a pair he had made for the late tollkeeper).

He was tried at Derby Assizes, found guilty and hanged. Afterwards, Lingard's corpse was brought back in a cart to a gibbet near Wardlow Mires under military escort. According to eyewitness accounts, there was something of a carnival atmosphere at Wardlow, with stalls and entertainers. A preacher called John Longden, who that day had walked 15 miles to preach at Tideswell only to find the chapel empty, carried on to Wardlow and instead conducted an impromptu outdoor sermon (curiously, he was later to become the landlord at the Snake Inn). Lingard's bones rattled in their metal cage in what is still known as Gibbet Field, near Peter's Stone, for eleven years.

More recently, in 1927, the landlady of the Lantern Pike Inn (then called the New Inn) at Little Hayfield, 36-year-old Amy Collinson, was brutally murdered on the premises. Her husband had gone out for the day, and when he arrived back he found Amos Dawson, one of the pub's regulars, standing puzzled on the doorstep wondering why the pub wasn't yet open. Inside they found Amy lying in a pool of blood, a knife stuck in her throat.

The police soon found that a small amount of money was missing (less than £40) and as they began to interview local men, including the pub's regular customers, suspicion began to fall on George Hayward. He was unemployed and in debt, and a witness remembered seeing Hayward on the morning of the murder wearing a black mac, even though it was dry. Hayward explained that he had called into the pub for cigarettes that morning before catching the bus to New Mills to collect his dole. However, another neighbour had seen Hayward cutting a lead pipe outside his home, and the matching length of piping was then located in the water cistern at the pub. There was also blood stains on Hayward's hat that matched the landlady's blood group, and a search of his house revealed money stuffed up the chimney. It seemed pretty conclusive.

In February 1928 Hayward was tried at Derby Assizes, and even though the trial had to be restarted after a juryman collapsed when listening to the gory details of the murder, Hayward was found guilty and was hanged by Thomas Pierrepoint in March 1928.

And to wrap up this grisly section we finish with a tale about some pub customers who really were out for the count. For many centuries the Chequers Inn below Froggatt Edge was a welcome stop-off for travellers on the long haul between the Derwent Valley and Sheffield; but in the 1800s there were some particularly unsavoury regulars. It was a time of the so-called body-snatchers, when surgeons and medical schools were looking for human cadavers for anatomy lectures and to practice dissection, resulting in an illicit but flourishing trade in stealing fresh corpses from burial sites. The Chequers Inn developed a reputation as a haunt for these resurrectionists, as they were sometimes called. It's said that they temporarily stashed

The Chequers Inn at Froggatt Edge was once frequented by body-snatchers.

some of the corpses in nearby Padley Wood, while at other times 'stiffs' were simply left in the cart outside. This could lead to unfortunate encounters, however. On one occasion the pub ostler went over to an unaccompanied passenger waiting in a trap outside the pub, but getting no response to his attempted conversation he gave the person a nudge – only for them to slump forward and reveal themselves as a dead body.

Odd and odder

Sometimes the goings-on at particular hostelries in the Peak District are not so much spooky or morbid as just plain weird, and there are several peculiar annual 'competitions' which are held at pubs that certainly do not feature at any Olympic Games.

It may be the effect of too much booze, but some distinctly odd sporting contests have been dreamt up by people in pubs. There's the annual man vs horse competition held for the last 40 years at the Neuadd Arms in Mid Wales (a 22-mile cross country marathon); the world gravy-wrestling championships held each year at the Rose 'n' Bowl pub in Lancashire; and the world conker championships that began as an idea at the Chequered Skipper pub in Northamptonshire back in 1965 when a group of regulars looked for something else to do as the weather was too bad to go fishing. To that bizarre list, Peak District pubs can proudly lay claim to toe wrestling and hen racing.

The toe-wrestling world championships originally began at the Olde Royal Oak at Wetton, a village south west of Hartington which is popular with walkers. However, in past years, if any had dropped by on a particular summer's weekend they would be surprised to find that they weren't the only ones massaging their hot and aching feet. In fact, they could well be treated to the sight of a large and animated group of people taking off their shoes and socks to see who had the most powerful toes in the world.

It is said that toe wrestling began in 1976 when regulars at the Olde Royal Oak decided to search for a game that the British could win. It loosely resembles arm wrestling (except with toes, of course), with competitors locking digits in an attempt to force over an opponent's foot on a 'toe-dium' in the best of three 'toe-downs.' Apparently, if a competitor is in too much pain he or she can give in by shouting out the words "Toe Much!"

The competition involves three rounds played with the right foot, then left and right again; and there are men's and ladies categories. Such is the publicity that the contest attracts entrants, not to mention the media, from around the world. According to local legend, the championships were abandoned in 1977 after a Canadian tourist rather unsportingly won the title; but they were resurrected in the 1990s when a new landlord at the Royal Oak discovered the original rules. Apparently in 1997 organisers applied for its inclusion in a future Olympic Games, but perhaps not surprisingly the International Olympic Committee turned the request down.

In 2004 the championships moved to the Bentley Brook Inn at Fenny Bentley, a few miles away, but the competition remains as fiercely-contested as ever and bruised and even broken digits are not uncommon. After winning his 14th world title in 2017, Alan 'Nasty' Nash explained that having long toes doesn't necessarily give you an advantage. He explained how his own were "short and stubby, which is good... because they don't snap as easily." One year he broke four toes in a semi-final bout, but still went on to win the championship. In 2019 the competition returned to the Royal Oak at Wetton and in 2020 transferred to a nearby holiday park.

The Peak District is generally not known for its race meetings, with just a handful of annual events like the point-to-point Flagg Races, and harness racing at Pikehall. (Regulars at the Horse and Jockey public house at Tideswell have quite a long trek to their nearest race course.) However, at the village of Bonsall, near Matlock, a more unusual type of racing takes place on the first Saturday of August every year, when chickens (yes – chickens) are raced across the car park outside the Barley Mow.

The 200-year-old pub holds regular live events (music, poetry, film) and they even brew their own beer (see Chapter 9), but a quirky and bohemian air runs throughout the pub, typified by its near obsession with chickens. It manifests itself in a wealth of hen memorabilia, including chicken wallpaper, all in homage to the annual spectacle of live hens racing each other in a competition that's free to watch and open to anyone with a hen. In past years as many as 30 birds have been lined up at the start and the fowl are very gently coerced down a narrow track between plastic safety fences, with their owners shouting and hollering encouragement and offering handfuls of feed at the far end beyond the winning line. It draws large crowds and considerable media interest. Landlord Mick Boam told me that an Iranian TV crew has even covered the event, although what on earth its domestic audience must make of it is anybody's guess.

Incidentally, the Barley Mow is also one of the few Peak District pubs specifically mentioned in a best-selling work of modern fiction. *Pastures Nouveaux* by Wendy Holden is about a young couple's ill-fated search for rustic bliss in the fictional village of Eight Mile Bottom ("but there are unexpected thrills in the hills...").

And proving that truth is sometimes stranger than fiction, the thrills at the Barley Mow don't end with chicken racing. The pub also organises its own 'Strong Man/Woman' competition, in which biceps ripple in an attempt to heave beer barrels, tractor tyres and telegraph poles around the pub car park. And then there are the UFOs...

Over the last few decades strange lights have been spotted above nearby Slaley Moor so often, and reported by so many different people, that Bonsall has made national news and UFO-spotters come to the location from all over the country to gaze up at the heavens. Over 100 unidentified sightings have been recorded in the skies above Bonsall and Slaley in the past 30 years and the previous landlord of the Barley Mow even led UFO tours around the area.

Toe-wrestling and hen-racing is matched by equally bizarre pub pursuits in the north of the Peak District. A peculiar challenge takes place inside the Peels Arms at Padfield, near Glossop. It began around the 1950s when workmen, who were staying in the area to erect new electricity pylons and had been 'relaxing' in the pub at the end of the day, dared each other to squeeze through a small hole in the wall to the side of the bar. The gap in question is through an interior wall next to the main bar, and measures roughly 27cm by 41cm, and is 47com deep (I measured it on my last visit). It's vaguely keyhole-shaped and was presumably left as a decorative feature

The Barley Mow, Bonsall, celebrates all things chicken.

Peels Arms landlord Phil Flanagan next to the celebrated hole in the wall.

and sometimes holds a vase of flowers.

After the workmen successfully squeezed through the tiny opening the new past-time of 'holing' was born. Although it seems so small only a child would fit through (and many do), apparently plenty of adults manage the feat, although one or two sometimes get stuck and need a helping hand. There's a special knack to holing. You have to go head-first, from one direction only (aiming towards the bar), and with one arm out front you twist your body through the fissure.

Successful 'holers' used to get a free pint of beer, but this was stopped after the pub's barrels began to empty rather too fast, and now you receive a certificate to commemorate your achievement instead. It's headed 'The Order of the Hole', and records that so and so '…has passed through the Hole under the watchful eyes of the Hole-Minders'. The Hole-Minders are, inevitably, the locals, who no doubt offer advice and encouragement.

A few miles away on the high moors an especially gruelling event involving pubs and beer has been occurring every October for the last few years. It all began one day in 1998 when local shepherd Geoff Townsend, a regular at the Old Nags Head in Edale, complained to the landlord that the pub had run out of his favourite beer. He jokingly offered to nip across the moors to the Snake Pass Inn and fetch a new barrel. The only problem was that, although the two pubs are less than four miles away as the crow flies, there's the small matter of the 2,000ft barrier of Kinder Scout in between, complete with steep slopes, as well as the peat hags and groughs of Kinder's infamous bog. However, the landlord told Geoff that if he succeeded he could enjoy the contents for free, so a small group set off for the Snake Pass and brought back a barrel strapped to a borrowed mountain rescue stretcher – and so the Great Kinder Beer Barrel Challenge was born.

Today, the annual competition sees teams of eight race between the Snake Inn and the Nag's Head carrying a nine-gallon beer barrel (called a firkin and weighing 98lb/44kg) on a home-made stretcher, ladder or similar contraption. The event raises money for local charities, with the aching winners coming away with a trophy and, most appropriately, a free firkin of beer for their efforts. Incidentally, the barrel that each team carries up and down Kinder Scout is full of water, not beer; and the rules stipulate that two team members must remain in contact with the barrel at all times, so it can't simply be rolled or slid down the hillside!

Another formidable pub-to-pub challenge is provided by the annual Four Inns race, which sees pre-registered teams of four setting off to complete a gruelling 45-mile hillwalk in 24 hours. The route was devised in 1922 by the legendary Fred Heardman, one-time landlord of both the Old Nag's Head and Rambler Inn at Edale.

In 1957, the 51st Derby Rover Scouts organised the first Four Inns race, which then as now begins at Holmbridge, on the southern edge of Holmfirth, and from the site of the long-disappeared Isle of Skye pub heads south across the windswept moors of Black Hill, Bleaklow and Kinder Scout, taking in the Snake Pass Inn and Old Nag's Head at Edale. The entire route is off-road, across high and often boggy moorland tracks where the weather can be unpredictable to say the least. Good map-reading and navigation skills are as important as fitness and stamina, as I found out when I tackled it (successfully) in 2016. The route continues via Chapel-en-le-Frith and the Goyt Valley to reach the last

In recent years, teams from Matlock Athletic Club have triumphed in the gruelling Kinder Beer Barrel Challenge (photo courtesy of Matlock Athletic Club).

pub, the Cat and Fiddle, high on the Cheshire moors, after which the weary and footsore walkers stagger down the old Roman road to finish at Harpur Hill on the edge of Buxton.

To give some idea of the seriousness of the challenge, three Rover Scouts died from fatigue and hypothermia while attempting the Four Inns Walk in March 1964. But out of this tragedy, the Peak District Mountain Rescue service was born.

Cuckoos and garlands

The Riverhead Brewery Tap at Marsden in West Yorkshire (see Chapter 9) has been involved in the annual celebration of Cuckoo Day each April. It remembers the old cuckoo legend, which tells how some people thought that if they captured a cuckoo they would also be able to usher in the spring, since the one is said to herald the other. So when a group of Marsden men saw a cuckoo in a tree they decided to build a wall around it in order to capture the bird, but just as they put the last stone in place it flew up and away. The men were understandably upset, but their leader turned round to the others and said that they must have built the wall too low.

Cuckoo Day begins with a walk to the purported birthplace of the Marsden cuckoo, then in the evening there is live music and, in the past, a specially-brewed Riverhead beer called Ruffled Feathers has been sold. Various activities and events are held on the Saturday, including craft fairs, clog dancing and a duck race, and it all culminates in the Grand Cuckoo Procession, with plenty of special cuckoo hats on show.

In Castleton, a long-established tradition known as Garland Day is enacted on 29th May each year. The origin of this popular, ritual procession around the village is thought to go back to the restoration of the monarchy in 1660, like similar Oak Apple Day commemorations that marked the end of the Puritan era; although some believe that it is actually much older and may stem from ancient pagan fertility rites. Either way, it requires the Garland King to wear an elaborate, wooden-framed and bell-shaped garland of flowers – which at 3ft high and weighing 30kg must be quite a task! Accompanied by his consort, crowds of onlookers and Castleton Band playing the Garland Tune, the King parades around the village on horseback and visits each of Castleton's six pubs in turn where there is a small dance (and invariably some beer consumed). At the end of Garland Day the garland is winched up the church tower and left there until the flowers have wilted.

The Derby Tup

There's a live performance that is believed to be unique to Derbyshire and its pubs, but sadly it is rarely seen these days. Until the 1960s it was still fairly common to encounter a group of four young men touring Derbyshire pubs around Christmas to earn some extra money by putting on the Derby Tup (also known as the Old Tup or Derby Ram). The performance involved miming and singing and began with a plea from the four men for beer:

> *Here comes me and my old lass,*
> *Short o'money, short o'brass;*
> *Pay for a pint and let's all sup,*
> *Then we'll show you our jolly Old Tup.*

The last two lines sometimes appeared as:

> *Gather around us and come close up,*
> *And we will perform you the Derby Tup.*

The origins of the performance are unknown, but the ballad was familiar as far back as the 18th century, and was particularly common in the north east of the county. Some have conjectured that its roots lie in a guising or mumming play.

The tale surrounds a mother and father taking a tup (a male sheep) to the butchers for slaughter. One of the four men would dress up as the ram, occasionally with just a sackcloth over his head, but at other times with a more elaborate costume involving a real sheep's skull. The second player acted out the part of the butcher, wielding a large stick or knife with which he would pretend to thump the unfortunate beast. The third dressed as a woman and the fourth player had a blackened face and carried a basin. The number of verses varied, but began in similar fashion:

> *As I was going to market upon a market day,*
> *I met the finest ram, Sir, that was ever fed on hay...*

The performance took between 10-15 minutes to complete, and involved the tup entering the slaughterhouse and threatening everyone within, while the others made claim and counter-claim about the animal's prowess:

> *This tup was fat behind,*
> *This tup was fat before,*
> *This tup was ten yards high,*
> *If not a little more.*

The wool that grew upon its back
It grew so mighty high,
That eagles built their nest in it
You could hear the young ones cry.

The words and even the verses tended to vary between locations, and no doubt there was some variation and elaboration depending on how much beer had been consumed; but the end result was usually that the unfortunate tup met his end, with everyone gathering around to discuss what was left:

All the boys in Derby,
Came begging for his eyes,
To punch them out for footballs,
For they were just a size.

And all the women in Derby,
Came begging for his ears,
To make their leather aprons of,
To last them forty years.

In Derby, people use to gild the horns of their rams when performing the play, which has prompted suggestions that it might have some distant connection with the Roman custom of gilding the horns of animals for sacrifice. The performance is rarely acted out these days, which is perhaps a reflection both on modern pubs and pub-goers as well as a waning interest in local traditions and customs. However, since the Derby Tup (or ram) is the mascot of Derby County Football Club, it's likely to remain lodged somewhere in the county's conscience for a while to come. Special thanks to Jim McIntosh, former Chairman of the Chesterfield and District CAMRA group, who was responsible for researching most of this information.

Another traditional performance that was acted out in certain pubs at Christmas and the New Year was the 'Old Horse'. This ancient folk play took the form of an unaccompanied ballad chanted by several men and enacted by one dressed in a black cloak topped by a symbolic, stylised horse's head. In later years the head was described as a large, fearsome-looking papier mâché construction formed around the skull of a blind pony killed when it fell down a quarry. It was fixed on to a broom handle so that the operator, hidden in the material, could work the head and snap the jaws as the story unfolded. The gallant animal would fall to the ground in the throes of death, then miraculously resurrected would rise once more in celebration.

When the enactment was over a hat was passed round, or the men would be offered drinks. The group would visit pubs, farms and well-to-do houses, and it seems to have been centred on north east Derbyshire, especially around Dronfield and what is today the Sheffield suburb of Dore (but part of Derbyshire until 1934). Indeed, the few details that survive are courtesy of the Dore Village Society.

Although its origins are unclear, the Old Horse appears to have survived well into the 20th century. As with many of these kinds of performances, there was much merry-making and a fair amount of heavy drinking, but on one occasion it ended in tragedy. A report in the *Derbyshire Times* from January 1869 described how a man was lost on the moors following a rendition:

> *A number of persons, including James Greenwood and Thomas Oxley, had left Dronfield the previous Thursday to go to Barlow and neighbouring villages, to act in what is well known in Derbyshire as the 'Old Horse'. On Friday evening Greenwood and his comrades visited the Bulls Head Inn, Calver. Words of an angry character are said to have passed between Greenwood and Oxley, which ultimately ended in a fight, and Greenwood leaving the party, as it is supposed, to go home. He was last seen as late as 12 o'clock at night, and being defective in sight and also worse for liquor at the time he left the Inn, it is supposed that he may have (being a stranger) missed his way, and perished on some part of the moors, or otherwise have got into the river Derwent, which was much swollen by the heavy rain falling at the time.*

The paper went on to describe his appearance:

> *He is of middle stature, with a scar on his left cheek near to the jaw, and had on two coats, one of fustian and a dark overcoat mended at the elbow of one of the sleeves, dark trousers and a pair of light clogs...*

The following issue of the *Derbyshire Times* reported that his body had been found in the River Derwent, only a quarter of a mile from the pub.

Out of place

Elsewhere, it's the pub itself, or what surrounds it, that can be rather unusual. An example is the Little Mill Inn at Rowarth, a hamlet tucked away in the rolling green upland between New Mills and Glossop.

There has been a mill at this location since the early 1600s, but the present building was built in 1781 as a candlewick mill. The pub was on the lower floor – where it still is today – together with a shop for the

The Little Mill Inn at Rowarth, complete with historic railway carriage.

millworkers, since there were several other mills in the area. Production ended in 1930 when a disastrous flood swept through, taking with it several buildings and the original water wheel. The replica wheel, 36ft high and with 32 spokes, can be viewed from the terrace by the side of the building and, now fully working once more, it's a great sight.

However, this splendid relic of the industrial age has a rival for customers' attention, for situated in the grounds at the other end of the pub is an authentic, 70ft-long Pullman railway carriage. The Derbyshire Belle once saw service on the London to Brighton line, and still retains its original Art Deco wood panelling and brass fittings. It's been used by the pub as a restaurant and deluxe B&B accommodation for guests.

Taking the pledge

As we've seen at Edale, when the barrel runs dry one solution is to hoof it over the moors to another pub and get a full one. But once there was a popular social movement whose aim was to get rid of the barrels entirely and encourage people to abstain from the demon drink. And one way of doing that was to establish temperance pubs and hotels.

Over the centuries there have been periodic attempts by the authorities to curb the numbers of alehouses, pubs, inns and taverns, amid concern at the harmful effects of alcohol on the population. This manifested itself in various ways, including trying to limit or reduce the alcoholic strength of the beer, restricting pub opening times, and so on. Of course, pubs and the brewing industry were important sources of revenue through taxes for the Government, and this ambivalent and arguably contradictory position for the authorities (that continues today) was evident in the see-sawing legislation from early times.

As far back as 1267 the Assize of Bread and Ale decreed a maximum price that beer could be sold that was linked to the price of barley. Over the following centuries various Acts attempted to impose some sort of authority over the spread of alehouses, until in 1619 a Royal Proclamation brought in much stricter requirement for would-be licensees to set up shop. It also acted to curb short measures and banned certain "sinful" games, such as dice, cards and skittles. However, the Beer Act of 1830 then served to relax many of the regulations and this led to a huge increase in beerhouses (where drink was consumed on the premises) and beershops (take away).

Almost certainly as a response, the London Temperance Society (later the British and Foreign Temperance Society) was founded in 1831, and people were urged to go teetotal and 'take the pledge'. What began as a largely working class movement soon attracted religious groups such as the Salvation Army and the Quakers, and before long there were numerous temperance societies, including the National Temperance Federation, Bands of Hope and the British Women's Temperance Association.

In the early days there was something of a split between those who favoured moderation, or just opposed drinking spirits, and sought to 'improve' public houses and those that frequented them, and the hard-liners who advocated total abstinence. But the Victorians' crusading morality helped usher in several Acts of Parliament which imposed tougher restrictions. The Licensing Acts of 1904 and 1910 began to rein in what many thought was an excessive and uncontrolled number of licensed establishments. There were new restrictions and regulations, and licensees were even offered compensation in return for not renewing their licences (see Chapter 8 on Glossop's former pubs). With the unfolding World War I as a sobering backdrop, the Intoxicating Liquor Act of 1914 went even further than previous Acts, increasing the tax on beer, reducing permitted opening hours, and even banning the buying of 'rounds' unless ordering with a meal.

Across the country, temperance inns and hotels were springing up to offer an alternative to the dens of iniquity that were pubs. There are plenty of examples throughout the Peak District, whether in towns such as Wirksworth, where old picture postcards show a temperance hotel above the shops in the main street, through to remote rural locations such as the Tollemarche Arms near Crowden in Longdendale, and Naylor's Temperance Hotel at Ecton Lea in the Manifold Valley.

The Red Lion (later Finderne House) in the village of Alstonefield became a temperance hotel, while the Travellers Rest Inn at Taddington was renamed Marlborough Temperance Hotel, and included a shop and café as well as accommodation.

As early as 1836, in Matlock, you could stay at Brown's Temperance Hotel and Family Boarding House on Dale Road. It was advertised as being close to Matlock Bridge Railway Station and was run by Miss H. Marriott. It had the added attraction, sadly for lady guests only, of 'Smedley's System of Hydropathic Treatment', the water treatment which had made the town famous.

In 1926, the Okeover Arms at Mappleton, near Ashbourne, decided to stop serving alcohol and become a temperance hotel, a situation only remedied in 1962 when brewers Ind Coope leased the premises. In Ashbourne itself, the town's Temperance Society was established in the 1840s, opening a coffee shop and gradually managing to cut the number of pubs.

The Victoria Cafe and Temperance Hotel on Market Street in Chapel-en-le-Frith advertised itself with the offer of "comfortable beds, always aired, at reasonable charges... every accommodation for cyclists, visitors and commercials".

Mind you, some individuals managed to see the error of their ways without any help. New Mills has always been a strong Methodist town, with almost as many chapels as there are pubs, but around Dye House Lane in particular there was a high concentration of licensed premises. Between what used to be the Pineapple Inn and the White Hart is a short and unremarkable-looking terraced row and it was here, in the last house, in the 1850s that a young stonemason called Thomas Handford put the demon drink behind him. On the wall of what was formerly New Mills Lock-up a plaque entitled 'A Drunkard's Reform' and dated 1854 explains more:

> *A working man, a teetotaller for ten years who was formerly a notorious drinker and notorious poacher, has recently invested his sober earnings in the purchase of the town prison which he converted into a comfortable dwelling house. Frequently an inmate of the prison whilst a drunkard and a poacher, he is now owner of the whole and occupier of the premises.*

A Drunkard's Reform – Thomas Handford's house in New Mills.

The original stone plaque is now in the New Mills Heritage Centre, where there is a fascinating exhibition charting the determined efforts of the New Mills temperance movement, which unsurprisingly seized upon Handford's miraculous conversion. Its newspaper *Sunday Companion* reported: "The man in question was so earnest in his teetotalism, and wanted his career as a drunkard to teach a valuable temperance object lesson, that he actually bought the prison in which he as confined scores of times for drunkenness and turned it into a house to live in."

Mind you, what it doesn't say is that according to one account Handford's conversion apparently followed a traumatic incident at the Cock Inn, which used to stand next to the prison, when his friend and drinking pal dropped dead beside him. After that Handford chose sobriety and never touched another drop. Let that be a lesson for us all!

CHAPTER SIX

Buildings Great and Small

The public houses of the Peak District come in all shapes, sizes and styles, from the traditional village hostelry through to the bustling urban tavern and elegant coaching inn. They occupy both humble cottages and opulent piles, sometimes merely functional but at other times designed to impress. Tracing the evolution of the pub as we know it today is an interesting exercise, stretching back as much as two millennia to Roman times when there was already a distinction between *diversoria* (drinking places) and *tabernae* (where travellers could stay). Over time this would set apart the alehouse, where brewing typically took place in people's own homes and where you went primarily to drink, and the inn or hotel where you went for lodgings. The term 'pub' or public house wasn't actually coined until the Victorian era.

Small and perfectly formed

What we consider today as the quintessential village pub can trace its roots back to traditional alehouses, where refreshment was served in basic household rooms through serving hatches or on simple counters. Over the years these private dwellings were converted or knocked through and became more respectable licensed premises. The Packhorse Inn at Little Longstone is typical. It began as a terraced row of two or possibly three miners' cottages, probably built in the 1600s, and became a pub in 1787, when its owner was recorded as a miner and innkeeper. The rooms are small, simple and cosy, and as its name suggests the pub was probably a regular stopping point for trains of packhorses and traders heading over Longstone Moor.

The Thorn Tree Inn at Matlock is a compact pub located amid the back streets high on the northern side of the town, and although not the easiest to find, it's definitely worth nosing out. The pub comprises two tiny bars – the 'smoke room' and 'public bar' – both of which are richly decorated by all manner of period memorabilia from the Edwardian

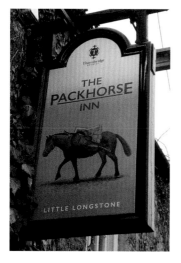

and Victorian eras. They're separated by the small entrance hall where, directly ahead, the serving hatch would have once dispensed off-sales.

Further down the Derwent valley is Crich, where the Cliff Inn was originally believed to have been built for the manager of the local quarry. Converted to a pub around in the middle of the 19th century, the two unpretentious bars are simply decorated and retain considerable character.

The Packhorse Inn at Little Longstone.

Connoisseurs of the pocket-sized rather than the pint-sized might also like to visit the Star Inn at Tideswell, Church Inn at Darley Dale and the White Hart at Bradwell. The Goyt Inn, at Whaley Bridge, is a cosy one-bar pub on a side-street near the canal basin, while a couple of miles away the earliest record of the Swan Inn at Kettleshulme apparently goes back to 1665. The roadside pub boasts two dark and atmospheric bars, with period seating and massive wooden beams. However, in 2015 the then owner decided to turn it into a house, but faced with the loss of their village local a consortium of regulars rallied around and raised enough funds and managed to buy it themselves and keep it open. Incidentally, the pub seems to have had a history of somewhat strong-minded landlords and landladies. According to an article in the *Guardian* from February 1962, the Ramblers' Association formally objected to the renewal of the licence of the Swan Inn on the ground that the licensee had refused to serve visiting ramblers. Landlady Mrs Ivy Kay said she had spent a lot of money on antique furniture and costly carpets throughout the pub and although the majority of ramblers were well-behaved there was a minority were "hooligans" and caused trouble. Macclesfield County Licensing Justices renewed the licence, but added: "We hope that a little more discretion will be shown in future by the licensee."

Like the Packhorse Inn at Little Longstone, the Red Lion at Litton is made up of three old cottages, in this case knocked through in 1787. It's a similar case at the Flying Childers at Stanton in Peak and the Ship Inn at Wincle (see Chapter 7 for more on both), two very traditional village pubs that ooze rustic charm.

Grand designs – coaching inns and hotels

Towards the other end of the scale are the traditional coaching inns, a few of which still survive reasonably intact. By their nature they tended to be large and busy affairs, with sizeable accommodation for guests and equally extensive stabling for their horses. The personnel needed to run such a place was considerable – from the publican, bar staff and maids, through to cooks, cellarmen and ostlers.

As we have seen in Chapter 3, many of these coaching inns have gone on to become popular modern hotels, but there are still some that stand out from the crowd because of their position and their history. Two of the most prominent, that in many ways dominate their respective towns, are the Rutland Arms in Bakewell and the Green Man and Black's Head Royal Hotel at Ashbourne.

The Rutland Arms Hotel, overlooking Rutland Square in the centre of Bakewell, boasts 33 en-suite rooms, including some annex rooms. It was built in 1804-05 on the site of the former White Horse Inn. The new building was an imposing Georgian construction, with the Tuscan portico carved by Bakewell sculptor White Watson. Railings lined the narrow front garden, matching those in Bath Gardens opposite, but all these were removed during the Second World War. For a few years the new tap room was known as the White Horse Bar; then later it became the Rutland Tavern before being sold off. The former stables, located across the road, were converted into extra accommodation.

It has been written that the hotel's distinguished past guests included Jane Austen, who is supposed to have stayed here in 1811 and used Bakewell as a model for the fictitious town of Lambton in *Pride and Prejudice* (the Rutland Arms being the inn where Elizabeth Bennett and Mr Bingley met). Unfortunately there's no evidence that any of this is true.

The Rutland Arms, here pictured in 1914, dominates the centre of Bakewell (copyright The Francis Frith Collection).

Far more certain, and for a lot of people I suspect of considerably more importance, is the fact that the Rutland Arms was where the Bakewell pudding was inadvertently created. The town's famous culinary export originated here in the 1850s, due to the carelessness of the hotel cook. Intending to prepare a strawberry tart, she poured the mixture of eggs over the strawberry jam instead of mixing it into the pastry, and what should have become a tart ended up a pudding. Luckily the result went down well with the guests, and a new gastronomic delicacy was established.

However, the content and whereabouts of the original recipe is hotly disputed, with at least one bakery/cafe claiming to have it locked away in a safe. Despite this, Bakewell puddings are widely available throughout the town, but do remember that they are not tarts, which are a completely different (and some would say inferior) product.

The Green Man and Black's Head Royal Hotel at Ashbourne (now reopened after a long closure and simply called The Green Man) is not especially notable for any culinary dish, but it does have several other claims to fame, and architecturally-speaking this 18th-century coaching inn is memorable for having one of the few surviving gallows signs left in England. It stretches right across St John Street, the main thoroughfare through the town centre, and although it's highly unlikely that it was ever used as a gallows the impressive and historic construction is certainly a rare sight these days. (Other surviving examples of gallows signs stretching across the road are Ye Olde Starre Inne in York and The George at Stamford.)

The Green Man's gallows sign across the road in Ashbourne, photographed in 2019, is one of the few of its kind left in Britain.

Perhaps not surprisingly most pub gallows signs have fallen victim to the changing shape and power of today's road vehicles, as well as stricter town planning laws. Although rare today, the gallows sign was once a fairly common sight and came about as publicans competed with each other to produce ever-more impressive and eye-catching advertisements for their premises. First, the swinging boards became larger and more prominent, then they began to stretch out into the highway.

Unfortunately other shopkeepers and traders did the same, and contemporary accounts suggest that simply negotiating the clutter of signs and notices festooned outside commercial premises could be an awkward and sometimes dangerous business. Early in the 1700s, for instance, a gallows sign outside a pub in London collapsed and dragged down the front of the house to which it was attached, killing two bystanders in the street below. Finally, in 1797, legislation was passed requiring the dismantling of signs considered a public hazard.

The Green Man at Ashbourne is famous for more than just its sign, however. Over the years the pubs of the Peak District have entertained many illustrious visitors, but two of Ashbourne's most notable were Dr Samuel Johnson and his companion and biographer James Boswell. Indeed, a plaque on the outside of the hotel wall records Boswell's visit in September 1777, not least because he afterwards praised the inn and the "mighty civil gentlewoman, curtseying very low." It is even conjectured that Dr Johnson had the Green Man in mind when he famously declared: "The tavern chair [is] the throne of human felicity. As soon as I enter the door of a tavern, I experience an oblivion of care, and a freedom from solicitude:"

Originally the full name of this historic Ashbourne establishment was the Royal Green Man and Blackamoor's Head Commercial and Family Hotel, which is surely one of the longest pub or hotel names in the country (it even beats a Stalybridge pub called the Old Thirteenth Cheshire Astley Volunteer Rifleman Corps Inn, which was often quoted as holding this record). The present, three-storey brick building is mainly Georgian and dates from around 1750. It is, in effect, the result of two separate inns coming together. In 1825 the then landlord bought up his nearest rival, the Blackmoor's Head, only to promptly close it down and add its sign to his own. The 'royal' was added after the young Princess Victoria, together with her mother the Duchess of Kent, briefly stopped at the pub for refreshment in 1832.

Without doubt it was a busy coaching inn, since Ashbourne was on the route from Derby to Manchester, and at the rear was a large yard with extensive stabling. When the stagecoaches began to decline there was an omnibus service from the inn to Derby for a while. At the back of the inn there was also a cockpit for cock-fighting, for this was a place that attracted a wide custom.

In addition to the high volume of passing trade, the hotel was an important venue for local events and served as a meeting place for numerous groups and societies. Local magistrates held Petty Sessions in its assembly rooms every Saturday morning; and every other week the Ashbourne Poor Law Board of Guardians and a local friendly society known as the Female Sick Club also met there to dispense poor relief.

Perhaps the oddest story connected with the Green Man concerns a visiting elephant, as described on the website www.ourashbourne.co.uk. In September 1830 a 7.5 ton elephant, called Mademoiselle d'Jacque, stayed in the Green Man yard whilst her master stayed in the Inn. The elephant was on her way to Birmingham and followed behind her master who rode on a pony. The elephant was reported to have bowed to the toll gate keeper when entering the town; and one man was so terrified that he froze to the spot and exclaimed "Will nobody tell me what it is? Will nobody stop it?"

There are plenty of other similarly old and imposing establishments across the Peak District. The Old Hall Hotel in Hope stands on the site of a medieval hall that once belonged to the Balguy family. The Royal Hotel at Hayfield was originally built as a parsonage in 1755, becoming the Shoulder of Mutton later that century. In 1805, it was bought by the Park Hall estate and the church-going squire returned it to a parsonage, only to revert to a pub a few years later when the landowner quarrelled with the church and turned the new vicar out!

A postcard of Hayfield from 1909 showing the Royal Hotel on the right (courtesy of Steve Lewis).

However, despite appearances to the contrary, not all of these handsome places started out as public houses. The Old Clubhouse in Buxton, next to the Opera House, was built in 1886 as the Union Club and served as a gentlemen's club. It also hosted formal meetings of upstanding local societies, such as Buxton Archaeological and Natural History Society which met there from 1922 and whose members attended lectures in black tie and dinner jacket. In 1969 the club closed and the building became a pub; and with its high-ceilings, lavish staircase and Opera House memorabilia, it's a popular venue for concert guests.

The Whitworth Hotel is part of the larger Whitworth Institute, named after the famous Victorian industrialist (see Chapter 4); while further south along the Derwent valley are a number of imposing hotels, most of which date from the rise of Matlock Bath as a spa resort in the mid 1800s. For a time, its five thermal springs were all the rage, with trainloads of unhealthy visitors heading for the new hydros and baths that lined the picturesque gorge. The New Bath Hotel and Spa continues to offer one of the UK's only natural spring water open air swimming pools, since the warm springs of Matlock Bath emerge at up to 20 degrees Celsius year-round. Meanwhile, the Temple Hotel was a popular coaching inn which in its day attracted such notables as Lord Byron who purportedly wrote a poem on one of its window panes.

Matlock Bath's success as a centre for the trendy new vogue of hydrotherapy inspired attempts elsewhere, but to no great success, including at Bradwell with the New Bath Hotel. This pub is now known as the Samuel Fox Country Inn, but despite its different name it still has a sort of watery connection. Bradwell was the birthplace of Samuel Fox, a Victorian industrialist and businessman who began his career as a wire drawer apprentice in Hathersage. He moved to Sheffield where he made his name and fortune by founding the Stocksbridge Steel Company, but today he is probably best known as the inventor of Fox's Paragon Umbrellas – the classic folding umbrella.

Keeping the faith

The Peak District doesn't boast too many castles, so it's no surprise to find that there are only a couple of pubs so-named. You can gaze up at the hilltop remains of the Norman Peveril Castle from the Castle pub on Castle Street in Castleton. Meanwhile Bakewell's Castle Inn remembers a motte and bailey castle which once stood on the small hill just across the bridge over the River Wye. The pub was previously called

Celebrations at the Church Inn, Darley Dale, c1929.

the Commercial and Castle, and for over 100 years hosted a regular horse market. Its three garages abutting the pavement were once stables.

In addition to two castle inns, there are two church inns at Darley Dale and Chelmorton, plus a Church House Inn sandwiched between terraced houses on Church Street in Bollington.

The Church Inn at Darley Dale is near St Helen's Church, with its ancient yew tree (see Chapter 4), while Chelmorton's is opposite the Church of St John the Baptist in this small village high on the limestone upland south of Buxton. So high is it, in fact, that Chelmorton's parish church is officially the highest in Derbyshire at 1,209ft (367m). The spire is topped by a locust weathervane, depicting St John's survival in the wilderness when he got by on locusts and honey. The bells were salvaged from the former church at the village of Derwent, which was dismantled in 1952 in order to build the Derwent Reservoir (more on this momentous event below). The pub was originally known as the Blacksmith's Arms and recorded as such in the 1870s when the landlord was also the village smithy.

Still on the subject of churches and pubs, there's an entertaining tale concerning the Miner's Arms at Eyam. In 1648 the Rev. Hunt was called to the pub to baptise the landlord's sick child. Unfortunately, the man of the cloth joined the assembled crowd afterwards and drank heavily, so much so that he ended up getting married there and then to Anne, the landlord's daughter. Alas, the reverend was already engaged to a lady from Derby, who when she heard about what had happened proceeded to sue him. As a result, Rev. Hunt was forced to flee the vicarage, and he and his new and possibly rather startled wife were forced to live in the church crypt, where they went on to bring up several children.

Bridges and reservoirs

Castles and churches are not the only man-made structures which are commemorated by Peak District pubs; bridges also feature quite prominently. The Bridge Inn at Calver is sited next to the historic crossing of the River Derwent which was originally a ford and then a wooden bridge. The old stone construction, which had stood for centuries, was joined by a graceless modern concrete affair in 1974.

Wye Bridge House at Buxton is located, as you would expect, near a crossing point over the infant River Wye; although with so much urban development, including a prominent railway viaduct, the actual bridge itself is almost forgotten. The river rises not far away at Poole's Cavern on the town's southern edge.

Perhaps the most famous named bridge in the Peak District, or at least the one that gives its name to a pub, is the Yorkshire Bridge, which dates from 1826. The pub is north of Bamford and named after a nearby packhorse bridge, still marked on Ordnance Survey maps, which at one time was said to be the only crossing point over the River Derwent for travellers between Derbyshire and the Yorkshire West Riding.

Nowadays you have to cross a wider expanse of water, as the Upper Derwent valley is dominated by three mighty reservoirs – Ladybower, Derwent and Howden – but, despite the changes, pubs still feature in the story of the valley.

After the Yorkshire Bridge Inn you come to the Ladybower Inn on the A57 Snake Road to Sheffield. It was originally a farmstead, but for a while in the 1700s served as a morgue after a series of local murders.

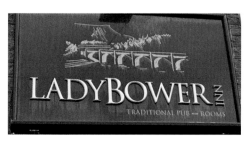

The present roadside inn was originally sited a little further up Ladybower

The sign for the Ladybower Inn depicts the famous viaduct across the reservoir.

Brook, but moved to its present position about a century ago. The interior of the pub includes prints and photographs connected with the valley and the reservoir; but if you think fishing and Lancaster bombers are odd bedfellows you must first understand a little more about the recent history of the Upper Derwent.

The three reservoirs you see today were built to provide drinking water for the growing cities of Sheffield and the East Midlands, and work started on the Howden and Derwent dams in 1901. Forty-four years later the last of the three (Ladybower) was officially opened, with King George VI and Queen Elizabeth unveiling the new, 140ft (43m) dam. However, the creation of these huge reservoirs came at a cost.

The village of Ashopton, including the historic Ashopton Inn, was demolished, and what little remains now sits beneath 6,310 million gallons (27.9 cubic metres) of water contained in the Ladybower reservoir. There's more on the demise of the Ashopton Inn in Chapter 8.

Inevitably, the first two masonry dams were such a huge construction project that a whole community of navvies was established in the valley, as well as a railway to bring in the stone and raw materials for the dams. The purpose-built settlement was called Birchinlee, but nicknamed 'Tin Town' after the artificial huts made out of corrugated iron in which some of the workers lived, and it survived for 15 years.

Although long-vanished, the outline of the 1,000-population 'village' can still be seen among the trees above the road on the west bank of Derwent reservoir. Perhaps most remarkably of all, for all its well-developed facilities, which included shops, school, mission and hospital, Birchinlee deliberately had no pub or alehouse, and beer was usually only served with meals in the canteen. In his excellent guide to the pubs of North Derbyshire (see Bibliography), Jim McIntosh wonders whether this was a case of owners Derwent Valley Water Board taking their social responsibilities seriously, or in fact a means of encouraging the hard-drinking navvies to spend their wages on site and so maximising the Board's return. Indeed, when the Temperance Society alleged that Birchinlee was awash with drunkenness the Board responded by extending the canteen to supposedly deal with overcrowding, but of course more beer was sold and profits grew even more. They also saw off licence applications by several enterprising private individuals to open new canteens for the workers in the area.

The Ladybower Inn, like the Yorkshire Bridge Inn and Bridge Inn at Calver, are all associated with the River Derwent, the Peak's mightiest waterway. It runs for around 50 miles from its source high up on the boggy, open waste of Featherbed Moss on Bleaklow all the way south to its confluence with the River Trent at Shardlow, near Derby. You can trace the river's journey on foot using the Derwent Valley Heritage Way and, perhaps not surprisingly, it goes past plenty of pubs.

In its journey through the Peak District, the River Derwent is marked by two former pubs bearing its name at Bamford and Whatstandwell, and quite a contrast they are too. The Derwent Hotel in the former is a high, twin-gabled building which was built around a century ago to catch the eye (if not the breath) and now is privately-run and offers group accommodation only; while the latter is around 300 years old and is thought to mark the spot of a much earlier river crossing. It's now a B&B and tea room.

Predictably, the many and often age-old crossings of the River Derwent inevitably gave rise to hamlets and small communities, although sometimes the origins of names have become a little muddied. There was certainly once a ford at Whatstandwell between Cromford and Ambergate, and according to one tale it was a Walter Stonewell who lived at the house on the bank and built the originally 14th-century bridge (hence the original name of 'Wattestanwell'). There again, others claim that a Walter Standwell was once a tollmaster and lived in part of the present building by the river. Either way, the former pub at Whatstandwell has stood for about three centuries and originally incorporated a toll house. It was once called the Bull's Head and served the coaches travelling the Derwent valley between Matlock and Derby.

Further upstream at Matlock, the Boat House Inn on Dale Road inevitably had a close association with the River Derwent, given its name and the fact that it is just a few yards from the river. According to an ex-landlord, the 280-year-old pub has at various times also served as a mortuary and a brothel. Regardless, the name definitely refers to the fact that trips by row boats and pleasure craft were made from here, since a foot ferry used to operate across the Derwent from this point. The pub is now a veterinary practice.

Gates, anchors and a question of style

'Gate' or 'gata' is an old Norse word for a road, and pubs and places of this name are still associated with many roads today. In terms of hostelries, rather than simply referring to any old field gate it can sometimes mean a specific barrier – and not just for passing through, either. There's still a Gate Inn at Tansley, in the centre of the village, plus a former one in Matlock; and likewise there's both a past and present Hanging Gate pub

The welcoming sign at the Hanging Gate at Chapel-en-le-Frith

elsewhere in the Peak District.

The surviving Hanging Gate pub is located just outside Chapel-en-le-Frith on the road to Whaley Bridge. It's already been mentioned in Chapter 2, since the location is known as Cockyard, which hints at what might have gone on at the pub in centuries gone by. Today it's a very pleasant place and sports a welcoming greeting inscribed on the pub sign which takes the style of a wooden bar gate: *This gate hangs free and hinders none, refresh yourself and travel on.*

Ironically, the gate in question used to be a toll gate, so travellers would have little option but to stop at this point. A similar story is associated with the Hanging Gate at Brassington (see Chapter 5), while the Hanging Gate pub that has recently closed and is now a private residence was at Higher Sutton, near Langley in Cheshire, on the upper side of Cophurst Edge. An inn since the 1600s, it's believed to be sited near the spot (the so-called Greenway Stone) where poachers and rustlers caught in the nearby Royal Macclesfield Forest were hanged.

Different again are former manorial buildings, such as the Peacock Hotel at Rowsley (Chapter 4) with its stately, ivy-clad exterior and association with the landed gentry. The Norfolk Arms at Ringinglow, on Sheffield's western moors, dates from the early 19th century and was built in the same Gothic style as the octagonal toll house erected across the road a few years earlier. Both buildings are listed and the pub, which was originally called the Ringinglow Arms, has a splendid castellated frontage, with triangular-headed windows and tall, narrow chimneys. It was a popular stopping point for travellers on the turnpike between Sheffield, Buxton and Chapel-en-le-Frith.

The Devonshire Arms at Pilsley and its namesake at nearby Beeley are two of only a very few true estate pubs left. They are owned (like much of the two villages) by the Chatsworth estate. The Pilsley pub dates from 1739 and is fronted by four distinctive window gables and exceptionally high

The Norfolk Arms at Ringinglow, with its distinctive castellated style.

chimneys, while Beeley's is an amalgam of three separate cottages, converted in 1747 and subsequently a well known coaching inn.

The neighbouring village of Edensor is also owned by the Chatsworth estate, and once sported a number of pubs and refreshment points for the large numbers of tourists that flocked to the stately home and its glorious grounds. They still come, of course, but at Edensor they have to make do with the Post Office tearooms. Nearby Cavendish Hall, a small Georgian mansion beside the main estate road, was originally designed as an inn, but in time became the village institute and is now the office for Chatsworth Estate.

At the recently refurbished Hope and Anchor in Wirksworth you have to go inside to admire its architectural claim to fame. The story goes that long before it became a town centre tavern the solid, three-storey building by the market place was originally the residence of a prison governor, because during the 17th century Wirksworth housed a large number of convicts. And it is these French prisoners of war that are possibly thought to be responsible for the intricately-carved wooden chimney piece in the snug of the pub, dating from around 1660, and which was originally the parlour of the house. In its centre is a pattern of four fleur-de-lis, flanked by two unicorns. At the bottom corners are what looks like Tudor roses. It's certainly an elaborate decoration in what is today just a small corner bar.

The original Hope and Anchor was further down the main street, and one of its more interesting features appears to have moved with it. As you walk through the grand main entrance of the present pub, with its open porch supported by Roman doric columns, look up at the ceiling. There's a small but beautifully-designed stained glass window directly above, depicting a Pre-Raphaelite-looking woman (long hair, flowing robes, wistful expression) draped around an anchor.

If you walk around the corner on to Coldwell Street, past the Red Lion, you come to another former pub with an interesting history. The Vaults was once the business premises of Charles Wright & Son, established around 200 years ago and an important wine and spirit merchants. At one time their operations included whisky-blending, and until it was demolished in the 1970s, there was a large warehouse to the back and extensive cellars or vaults under the centre of the town.

It's surprising what sometimes lurks inside other ostensibly unremarkable-looking pubs. For instance, the bar of the Waterloo Inn at Biggin used to sport an authentic Midland Railway bench which could once be found on Derby Railway Station; and the Bridge Inn at Calver used to boast a collection of antique fire-fighting equipment, with unusual copper extinguishers. A vast array of Toby jugs still adorns the Angler's Rest at Miller's Dale, petwer mugs hang from the beams of the Olde Gate at Brassington and bank notes from around the world are pinned to the ceiling at the George at Alstonefield.

The Cock and Pullet at Sheldon (Chapter 8) is full of clocks, while the Cockerel Wine Bar at the Old Hall Hotel (Buxton) and the Barley Mow at Bonsall are crammed full of chicken memorabilia. A few pubs still retain traditional snug bars, intimate little side or back rooms, perhaps most notably the Bell Inn at Cromford.

Then there are some pubs, in terms of built style, that either look a little out of place or rather confusing in appearance. The date above the door of the Shoulder of Mutton in Bradwell reads 1937 and, as explained in Chapter 8, the pub replaced another that closed when the road was widened. However, this ostentatious and obviously 20th-century-looking building seems totally out of place amid the traditional stone cottages, not least because it's built of brick and its style is so evidently modern. Some conjecture that it was built as a grand entrance to the village to match the new and improved road. However, another version told locally is how the architect's plans became mixed up with those for a new pub intended for a Sheffield estate and what was designed for a city suburb ended up in a Derbyshire village! It's tempting, therefore, to imagine that amid the flats and semis of suburban Sheffield is a rustic Peak District pub, but unfortunately there's no evidence to suggest that any of this is true.

Other Peak District pubs that seem a little out of keeping with their surroundings include the Monsal Head Hotel, with its Alpine connotations (see Chapter 3), and the Millstone Inn above Hathersage. This prominent roadside building appears to incorporate no less than three different architectural styles. It's perhaps more remarkable still when you see a photograph of the original inn, a traditional two-storey farmhouse which was believed to date as far back as the 1630s. It was first licensed in 1820 and run by a Thomas Wilkin, who like so many other

The Shoulder
of Mutton at
Bradwell – should
it have been built
in Sheffield?!

publicans at that time continued to farm. The attractive, whitewashed building was established on the Sheffield to Chapel turnpike, handily close to Surprise View where travellers from Yorkshire are treated to a sudden and dramatic view across the valley. Sadly, the old building was knocked down in 1929 and replaced by a three-storey, half-timbered roadhouse that presumably was all the rage at the time (the nearby Scotsman's Pack suffered a similar fate). If you look closely you can tick mock Tudor, Georgian and even a bit of Regency in the styles.

The Millstone Country Inn, as it styles itself these days, takes its name from the millstones which were quarried from above the Derwent valley and which are now used as the symbol of the Peak District National Park. It's a friendly and comfortable place, offering good food and drink, but perhaps an example of where the best view is *from* the pub rather than *of* the pub.

The Millstone
Country Inn
displays an
interesting
blend of
architectural styles.

Pub royalty in the Peak District comes in all forms: The Royal Cottage beside the A53 on the Staffordshire Moorlands and the Royal Hotel at Hayfield.

Excursion carriages outside the Cat and Fiddle Inn in the 1930s
(© picturethepast.org.uk).

At 1,690ft (515m), the Cat and Fiddle's high and exposed location makes it
vulnerable to wintry weather, such as here in January 2010 (photo courtesy of
Colin Townend/maccinfo.com).

Not surprisingly for a rural area, one of the most common pub names in the Peak District is the Bulls Head (from top left): Castleton, Ashford in the Water, Foolow and Youlgrave.

The Marquis of Granby Hotel, near Bamford, had graced the Hope Valley since the mid 1800s and is pictured here around 1960 (copyright the Francis Frith Collection). In 2001 it was sold, closed and subsequently demolished, to make way for a new hotel that so far has not been built.

The Red Lion once stood in the centre of Stoke-on-Trent, but after closing it was dismantled and later rebuilt at Crich Tramway Village, where it is once more a functioning pub and part of the period streetscene at this popular visitor attraction (photos courtesy of Crich Tramway Village).

The 18th-century George Hotel at Tideswell and morris dancers outside the Red Lion at nearby Litton (both photos by Karen Frenkel).

Among the Peak District's pubs that have closed In just the last few years are (from top left) the Tunnel End Inn, Marsden; George and Dragon, Old Brampton; Crewe & Harpur Arms, Longnor; Hanging Gate, Higher Sutton; Highwayman, Rainow; and Navigation Inn, Whaley Bridge.

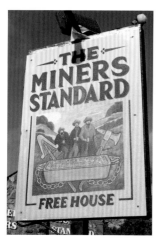

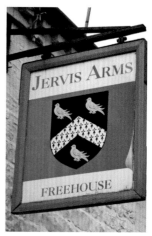

One of a kind (from top left): Flying Childers at Stanton in Peak, 19th Hole at Buxton, Staffordshire Knot at Sheen, Knockerdown Inn near Carsington Water, Drum and Monkey at Whaley Bridge, Ship Inn at Wincle, Miners Standard at Winster, Druid Inn at Birchover and Jervis Arms at Onecote.

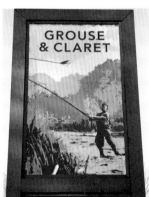

Unique in the Peak (from top left): Winking Man on the A53 near Upper Hulme, Lazy Trout at Meerbrook, Waltzing Weasel at Birch Vale, Grouse and Claret at Rowsley, Farmyard Inn at Youlgrave, Fishpond at Matlock Bath, Dandy Cock at Disley, Woodroffe Arms at Hope and Quiet Woman at Earl Sterndale.

Peak District pubs vary enormously in size and style: The Rutland Arms Hotel, with its elegant Georgian features, has dominated the centre of Bakewell for 200 years; Smiths Tavern is a handsome brick-built town pub in the centre of Ashbourne; while at 1,250ft (381m) and Derbyshire's highest pub, the Barrel Inn at Bretton is a sturdy rural farmstead built to withstand the elements.

The Green Man and Blacks Head Royal Hotel, Ashbourne, pictured some time
in the 1880s–90s, has one of the few surviving 'gallows' pub signs left in the
country (image courtesy of Brett Payne/Photo-Sleuth).

Along with the rest of the village, Ashopton Inn in the Upper Derwent Valley
was demolished in the early 1940s to make way for Ladybower Reservoir
(© picturethepast.org.uk).

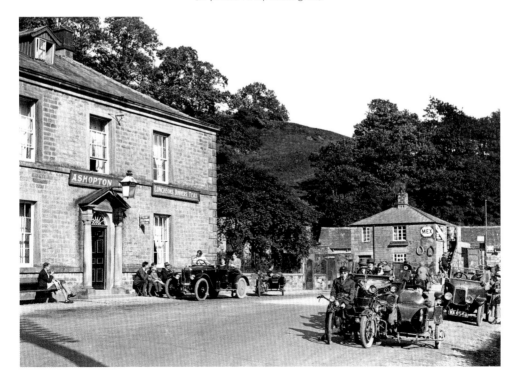

The 16th-century Old Hall Hotel at Hope was formerly home to the Balguy family when it was known as Hope Hall. The Rambler Inn at Edale sits at the foot of Kinder Scout and has been welcoming outdoor enthusiasts for many years.

Located prominently on the Market Place at Cromford, the ostentatious Greyhound Hotel was built in 1778 for the mill bosses to entertain important guests. The mill workers, on the other hand, supped at the Boat Inn on Scarthin, largely out of sight and a discreet distance away.

Pursuant to the licensing act
1910-1921 intoxicating liquors
are permitted to be sold & supplied
in these premises between the
hours of 3 to 4 in the afternoon
any Market day except

Sunday
Good Friday
Christmas Day

for the accommodation of
Persons attending market

ANGLERS
REST
FREE HOUSE

LOUNGE

WELCOME TO THE
QUIET WOMAN
INN
REAL ALE ON HAND PUMPS

FEATURED IN THE AS SEEN ON
GOOD BEER AND PLAIN PRACTICE and
GOOD PUB GUIDE

ROBINSONS
BREWING EXCELLENCE

SHOP
IN THE PUB
OPEN

Mon Tues Wed 10-2 7-9
Thur-Fri 10-2 6-9
Sat-Sun 10am-9pm

MINERS
ARMS

THE NEW INN
Britains highest
Village pub
1518ft

The Old Bulls Head at Little Hucklow was closed for many years, but after extensive renovation it re-opened in 2020 as the Blind Bull. Purportedly one of the Peak District's oldest pubs is now its newest.

Supporters gathering outside the Anglers Rest in Bamford during the community's fundraising efforts in 2013. The pub now incorporates a cafe and the village post office and is a popular destination for locals and visitors alike.

CHAPTER SEVEN

What's Inn a Name?

Beating a path to the door

There are a wide variety of names across the 40,000 or so pubs of Great Britain and they can tell us a great deal about the history and make-up of a specific area – everything from local trades and professions through to leading local families and past political allegiances. The Peak District has its fair share of familiar pub names, but also some relating directly to local families, plus some rather unusual and even unique examples.

Going back to the beginning, in Roman times taverns would be symbolised by vine leaves hanging outside the door to show that they sold wine, from where the phrase 'a good wine needs no bush' originates. In this country, vines were replaced by the more hardy ivy or an evergreen bush hanging from a pole, and this is still remembered by the name of the Hollybush Inn, which can be found at Grangemill and Bollington.

The Holly Bush Inn on Palmerston Street, Bollington in 1905 (photo courtesy of Bollington Civic Society collection).

A bundle of barley was another obvious symbol that was displayed outside or above the door. Until recently, it was customary at the unveiling of a new pub for a cluster of greenery, called an ale garland, to be hung at the door.

Another pub sign around today that dates from the same era is the Chequers, and proof of this has been provided by excavations of the Roman town of *Herculaneum*, buried by the eruption of Vesuvius in AD79. Chequered signs have been unearthed that were displayed outside wine shops and taverns, and in today's Peak District you can visit the Chequers Inn at Froggatt, near Calver. Board games such as draughts and chess were popular in ancient Rome, and evidently widely played in taverns. However, the chequers symbol was also the emblem of money-lenders in medieval times.

Biblical references and saintly legends

Many early pubs had a religious or sometimes a specific biblical subject as their name, such as the crossed keys (the emblem of St Peter, the keeper of the keys to Heaven) which until a few years lived on at Chapel Milton, near Chapel-en-le-Frith. The Lamb (for instance, at Chinley Head, near Hayfield, and on the extreme eastern edge of the Peak at Holymoorside) is often a reference to Christ; and the origin of others like the Mitre and the Angel is also obvious.

In addition to the biblical names, there are also a couple of saints amid the pub names of the Peak District. The Crispin Inn at Great Longstone, north of Bakewell, takes its name from St Crispin, patron saint of cobblers, shoe-makers and leather-workers. Boot and shoe making was a traditional village craft in Longstone.

As with so many of the saints, there are numerous legends told about Crispin, and the English version tells how he was born in Canterbury to the queen of Logia (Kent). In an attempt to avoid persecution by the anti-Christian Romans, Crispin and his brothers dressed in everyday clothes and fled to nearby Faversham. In the middle of the night and with nowhere to stay, they heard music and song from behind a door, and knocking they asked whether they could come in. The house belonged to a master shoemaker named Robards, who took pity on them, and before you know it they all moved in and Crispin began a seven-year apprenticeship. So good was their work that Robards found himself appointed shoemaker to Roman Emperor Maximinus. Crispin was commanded to make shoes for Ursula, the Emperor's daughter, and while presenting

The Crispin at Great Longstone is named after the patron saint of shoe-makers.

them to her in Canterbury he was struck by her beauty and fell in love with her. They ended up marrying in secret, and when Maximinus discovered Crispin's high birth he eventually acquiesced to their marriage, saying: "A shoemaker's son is a prince born." Their wedding took place on 25th October, since when it has become the Shoemakers' Feast Day.

However, it seems that the real St Crispin and his brother, St Crispinian, were martyred in about AD287. They were Christians who fled persecution in Rome, and supposedly provided the poor with shoes, taking no payment unless it was offered. Such was Crispin's benevolence that he even stole leather to make shoes for the poor.

St Crispin's Day is also the date of the Battle of Agincourt in 1415. The Crispin public house in Ashover reputedly gained its licence the year after Agincourt. A sign outside the pub explains how Thomas Babbington, Lord of the Manor, and 'several men of Asher' returned victorious from the battlefield, and how they regarded St Crispin as their saviour.

Unfortunately there were less than saintly goings-on when Royalists troops were billeted in Ashover in 1646, as the sign also relates. They were there to patrol the Chesterfield to Matlock road, but according to eyewitness accounts the men were more interested in supping ale at the Crispin Inn. The landlord, Job Wall, blocked the doorway, telling them they had had quite enough already and they should be on their way. Unfortunately for him they 'turned him out and set watch at the door while the ale was drunk or wasted.'

Another saint has even stronger English credentials. Although pubs called the George sometimes refer to one of the English kings of that name, it is also associated with St George, and as at the village pub at

Alstonefield the sign depicts not a sombre monarch but the dragon-slaying saint.

The George and Dragon (in Ashbourne and Charlesworth, Glossop) is the more common pub name associated with this famous legend, of course, which saw George kill the dragon and save the life of the King's daughter, resulting in the heathen King converting to Christianity. Some time later, in the Crusades, it was reported that a vision of the saint appeared before the Christians during the siege of Antioch. Richard I immediately placed his army under the protection of St George, and went on to defeat the Saracens.

St Dunstan is also remembered in the Peak District, giving his name to a pub located amid a row of terraced cottages in Langley, near Macclesfield. Just as St Crispin has no known connection with Derbyshire, St Dunstan is unlikely to have visited this tiny Cheshire village. He began as a Benedictine monk at Glastonbury Abbey and went on to become Archbishop of Canterbury. Dunstan was notable for his artistic skills, such as painting and embroidery and working with precious metals. Today he is considered the patron saint of goldsmiths, as well as blind people and bell ringers.

By Royal Appointment

Although by the Middle Ages many inns and taverns had specific names, they needed to also have easily-recognisable signs which were strong on visual imagery, since the majority of the population could not read.

One of these was a white stag, which was a reference to King Richard II whose coat of arms featured a swan and an antelope with a collar. This became a white stag or hart on most signs. The story can be traced back to Alexander the Great, who is reputed to have caught a pure white stag and placed a gold collar around its neck.

It was in 1393, during Richard's reign, that pubs were ordered to display a sign so that they could be identified by the official ale taster. Not surprisingly, the white hart was immediately adopted by many establishments, and it soon became a generic term for a tavern in the Middle Ages. There are still over 300 pubs of this name across the UK that bear this name, and in the Peak District you can find White Hart Inns at Bradwell and Whaley Bridge, and until a few years ago in Ashbourne and New Mills as well.

Together with the Church, the monarchy was the main influence on early pub names, and after Henry VIII split with Rome it's quite

The White Hart at Bradwell.

likely that a number of pubs (perhaps wisely) changed their name to demonstrate their loyalty to the monarch. Today there are still a huge number of pubs with royal connections, even though the face of the actual king or queen depicted on their signs tended to change with the fluctuating fortunes of the individual monarchs or royal houses.

The names which are still common today include general ones, such as the King's Head (Bonsall and Buxton), King's Arms (Crich and Chapel-en-le-Frith) and the Queen's Arms (Bakewell and Taddington). Incidentally, this last name became something of a joke among former commercial travellers. When asked where they had stayed in a certain town, if they lived there and in fact had stayed at home they used to reply: "In the Queen's Arms".

The King's Head at Bonsall is believed to be the village's oldest pub, established in 1649, since the name usually commemorates Charles I who, of course, famously lost his own head. However, a plaque on the wall outside dates the current pub from 1677, which certainly places it post-Restoration; and the sign itself appears to resemble Charles II. It's more surprising, still, when you consider that the powerful Parliamentarian supporter John Gell lived not too far away at Hopton, near Wirksworth.

Mind you, Bonsall seemed to be a law unto itself, especially when you learn that at one stage there was even a Queen's Head to match the King's Head. The two pubs were next door to each other on the main square, and it is thought that, since there were stables behind the Queen's Head, perhaps the ostlers, coach drivers and servants used this pub, while the passengers stayed at the King's Head.

Three pubs are simply called the Royal: the handsome 18th-century hotel next to the River Sett at Hayfield; the village pub at Dungworth, near Bradfield; and a pub overlooking the market place in

The name of the 17th-century King's Head, Bonsall, suggests royalist sympathies, but the area was strongly Parliamentarian.

Chapel-en-le-Frith (which always used to be called the Royal Oak – see below).

However, when it comes to the most popular pub names, in general, there are three that are out in front, and they all have royal origins: the Red Lion, Crown and the Royal Oak.

According to the Pubs Galore website (www.pubsgalore.co.uk), the most common pub name is the Red Lion, with over 550 throughout Britain. It symbolises the badge of John o' Gaunt, Duke of Lancaster (1340-99), although it also crops up in Scottish heraldry after James I (James VI of Scotland) ordered that it should be included on his coat of arms and displayed on all important public buildings, including pubs. It certainly is prolific in the Peak District, with Red Lions at Bakewell, Birchover, Hognaston, Kniveton, Litton, Matlock Green, Stone Edge, Waterfall and Wirksworth.

Meanwhile, the less widespread White Lion dates from the time of Edward IV, and there are pubs of this name at Disley, Great Longstone and Starkholmes, near Matlock. But, as with many heraldic pub signs, there is an alternative explanation, since a white lion also featured on the badge of the Duke of Norfolk who owned land in the Peak District. Likewise, the Black Lion can refer to Queen Philippa of Hainault, wife of

Edward III; or alternatively to the 14th-century Welsh freedom-fighter Owain Glyndwr, Prince of Wales.

The next most popular pub name nationally is the Crown, with just over 500 at the last count. Ironically, only a handful are located in the Peak District, including the popular Wetherspoon pub on Matlock's Crown Square. It is, in fact, the third establishment on or near this location to bear this name, beginning with a seedy lodging house that was demolished in 1906.

There is a Crown Inn that occupies an unspoilt end-of-terrace position on Victoria Street in Glossop and has a distinctive curved bar; and equally noteworthy is Ye Olde Crown in Waterhouses, Staffordshire, an imposing Grade II listed building dating from 1647 and which served as a coaching inn for Ashbourne to Manchester travellers. The name was widespread, probably because the royal crown was a clear and unambiguous visual symbol, and of course represented loyalty to the monarchy in general rather than an allegiance to any one particular sovereign – a clear case of hedging your bets. As with other royal pub signs, it is believed that many made a swift and tactful change of name during England's short lived republic in the 1650s; but the fact that so many have survived to this day must surely be some sort of testimony to the country's enduring relationship with its monarchy. In the case of the Crown, the name was often given to a place after it received some sort of royal patronage, or if it stood on royal land.

There are plenty of pub names where the crown is crossed with something else. The ubiquitous Crown and Anchor, for instance, is the badge of the lord high admiral, and a favourite with retiring seamen who become innkeepers. The Rose and Crown, such as at Allgreave on the Buxton-Congleton road, clearly indicates loyalty to the mother country, but it also symbolised the end of the Wars of the Roses which had divided the nation for many years. The Crown and Mitre (there used to be one in the Peak District near Chinley) represents the not always easy relationship between government and the Church.

The third most popular pub name in Britain remembers the dramatic escape of Charles II after defeat at the Battle of Worcester in 1651, and at the last count there were over 420 Royal Oaks dotted about the country. The name tells how the deposed monarch famously hid from his pursuers in the cavity of an old oak tree (the Boscobel Oak) in Shropshire. Following the Restoration of the Monarchy, Charles II declared that 29th May, the King's birthday, should be celebrated as Royal Oak Day or Oak Apple Day. In the Peak District you can toast the moustachioed and be-wigged King in Royal Oaks at Chapel-en-le-Frith, Hurdlow, Millthorpe, New Mills, Old Brampton and Wirksworth. There was also a Royal Oak at Tansley until a few years ago until it turned into an Indian restaurant.

It's said that Royal Oak pubs were often run by Royalists, while King's Head pubs were frequently occupied by supporters of Parliament (because the King's head is what they wanted). Supporters of either side claimed they would not enter a pub which indicated support for the other.

The Rising Sun, suggesting a new dawn and a bright future, is depicted on the coat of arms of Edward III, William II and William III. There's a Rising Sun pub at Middleton by Wirksworth, plus another that used to stand on the A6187 between Hope and Bamford.

The White Boar, emblem of Richard III, was a popular inn sign during his reign in the mid 15th century, and as C. Lamb points out in his guidebook to inn signs, these particular publicans must have thanked the Earl of Oxford, whose crest was a blue boar, for supporting Henry Tudor (who defeated Richard III at the Battle of Bosworth). 'They had only to paint the boar blue to show a healthy respect for the new reign,' he observes.

Clearly a knowledge of heraldry is useful when it comes to deciphering some royal pub signs, but luckily others are much more comprehensible. The Queen Anne at Great Hucklow appears to be named after the last Stuart monarch, who died in 1714, although records from 1851 show that it was formerly called the Queen's Head and the landlord went by the splendid name of Caleb Higinbottom.

A more recent and longer-reigning monarch used to be remembered in the names of two former pubs. The Princess Victoria formerly occupied a terrace row of shops on South Parade in Matlock Bath and commemorated

The former sign at the George Hotel in Youlgrave celebrates four separate monarchs.

the visit to the resort of (Princess) Victoria in 1832 before she reached the throne. Meanwhile, her Prince Consort has fared a little better and is remembered by the red-brick Albert Hotel at Disley.

Other royal figures featured in Peak pubs include the Duke of York, although of course there are a number of different ones. You can find local examples at Elton and Pomeroy.

Another common royal pub name is the George, with pubs bearing this name at Hathersage, Hayfield, Tideswell and Youlgrave. Of course, there were several kings of that name, and at the George Hotel at Youlgrave they used to get round the problem of identification by depicting four separate Georges on the pub sign outside (their new sign plumps for just one).

The royal House of Hanover is remembered in the White Horse, a Saxon motif, and in the Peak District there's one at Disley and there used to be another until recently in Whaley Bridge. Baslow has a Prince of Wales pub and it's a name that often refers to Edward VII, who became King in 1901, although sometimes it can refer Edward II who held the title in the 14th century. Another former pub of the same name used to exist on Fairfield Road in Buxton.

A military connection

Well-known military battles are also represented by pub names, with the Waterloo Hotel near Taddington and the Waterloo Inn at Biggin. The famous victory of the Duke of Wellington against Napoleon in 1815 gave rise to numerous pubs bearing the name of this location in what is now Belgium; and of course it also paved the way for the victorious commander to be remembered in pub names the length of this country.

In the Peak District you can raise a glass to the Duke of Wellington on Wellington Street in Matlock; and until around 2007 at the Wellington in Ashbourne (which changed its name from the Nags Head to celebrate the beating of the French). In fact, the Iron Duke, who after his success went on to become foreign secretary and prime minister, appears in more English pub signs than any other military figure apart from Admiral Nelson.

Until fairly recently, one Peak District community celebrated both of these military heroes through their pubs. There was once a Duke of Wellington on Duke Street in Middleton by Wirksworth, while just around the corner stood the Nelson Arms on Main Street. The latter is still there, and a good pub it is too, although according to the present

The Waterloo Inn at Biggin.

landlady the pub's original name was believed to be the Messenger before being changed to honour the hero of Trafalgar. One of the most noteworthy guests at the pub was Eleanor Marx, daughter of Karl, who stayed while on a visit to the Peak District in July 1884 and apparently left without paying her bill!

Another naval man is celebrated by the name of the village pub at Onecote on the Staffordshire Moorlands. The Jervis Arms commemorates Admiral Jervis, whose name I am reliably informed is pronounced 'Jarvis'. According to the pub's website, he was born in Meaford near Stone, Staffordshire, in 1734, and as well as being an MP he was First Lord of the Admiralty and a distinguished naval commander, helping to lead the British fleet to victory over French and Spanish ships in the Battle of Cape Vincent in 1797 (from which he earned his titles). He even commanded the young Horatio Nelson.

However, it's not just the powerful few at the very top that are commemorated. On the Buxton Road in Furness Vale, near New Mills, is a pub called the Soldier Dick. The sign outside depicts a wounded soldier, bandaged and supported by a crutch. The story goes that, some time in the 1600s, the landlord took in an injured soldier (possibly a deserter) returning from a distant battle, and his wife nursed him back to health. The man stayed on and became a popular and colourful local character, taking up painting and recounting stirring and often blood-curling tales of his adventures for the pub's customers. The name Soldier Dick is also sometimes said to stand for Richard Cromwell, Oliver Cromwell's son.

Another interesting tale concerns John Manners, Marquis of Granby (1721-70). He was the eldest son of the third Duke of Rutland and was the distinguished Commander-in-Chief in Germany during the Seven Years' War, famed in particular for the way he led his cavalry against the French at the Battle of Warburg.

The Soldier Dick at Furness Vale is supposedly named after a wounded soldier cared for by the pub.

At the Battle of Minden he was leading a charge when both his hat and wig flew off, but despite this he continued the assault with gusto, thus giving the English language the immortal phrase 'going for the enemy bald-headed'. By all accounts he was a popular leader, once described as 'brave to a fault, skilful, generous to profuseness, careful to his men and beloved by them'. After his campaigns he rewarded his senior non-commissioned officers who had been injured or disabled with a gratuity for them to set themselves up as innkeepers, hence the enduring popularity of the pub name around the country today. Indeed, one epitaph for the Marquis Granby reads:

> *What conquest now will Britain boast,*
> *Or where displays her banners?*
> *Alas, in Granby she has lost*
> *True courage and good manners.*

John Manners (once the Lord Lieutenant of Derbyshire) died leaving debts of £37,000. He was painted a dozen times by Sir Joshua Reynolds, and most of the surviving pub signs are based on these portraits.

There was once a Marquis of Granby pub in both Ashbourne and Tideswell; and, until 2001, a handsome old hotel of the same name in the Hope Valley near Bamford that dated from the mid 1800s. It was particularly notable for its Olympic Room, which was fitted out with decorative woodwork from the White Star liner RMS Olympic. She was the lesser-known sister ship of the Titanic, and after a long life during which she managed to successfully dodge icebergs and enemy bombs, she was broken up on the Clyde in the 1930s. Her luxurious interior fittings were then sold off, some of which supposedly found their way to the Marquis of Granby in Derbyshire; and even now I can remember admiring the wooden panelling when I first paid it a visit. Sadly, it was all removed and sold, following the pub's sale in 2001, after which it was promptly closed and the building demolished. Planning permission was granted for a new hotel on the site, but at the time of writing (almost two decades later) the site is still an untidy pile of rubble.

Other pubs have their own story to tell, but like so many rooted far back in the past, it is not always easy to separate fact and fiction. The former village pub at Grindon, a small village high above the Manifold valley in Staffordshire, used to occupy a 400-year-old building that started off as the village smithy and was once called the Shoulder of Mutton, but at the some point the name was changed to the Cavalier. It was a term given to a Royalist who fought for King Charles I during the English Civil War, of course, and indeed the pub sign depicted a dapper and smiling fellow straight from that era. However, some say that the new name was possibly bestowed in honour of Bonnie Prince Charlie, who is said to have stayed in the village during his march south from Scotland in the 1745 Rebellion. Other Peak District pubs that he or his followers are supposed to have stayed in include the Ship at Wincle, and the Royal Cottage on the Staffordshire moors (see Chapter 2).

Odd and unusual names

A highly distinctive pub name can be found in the Staffordshire hamlet of Sheen, perched on a low ridge separating the valleys of the Dove and Manifold near Hartington. The Staffordshire Knot Inn takes its name from the county emblem, which is incorporated in the county council's logo and the badge worn by the Staffordshire police force, and it originated around 1400 with the Earls of Stafford. However, there's another tale suggesting that a former Sheriff of Stafford devised the triple knot as a means of hanging three men at once.

The Staffordshire Knots was also the nickname of the South Staffordshire Regiment, and the story of how they supposedly acquired this moniker is intriguing. The 38th Foot Regiment was sent to Antigua in 1706, but for several decades the War Office effectively forgot all about them. With no new uniforms sent out they were forced to patch their increasingly threadbare tunics with brown holland (a coarse linen cloth that took its name from the country where it originated). Thereafter it was customary to wear a piece of this cloth behind the cap badge to commemorate this period, which soon became known as the Staffordshire Knot.

Some pub names, like the Staffordshire Knot, you can perhaps guess at, but there are others that unless you have the benefit of some specialist knowledge can leave you bewildered, such as the Grouse and Claret at Rowsley, which refers to an imitation fly used by fly fishermen (see Chapter 2).

Only a couple of miles from Rowsley is the hilltop village of Stanton in Peak, where you will find the Flying Childers pub. Converted several centuries ago from four cottages, it's a timeless, unspoilt two-room pub that in 2019 won the Good Pub Guide's Unspoilt Pub of the Year award.

Despite all the photographs of cricket teams in the bar, the pub takes its name from a champion racehorse from the 1720s and '30s, owned by the 4th Duke of Devonshire and trained by Sir Hugh Childers. He was said to be the first thoroughbred racehorse in England, sired by an import from Syria named Arabian. By all accounts the Flying Childers was a handsome animal, with a distinctive white flash, and he could also go like the clappers. He so daunted the opposition in his first race at Newmarket in 1721 that in his second race, six months later, all the other horses were withdrawn and he won in a walkover. He was often known as the Devonshire Childers, after his owner, who refused several offers for the prize-winning animal, including one reputed to have been the equivalent weight of the horse in gold crowns. Flying Childers retired undefeated to the Duke's stud at nearby Chatsworth when his racing career ended. There is also another pub named after this racehorse at Kirby Bellars in Leicestershire.

An equally distinctive name is the Quiet Woman at Earl Sterndale. The sign outside this unpretentious village pub, south of Buxton, bears the picture of a decapitated woman with the motto: 'Soft words turneth away wrath.' There are several stories about its origin, but the one told most often is of a former landlord who, returning from market at nearby Longnor and fed up with his wife's constant nagging, decided to have a quiet woman outside if he couldn't have one in. She is said to have had the nickname 'Chattering Charteris', and the tale relates how he chopped off her head after she wouldn't stop talking. But rather than condemn the landlord's actions, the other villagers were said to have had a collection to buy her a headstone and given what remained to the husband.

There are other examples of this pub name around the country, often with variations such as Silent Woman, and indeed one such used to exist in Calver. Another version is the Headless Woman, and all allude to what may happen to over-talkative women. As the old rhyme goes:

Here is a woman who has lost her head
She's quiet now – you see, she's dead.

Eric Delderfield, author of a series of seminal books in the 1960s and '70s on the history of British pub signs, believes that this notable pub name may have originated during the reign of Henry VIII and referred, of course, to the beheading of Anne Boleyn.

A long-gone pub at Horwich End in Whaley Bridge was also known as the Quiet Woman, but for a much more benign reason. A news item in the *Ashton Reporter* of 6th April 1889 explains why:

> *DEATH OF MRS MARY BENNETT: During the week a link, connecting the past with the present, has been severed. On Wednesday morning, Mrs Mary Bennett of Horwich End passed away. The deceased, who was 90 years of age last February, came with her husband from Hilton near Chatsworth, 60 years ago. The house at which she resided was best known as 'the quiet woman', but the proper name of the hostelry is 'The Nelson Arms', a fact known only to a few. The house was one of the most respectably conducted in the Peak District, and the kindly old hostess was warmly respected by all.*

There is another Quiet Woman pub on St Edward Street in Leek (which at the time of writing is currently closed); and further back still also one on the southern edge of Beeley Moor, a rather bleak expanse of upland high above the Derwent Valley near Chatsworth. The pub was located on

Flash Lane in the middle of the unpopulated moorland, and although it is now partly surrounded by woodland, it's not hard to imagine what an unwelcoming and dangerous place it could be for passing travellers. Of course, it doesn't help matters if the pub landlady goes in for a spot of robbery herself, for according to one report in this case she not only relieved them of their valuables but also polished some of her customers off and

The sign for the Quiet Woman at Earl Sterndale.

then buried them under the cellar floor. She was eventually arrested and hanged for her crimes, but not surprisingly the premises retained a sinister air and appeared to be plagued by mysterious goings-on, including unexplained fires.

The last pub buildings here were believed to have been erected in 1874 after a fire, and even when it was turned into a farm the problems persisted. As recently as 1966 a country club built on the site went up in flames, and when the owner began to rebuild the premises his temporary caravan located on the site was destroyed by fire. Another account, related in Clarence Daniel's *Ghosts of Derbyshire* and which apparently goes back to Elizabethan times, tells how the moorland inn was in fact haunted by a female ghost with a reputation for arson. She was the surly and ill-tempered daughter of the landlord, who unwittingly drove her father to burn down the pub – unfortunately with him inside it. The tragedy left her unhinged and she was found dead on the moors some time later.

Now, if you think this is a little eerie, consider once again the Quiet Woman at Earl Sterndale. Half a century ago, the village church had the dubious distinction of being the only one in the whole of Derbyshire to be bombed during the Second World War. In June 1941 a German plane believed to be returning from a raid on Manchester dumped its incendiary bombs over the village and scored a direct hit on the church. According to eyewitness accounts, the men of the village emptied out of the Quiet Woman opposite and rushed over to extinguish the flames, but such was the ferocity of the fire that the roof was completely burnt down, all the windows smashed and even the Saxon font broken. Miraculously, though, most of the walls remained standing, and a wedding booked for 11am the next day between William Wain and Annie Harrison actually went ahead in the open and gutted building. Perhaps the Quiet Woman was having her say, after all?

Interestingly, a wartime bomb just missed the next pub with an unusual name. One night towards the end of the Second World War, fire-watchers on Axe Edge above the Goyt Valley had a narrow escape when an enemy flying bomb passed close above their heads. It landed just beyond the Cat and Fiddle Inn with a mighty explosion, and a crater is still visible in the ground.

But let's return to names. On the face of it, the Cat and Fiddle presents a much more straightforward case, but in fact here again there are various accounts of its origin. The fire-watchers, huddling on the moors 50 years ago, were there for a reason, for the pub sits 1,690ft (515m) high up on a breezy ridge mid-way between Buxton and Macclesfield on the A537 and enjoys spectacular views. For everyone from map-makers to holidaymakers, location and pub name are synonymous, and for motorists in particular the winding and sometimes treacherous road can be notorious and the inn a welcome and reassuring sight.

This was almost certainly in the mind of John Ryle, a local silk merchant, who in 1813 purchased a plot of land beside the new turnpike road. The hilltop pub that he built soon became an essential stop for travellers, including a Mr Charles Rolls who often used to call in while testing cars for his new business with a certain Mr Royce. But why the pub's unusual name? The obvious answer is that it comes from the popular nursery rhyme that is believed to be hundreds of years old:

> *Hey diddle diddle*
> *The cat and the fiddle*
> *The cow jumped over the moon*
> *The little dog laughed to see such craft*
> *And the fork ran away with the spoon.*

However, another version suggests that the name of the pub was introduced in the 1850s after the Duke of Devonshire presented the landlord with a picture of a cat playing a violin. A sculptured relief still sits in the wall by the main porch.

Some pub historians believe that the name originates with Caterine la Fidele, or Catherine of Aragon, the first wife of Henry VIII (and

that Edward I's queen, Infanta de Castille, is likewise remembered today in the equally prosaic name Elephant and Castle); or that it relates to Caton de Fidele, the 14th-century governor of the English-held town of Calais.

Whatever the origin of the name, running such a remote and isolated establishment can be really tough – see Neil Hanson's experience of managing the even

A sculptured stone relief of a cat and fiddle on the outside wall of the famous hilltop pub.

more out-of-the-way Tan Hill Inn high up on the Pennines during the 1970s, as immortalised in his book *The Inn at the Top*. In recent years the Cat and Fiddle has been closed and deserted. However, in 2019 the Forest Distillery in nearby Macclesfield Forest announced plans to develop and re-open the pub as a whisky and gin distillery, complete with visitor experience. It seems that the Cat and Fiddle is to have another life, yet.

Oddly enough, the Cat and Fiddle rhyme is referenced by another Peak District pub – see Chapter 8 for details of the former Children's Inn at Rowarth.

All at sea in the Peak

For a region entirely landlocked, it might come as a surprise to learn that there are several pubs bearing nautical names in the Peak District. The Anchor Inn, above Tideswell and at Hadfield, near Glossop, seems as far adrift from the ocean as you could possibly get in England, but originally the anchor in question did not necessarily belong to a ship. The earliest records of the former show that it was a licensed ale house as long ago as 1699 and its continued success was due to its location on the well-used turnpike, with stagecoaches stopping here throughout the week.

Of course, there were plenty of ex-mariners who retired to take up innkeeping (see the earlier reference to the common name Crown and Anchor), and of course an anchor, like a crown, was a strong but simple visual symbol. But there was another meaning attached to the anchor, stemming from the words of St Paul (Hebrews 6:19): "We have this as a sure and steadfast anchor of the soul…" A boat's spare anchor was often known as the (last) hope anchor; and the colour blue was regarded as the emblematic anchor of hope. Hence there are many pubs called the Blue Anchor or, as at Wirksworth, the Hope and Anchor (see Chapter 6).

The origin of the name of the Ship Inn at Wincle, in Cheshire, is much more straightforward. The pub dates from the 16th century and was created when three small cottages were knocked into one. It was renamed early in the 20th century in honour of Ernest Shackleton's successful expedition to the Antarctic in 1907-09, because his team included Sir Philip Lee Brocklehurst of nearby Swythamley Hall. The expedition's ship, a small whaler called Nimrod, is depicted stuck in the ice on one side of the pub sign, while the coat of arms of the Brocklehurst family is on the other.

The Ship Inn is named in honour of Shackleton's Antarctic expedition.

One story has it that a ship-builder friend of the Brocklehursts named a new ship Swythamley, after their family home, but the sailors had such trouble pronouncing the name they re-Christened her 'the Sweet Emily'.

The animal world

The Greyhound Inn is a 250-year-old coaching inn in the former estate village of Warslow, near the Manifold valley. According to one account, the name refers to a local stagecoach, but since the pub used to be called the Greyhound and Hare (or Hare and Hounds according to another source), perhaps the name has more to do with hare coursing?

Other animals that feature in Peak District pub names include, as we have already seen, the Lamb at Chinley Head and Holymoorside and the Bear at Alderwasley; and you could once visit a Squirrel at New Mills. There's a muster of Peacocks (Bakewell, Owler Bar and Rowsley); a small herd of Packhorses (including Crowdecote, Hayfield, Little Longstone and New Mills); a Roebuck at Chapel-en-le-Frith; and an Eagle in Buxton. The Swan (Buxton and Kettleshulme) can also come either White (Ashbourne) or Black (Ashover, Crich and Idridgehay); and of course there are various farmyard animals such as horses (nags), bulls and rams.

However, like royal pub names, some animal references can be misleading. Although there are just under 300 pubs in Britain called the Swan, for instance, quite a few reflect an heraldic significance rather than a landlord's ornithological preferences, whether it relates to a specific coat of arms or perhaps a recognition that swans have traditionally been the property of the reigning monarch. For most regulars, though, the origin of the name isn't especially important, nor perhaps to most publicans either. According to the victuallers' records for the Black Swan at Idridgehay, south of Wirksworth, between 1827-1901 the name of the pub switched back and forth from 'Swan' to 'Black Swan' several times.

A unique name is the Setter Dog, a pub which sadly closed a couple of years before the first edition of this book was written. It stood on the Buxton to Macclesfield turnpike (the Cat and Fiddle road) at Walker Barn, and according to folklore was a popular haunt of highwaymen. As Louis McMeeken suggests in his book on place names of the Peak District, the name of the pub may refer to the slang term for a lookout, or the highwayman's accomplice who would keep an eye open for approaching coaches.

As mentioned earlier, the White Lion is usually a name associated with Edward V, but Disley's version sports what must be one of the most tongue-in-cheek pub signs in the Peak District, since the painting actually depicts a zebra!

A case of mistaken identity at the White Lion, Disley.

The only one of its kind?

Finally, a clutch of very unusual and perhaps unique pubs names, one of which still defies a convincing explanation. The pub in question is the Flouch Inn, which when the first edition of this book was published stood near the junction of the A628 and A616 between Langsett and Hazlehead, in the north east corner of the Peak District. It opened in 1827 as the New Inn, but why or when it was renamed, and what 'flouch' actually means, has left everyone mystified. The most common suggestion is that it refers to a speech impediment suffered by the first landlord, since a flouch lip was said to be a slang term for a speech defect. Another, rather more simple explanation, is that the pub may have once been called the Plough and the letters fell off or got twisted. The pub was demolished in 2013 to make way for new housing.

Alongside the conventionally-named Black Swan, Cliff Inn and King's Arms at Crich, was a pub called the Jovial Dutchman. Originally a thatched building, it was largely rebuilt in 1904, and is said to have taken its name from a Dutch engineer who, like many of his fellow countrymen, came to Derbyshire to work on the Cromford Canal in the Derwent valley below (although some believe he may have been employed to drain the lead mines). The canal was connected to the quarry at the top of the hill by a light railway, so no doubt some of the workforce stayed in Crich, including this particular fellow who became the pub's first landlord. The Jovial Dutchman closed in 2009 and is now a private dwelling.

Another unique name in the Peak is the Druid Inn, an attractive, ivy-covered building in Birchover. It's purported to be named after the Druidical, a quasi-religious group who once worshipped on Rowtor Rocks behind the inn. What is more certain is that the gritstone outcrop, half hidden among trees, is reachable via a small path which, together with a series of steps, seats and caves, was carved into the stone around 300 years ago under the direction of the Rev. Thomas Eyre of Rowtor Hall. It is said that he sat up there, high among the rocks, composing his sermons which he later delivered in the small church below. As if to compound the vague sense of mysticism, above the village is Stanton Moor which contains a well-known stone circle called Nine Ladies. According to local legend shared with many other stone circles, these nine stone stumps are the remains of local women who were turned to stone while dancing on the Sabbath, while a separate stone – the King Stone – is all that remains of the fiddler who accompanied them.

The Knockerdown Inn, near Carsington Water, began life as a 17th-century farm and became a pub in the 1830s. It was originally called the Greyhound but for many years has been known by the much more memorable name Knockerdown, for which there appear to be two possible explanations. The first supposedly relates to an old 19th-century Derbyshire term 'knock-a-down', meaning a group of dilapidated buildings, although evidence for this is sketchy. The second, suggested by the pub sign and the favoured by the present landlady, makes a link with local lead mining and the practice of knocking out ore from the roof of the shaft (a crude and risky procedure known as overhand stoping). However, a knocker was also the name given to malevolent or mystical spirits that could be heard knocking on the walls or creaking the timbers before the roof crashed down. Miners were a superstitious lot and some believed that this mysterious knocking sound would even lead them to rich veins of lead and personal riches. See Chapter 9 for more about this pub, which has given its name to the location.

Other unusual pub names include the Friendship Inn, an unassuming corner pub on the back streets of Glossop, and Ye Olde Mustard Pot in Midhopestones. Another unique name is the Wanted Inn, with a suitably unusual story behind it. The pub is located at Sparrowpit, a hamlet on the A623 east of Chapel-en-le-Frith. Originally called the Three Tuns, it changed its name to the Devonshire Arms in 1839 to reflect its new owner. But when the 10th Duke tried to sell it in 1956 there were no takers, since it is, after all, in quite a remote spot. Two years went by with hardly any interest and not a single bid, and when new owners eventually took it over the pub was renamed the Wanted Inn – "the pub that nobody wanted." In 2020 the pub changed its name to the Olive Tree cafe and bar and now incorporates a farm shop.

The Friendship Inn at Glossop.

The name game

A common if rather unimaginative pub name is the New Inn. It was usually given to a pub that replaced an older establishment, and it is reckoned there are just under 250 New Inns around the UK. Of course, plenty of these New Inns are themselves quite old and historic. There are pubs of this name at Chapel-en-le-Frith and in the village of Flash, high on the moors south of Buxton. In fact the village is *very* high, and evidently proud of it, since a sign on the outside of the New Inn proudly proclaims that it is Britain's highest village pub at 1,518ft (above sea level).

However, the elevation of both the pub and indeed the village has been the source of some fierce disagreement with Wanlockhead, in Dumfries and Galloway, which also lays claim to the title of Britain's highest village. In 2007, the BBC One Show attempted to settle the quarrel by calling in the Ordnance Survey to measure the height of the highest house in each village. It found that Flash was higher by almost 100 feet. This didn't go down well with the residents of Wanlockhead who claimed that the report was biased towards the English and disputed the findings. There was understandably also great interest in the story among the 200 or so inhabitants of Flash. Landlady of the New Inn, Diane Phillips, told the *Macclesfield Express*: "Loads of the villagers came in and watched the programme and since it's been on everyone's been talking about it." One of those was the owner of what was now officially the highest cottage in the highest village in Britain, and it's fair to say that 54-year-old John Higginbotham took a slightly more triumphal line: "This is good news and gets one over on the Scots. They tried to take Robin Hood off us, but they're not having the highest village."

Elsewhere, for some people at least, the unusual and historic names of one or two pubs, while a product of their age, don't sit altogether easily in today's more enlightened times. A few years ago a complaint was received by the local council about the pub sign for the Black's Head in Wirksworth, which depicted a smiling and caricatured, black-skinned child in a turban. After some wrangling, owners Greene King took down the sign, which is now on the wall inside the pub next to the main bar. In fact, the picture of the boy on the pub sign is modelled directly on the bottle label for Hardy's Blackamoor Sweet Stout once produced by Hardy and Hanson's Kimberley Brewery of Nottinghamshire.

It's said that the pub was once called the Blackamoor's Head and some believe that it was named after African men who worked in the local Derbyshire mines. An alternative version is that the name is simply a

The Blacks Head
at Wirksworth.

variation on the ancient inn name the Turk's Head or Saracen's Head, and refers to the times of the Crusades, when anyone of a darker skin was considered an infidel and unholy.

Similar controversy has lately surrounded the historic sign for the Green Man Royal Hotel in Ashbourne, which incorporated the name Blackamoor's Head when the pub merged with premises next door in 1825 (see Chapter 6). However, in 2020, against the backdrop of the Black Lives Matters movement, the carved bust of a black man's head which had sat on top of the pub's gallows sign spanning the road for many years was removed following protests over racism. As at Wirksworth, the origin of both the pub name and symbol is a matter of some conjecture.

One widely-held local tale is that the carved wooden head represents a young servant boy who accompanied Sir Walter Raleigh on his visits to Ashbourne. But local author and historian Maxwell Craven, interviewed in the *Derby Telegraph* in June 2020, believes that the carved bust relates to the former Blackamoor's Head pub and is derived from the family crest of the Shirley family, later Earls Ferrers, who were local landowners. He says that a family member probably went on an early Crusade, which mostly took place in the 11th, 12th and 13th centuries (before the transatlantic Slave Trade started mid 15th century), and the head probably represents a Saracen or Arab Muslim. The family's Derbyshire estate was centred on Shirley, near Ashbourne, where the estate pub is still called the Saracen's Head. Either way, the cultural sensitivity of the depiction is obvious and it's highly unlikely that the controversial carving will return to Ashbourne's most famous pub sign, which in fact belongs to the local council and has nothing to do with the owners of the present pub. Instead, it's been suggested that that it might go on display as an historical artefact and educational tool in a local museum or heritage centre.

The Red Lion at Thorncliffe, near Leek, closed for refurbishment in 2018 and when it reopened some months later it had been re-named the Reform Inn. In fact, research by the new owners had revealed that this was the name of the pub when it first opened in 1851. There can't be too many instances of a pub reverting to its original name 150 years later.

Mind you, even though it's said to be unlucky to change the name of a pub this hasn't stopped countless places trying to switch their identity over the years – and some of the changes have certainly not been for the better. By and large, the Peak District has resisted the trend (mostly urban, it has to be said) that in recent years has seen an influx of new and supposedly humorous names like the Slug and Lettuce and Brahms and Liszt. For a while Monyash residents had to put up with the name of the Bull's Head (one of the most authentic English pub names) somewhat bizarrely being changed to the Hobbit. What connection a diminutive character from Middle Earth has with a Derbyshire lead mining village is unclear, but the Tolkien theme was echoed at the former Royal Oak at Eyam that for a while in the 1980s was renamed the Prancing Pony, after the fictitious inn from Lord of the Rings. Not surprisingly, this went down badly with the locals, who promptly nicknamed the pub the 'Bonking Donkey'.

Another Bull's Head, this time at Foolow, became the Lazy Landlord for a time in the 1990s, and the equally historic Ram's Head at Disley was briefly the Hungry Horse, but fortunately both have gone back to their roots. The Lazy Trout at Meerbrook was probably not its original name; and according to one (admittedly unconfirmed) account, a pub in Longnor once had its name changed to the Train Robbers Den by a new landlord keen to display his collection of dodgy mementoes. It didn't last long.

As mentioned earlier, the name of the Nelson Arms at Middleton by Wirksworth remembers the great naval figure, but a few years it was changed to the Wildlifers, for no other reason, it seems, than to honour one of the regulars who was a budding naturalist. Today it's once again the Nelson Arms.

The Waltzing Weasel at Birch Vale, between Hayfield and New Mills, would seem to be a name more in keeping with a city centre student bar. For 200 years the Waltzing Weasel was called the Birch Hall Inn, but its name change was not as recent as you might think.

You have to go back to 1965 to find the then landlady telling the local magistrates why she thought the name should be altered: "It sounds more rural in character," she said, "it has more scientific foundation, and it's a far more entertaining title than the present Birch Hall Inn!" The "scientific foundation" she mentions refers to the way in which weasels mesmerise their prey by appearing to dance or gyrate around them. In fact, there is also a pub in Manchester called the Dancing Weasel.

Most pub names appear to be changed by impulsive new landlords, or some distant marketing director of a faceless pub chain. In most cases, if they consulted the actual punters – the regulars – the answers might surprise them. In 2003 the new landlord of the Queen's Arms at Taddington, 37-year-old Nathan Gale, decided to revert to the original name of the Miner's Arms. It had been renamed the Queen's Arms to celebrate Queen Victoria's Golden Jubilee in 1887. To his credit, he put the name change to a referendum of Taddington residents, sending out voting slips to everyone in the village and also giving them out to customers (250 were handed out across the bar alone). "Is the Queen's Arm's name old and tired or is it still young and fresh?" he was quoted as asking in a local newspaper. "Instead of imposing a change I thought I'd ask the villagers what they think." Around two thirds of them rejected the original name in favour of the Queen's Arms. "I'm pleased that so many people were kind enough to vote," the landlord said afterwards. "We now have a corporate identity and can forge ahead with that." Unfortunately he left not long after, when his application to establish a brewery at the pub was rejected by the planning authority.

CHAPTER EIGHT

Lost to History

"Change your hearts, or you will lose your inns, and you will deserve to have lost them. But when you have lost your inns, drown your empty selves – for you will have lost the last of England" – Hilaire Belloc.

Whether you're a pub aficionado or simply someone who enjoys an occasional trip to their local, it's an inescapable fact that British pubs and inns have spent most of the last century in a gentle (and latterly not so gentle) decline. Of course, pubs are no different to any other business. For most landlords and landladies the pub is their livelihood, and in the case of national chains it is often run on strict commercial lines where figures on the balance sheet or the whims of a marketing strategy counts for much.

Inevitably, pubs come and go (usually go, it must be said) and long gone are the days when comparatively small villages like Winster could boast over 20 pubs and alehouses; and even a modest town like Wirksworth had as many as 50 at one time. Indeed, a small but significant number of Peak District pubs have disappeared since the first edition of this book came out.

Although this reflects the decline in traditional Peak District industries and occupations like lead mining, it's also a reflection of changing lifestyles and social patterns which began 150 years ago with a reaction against soaring levels of alcoholism and the unchecked proliferation of pubs and beerhouses. Lately pubs have had to compete with the growth of home entertainment and the rise of new media, which is why traditional village cinemas and picture houses have also largely vanished. Cheap alcohol from shops and supermarkets has also played its part, encouraging people to drink at home. In addition, latest research shows that young people in particular are drinking less alcohol, so in all likelihood visiting pubs less that they might have done as a result. In short, people are socialising in different ways these days and for many the public house is no longer where they go for a night out. Perhaps the decline in the number of pubs is simply the natural consequence of this and ultimately we will be left with a smaller number of leaner but well-run establishments that is more sustainable in the long run? Let's hope so.

On top of all this, of course, is the impact of the Covid-19 pandemic and ensuing recession. While the long term effect on pub numbers is still unclear, it's inevitable that the pressure on pubs and breweries alike to remain economically viable is only likely to grow; and the loss of more rural pubs seems a distinct possibility.

Once upon a time there were reckoned to be the 'four Ps' which underpinned rural communities: the post office, the pub, the police station and the parish church. The police station has long gone, the post office has been disappearing fast, and in too many cases the pub isn't far behind. Plenty have disappeared over the years, and while some of them are long gone, often centuries ago, there are others that have vanished far more recently – and for a variety of reasons.

Before we begin our lament it's worth stating a couple of fairly obvious points. First, bear in mind that in previous centuries some pubs (and especially alehouses and beerhouses) might only have been in existence for a short time, plus it was not uncommon for some to change their name or re-open some time later under a new name, and for licensees to move between different establishments, even taking the name of the pub with them. Some of the pubs that follow may have had only a brief life before last orders was called and they were consigned to the great brewery wagon in the sky; and given often sketchy historical records it's quite possible that some pubs listed separately here might actually be one and the same – just with a different name and under new management. So apologies in advance for any errors that have crept in.

Secondly, this does not pretend to be a definitive or comprehensive list of all the former pubs of the Peak District. Many towns and villages deserve their own dedicated volumes and in some cases authors or local history societies have provided just that. When I've come across their work I've gratefully acknowledged it in the text and provided details in the Bibliography at the end so you, too, can delve into this source material. Indeed, to comprehensively research the subject you need to do some serious investigative work. Since the 1500s any individual who wanted to serve food and alcoholic beverages in a public house had to apply for a victualler's licence, plus there are trade directories, valuation records, local maps, and so on, so there are detailed records out there for budding pub historians to pore over. Regardless, what follows is a round-up of some of the more notable casualties over the last few centuries and a short homage to them all.

"Time Gentleman, please!"

We begin our sorry stagger on the southern edge of the Peak District, working gradually northwards with a little gentle swaying and perhaps the odd stumble. The historic market town of **Ashbourne** is said to have had as many as 36 named inns and pubs in Victorian times, as well as a fluctuating number of alehouses. They included the White Lion, Hare and Hounds, White Horse, Royal Oak, King's Head, Steam Engine (or Tailor's Arms), Red Lion, Barley Mow, Horse and Jockey, and Marquis of Granby – to name but a few. Among the more unusually-named former pubs were the Tiger, near the Vaults off the Market Place, the Ostrich (or Gaping Goose), and the Old Bear on Church Street; while the Talbot Inn was replaced by the Market Hall in 1850s.

Heading north, in the village of **Alstonefield** the Red Lion became Finderne House in the 1830s, and it is thought that the Black Lion could have become the village workhouse around the same time, but nothing remains of the Harpur's Arms.

In addition to the Sycamore Inn, at the end of the 18th century **Parwich** also had the Crown Inn (now Crown House) and the Wheatsheaf (now Wheatsheaf and Hallgates Cottages).

As of mid 2020, the Bluebell Inn on the A515 at **Tissington** continues to remain empty.

A shop in **Hartington**, between Dig Street and Hide Lane, was also once a pub called the Volunteer Arms, but in 1839 three people were killed when a barrel of gunpowder exploded in the rear of the premises. Until 1951 the Red Lion used to be found at the bottom of Hall Bank and was once notable for its bowling green, as well as its long-time licensee Annie Harrison who spent almost her entire life living there. According to Hartington History Group's engrossing account of village life between 1933-55, "Annie is also remembered as a small lady who nevertheless had a firm manner when it came to dealing with over-enthusiastic drinkers". Apparently there was once another pub almost immediately adjacent to the Red Lion called the Snake and Diamond, but little is known about it.

The George and Dragon at **Brassington** closed in the 1920s, and was divided into two properties: Dragon House and Dragon Cottage. The village website also records the Red Lion, Royal Oak, Wheatsheaf, New Inn and Thorn Tree as former village pubs.

Kirk Ireton lost the Bull's Head, while at **Hognaston** former pubs include the Pack Horse and Bull's Head. The latter shut up shop in the 1880s, and it is said that landlord, Samuel Hardy, closed the premises after a fight in the bar during which he was hit by a bottle, receiving cuts. Furious, he proceeded to open all the beer barrels and pour the demon drink away!

In the mid 19th century the village of **Crich** supported 11 inns and 13 alehouses. The Wheatsheaf once stood at the top of Wheatsheaf Lane, and it is said that George Stephenson stayed here while working on the construction of the mineral railway between Ambergate and Cliff Quarry. The Greyhound could once be found in Roe's Lane, while the White Swan was located on the Market Place and was supposedly linked to the (existing) Black Swan by an underground passage. The Royal Oak and the Blue Bell (now Church Farm) have both gone, as has the Bull's Head (in 1954), plus the Shoulder of Mutton and Rising Sun (both in the 1970s). Records have also been found of a pub called the Last Drink Out near Causeway Lane. The Jovial Dutchman (see Chapter 7) closed in 2009 and became a private 6-bedroom property. Crich's parish website has some splendid archive photos and more details about many of these former hostelries (see Bibliography).

At **Ashover** you could once sup at the White Lion, Yew Tree, Hand and Shears, Boot and Slipper, and Packhorse Inn, although most had gone long before 1900.

The Junction Inn is recorded to have been in existence for about 40 years at **Lea Mills**, and was owned by the Arkwright family. It was located at High Peak Junction, where the Cromford and High Peak Railway met the Cromford Canal. The pub was reported to stand on a narrow strip of land between the canal and the railway and was demolished when the Midland Railway decided to straighten the track.

At the time of writing the Yew Tree Inn at **Holloway** has been closed since 2008, with the owner repeatedly trying to get permission to turn the 19th-century pub into a private house.

Archive photos on the Crich parish website show that **Whatstandwell**'s former pubs included the Iron Grates and the Wheatsheaf. It is said that Florence Nightingale once considered purchasing the latter in order to convert it into a coffee house and reading room. However, this fate more or less befell the last remaining pub, the Derwent Hotel (previously the Bull's Head) next to the bridge over the River Derwent, which closed around 2015 to become a coffee lounge, tea room and bed and breakfast establishment. Less than a mile north along the A6, the **Homesford Cottage Inn** closed some years ago and now offers holiday accommodation, although the names of the pub and brewery (Kimberley Ale) have lived on as large, white painted letters across the tiled roof of an outbuilding across the road.

The Queen's Head Hotel at Matlock, c1870
(copyright the Francis Frith Collection).

Among **Matlock's** long gone pubs are the Wheatsheaf and King's Head in Old Matlock (the area from Matlock Green up to St Giles Church). The first pub once stood opposite the present Duke William and the second next to it. For some years the Queen's Head Hotel was prominent on the corner of Dale Road and Snitterton Road, opposite Matlock Bridge. Although now occupied by shops, the building is still known as the Queen's Head and the hotel is believed to date from the 1780s, with possibly a simple hostelry on the same site before that, since it's said that it was ideally placed to serve the drovers who came down Steep Turnpike at that time.

A curious pub that existed a century ago in the town was the Hole in the Wall. It was located on Jackson Road, near the Friends' Meeting House, and there is speculation that its unusual name came from the activities of some of its rather shady customers. It's been suggested that the pub was used for selling on stolen goods, perhaps hidden in a hole in a wall. Indeed, in his book on Matlock (see Bibliography) local author M. J. Arkle says that the pub was never listed in any trade directories. "It was one of a number of small pubs which dotted the Bank, whose opening hours were flexible and whose patrons sometimes preferred the comfort of an alias such as Duck Jack, Ribs, Smack, Crack and Gentleman Bill.

These nicknames were very much part of the local folklore and often accurately described the personality, background or occupation of the owner. Other nicknames included Tramfat, Putty, Gammy, Cartoil and Nightsoil."

However, an entirely different tale links the pub to the so-called Great Matlock Will Case of the 1860s. It concerned a will involving a piece of land off Snitterton Road that was challenged by three codicils, one of which was supposedly found in a hole in the wall. (Elsewhere in the country, the pub name 'hole in the wall' is thought to directly refer to the means by which regulars could make a hasty exit, either from officers of the law, a press gang, and so on.)

Other pubs that have vanished from Matlock include the Willows and Gate Hotel, both on Smedley Street. The Boathouse on Dale Road closed to become a veterinary practice; and at the time of writing (2020) the Railway Inn on Bakewell Road remains empty.

At **Matlock Green** the Horseshoe pub closed in around 2010; and in just the last few years the popular visitor destination of **Matlock Bath** has lost both the Princess Victoria and the County and Station.

Beyond Matlock is **Tansley**, where today's Tavern at Tansley used to be called the George and Dragon. To local people it was known as the "Big Dragon", and the nearby Royal Oak was the "Small Dragon". An alehouse called the Dyers Arms, on South View, is believed to have closed around the 1850s.

"Last orders at the bar"

On the Staffordshire Moorlands you could once find the Butcher's Arms (now Newhouse Farm) and the Dog and Partridge (now Moorland House) at **Onecote**; and there is mention of the Royal Arms at nearby **Butterton**. The Cavalier at **Grindon** ceased trading in 2006 and is now a private dwelling, while the Bulls Head used to occupy part of what is today called White House but closed before the Second World War.

The Red Bull Inn was once a colourful hostelry in the centre of **Longnor** at a time when there were as many as eight licensed alehouses in the village, but is now a private gallery. In 2018 the Horseshoe Inn closed its doors for the last time and became a private residence, while in recent years the Grapes Inn on the Market Square has periodically closed and at the time of writing is now the newly-launched Merchant's House 'hotel, bar and kitchen.' Meanwhile, a few years ago the Crewe and Harpur Arms, a handsome redbrick building also on the Square, ceased

The Horseshoe Inn at Longnor closed in 2018.

being a public house and now offers private accommodation for groups (see later on in this chapter).

A record of many of **Leek's** former pubs has been compiled by local historian Neil Collingwood (see Bibliography). They include the Railway Tavern, Crown and Anchor, two separate Black Lions, Churnet Valley (near the railway station and now the site of a supermarket car park), Cock Inn, Jolly Sailor, Merry Monk, Cheshire Cheese, Royal Oak, Talbot (now the town's Premier Inn), Sea Lion and Unicorn. Another that disappeared, about a century ago, was the Raglan Arms on the corner of Brook Street and Compton. This was named in memory of Lord Raglan who in 1854 commanded the British forces at the Battle of Balaclava in the Crimean War and who gave the fateful order for the Light Brigade to charge, resulting in heavy casualties. Sergeant Major John Allen, who rode in the ill-fated cavalry charge, survived to tell the tale and returned home to become landlord of the Queen's Arms on Osborne Street in Leek (later renamed the Blue Mugge), as well as drill instructor for the Leek and Biddulph Queen's Own Yeomanry. He later became the licensee of the Swan Hotel on Edward Street (later the Green Dragon) until his death in 1894.

For an authoritative guide to the lost pubs of **Wirksworth** you must turn to Gavin Repton who discovered a list, dated 1840, of over 50 pubs in the town. He used this to make a superb documentary short film, available on a DVD from Wirksworth Heritage Centre, in which he explores the town and its buildings in search of its former watering holes, talking to a wide range of people and unearthing some splendid stories. It's a fascinating look at the social history of the town, including an exploration of the cellars, hidden doors and secret tunnels which appeared to link many of its former pubs. From it we learn that the Crown Inn used to be found on the Market Place opposite the Hope and

Anchor. It was a coaching inn first mentioned in 1758, but closed around 1910. The Green Man, Cheshire Cheese and the Three Tuns once stood on West End, while the Rose and Crown public house closed in 1876. There are records of other town pubs long since vanished, including the Angel on Coldwell Street, the Bell on St John's Street, and the Cock, Crown, and Dog and Partridge, Glazier's Arms, Greyhound, White Lion, Tiger, Spreadeagle, Recruiting Sergeant and Lord Nelson. More unusual names include the Boggart's Inn and Gaggler's Arms. A far more recent casualty was the Vaults on Coldwell Street which closed in 2008 and the Kingsfield which was demolished to make way for a housing development two years later. Where once there were 50 pubs there are now only seven. For more information on the town and its history make sure to visit Wirksworth Heritage Centre on St John's Street.

At nearby **Wirksworth Moor**, the Noah's Ark Inn closed in 1918; while at the small mining community of Bolehill there were once four hostelries. Apart from the Miner's Standard, you could once get a drink at the Hollybush Inn (now the location for the stables of Bolehill House) and the New Inn (next to Bage Mine).

In much more recent times the Duke of Wellington at **Middleton by Wirksworth** closed and is now private housing.

Bonsall is another village steeped in mining history, and according to research by Peter Fellows via the Bonsall History Project, there were once as many as 12 pubs in or close to the parish, including nine actually in the village. Today only the King's Head and Barley Mow remain, but as we have seen in the previous chapter, the Queen's Head used to stand next to the King's Head (it closed in 1817 and for a time became a fish and chip shop) and the house still bears the name of the former pub. The former Miners' Standard (in the High Street until around 1908) and Pig o'Lead at the Via Gellia junction (which closed in 1995) both recall the days of lead mining. Another High Street pub was the

The former Duke of Wellington at Middleton by Wirksworth.

Britannia Inn, which disappeared in the 1870s; and Briars Inn, off Black Tor Road, is now known as Briars Inn Farmhouse. The New Inn, on Yeoman Street, was renamed the Fountain. It finally closed in 1983 and is now a tearoom and B&B.

Records from 1870 show a pub called the Lillies Inn existed at the hamlet of **Ible** and was probably named after the plant that was once plentiful in the valley, but it's believed to have closed in the 1950s; and there were supposedly several pubs up on the moors above Bonsall, including the Gate Inn at Slaley, but little or no records exist.

On the other side of Slaley Moor lies **Winster**, which in 1750 had two dozen inns and alehouses. Long-lost venues include the Bull's Head (East Bank), the Crown (Main Street), Shoulder of Mutton (West Bank), and also the Wheatsheaf. A pub or alehouse called the Derbyshire Sally came to a conclusive end in 1785, when it was blown up after an accident thought to involve mining explosives.

Winster Hall became a pub in 1984, after operating as a B&B, but then after changing hands several times it reverted to a private residence. The original pub sign depicted a group of Morris Dancers that was styled on a photograph of the famous local Winster Morris men. Another well-known inn was the Angel, opposite the Old Hall, and both this and Winster Hall were reputedly haunted (see Chapter 5 for the full story).

Just along from Winster is the village of **Wensley**, which waved goodbye to the Crown in 1997 and the Red Lion a decade later (see Chapter 2).

On the nearby B5056 you could once knock back a pint at the Piper Inn until it fell derelict in the 1930s. Turning right at Grangemill, on to the A5012, Pikehall Farm at the hamlet of **Pikehall** was formerly the

Pikeham Inn, once a well known roadside stop for travellers.

Back along the same road at **Cromford**, pubs that have long vanished include the Bull's Head, which stood by the Market

The Red Lion at Wensley.

Place at the end of Scarthin until it was demolished in the late 1800s. The Cock Inn was situated on North Street (Cromford Hill), opposite the Bell Inn, which is still there. Further down the hill stood the Crown, which became a butchers and ended up a private residence. At the very top of the long slope was the Cromford and High Peak Railway Inn, which not surprisingly became shortened to the Railway Inn.

The King's Head, described as a three-storey Georgian inn, once stood next to Masson Mill and served as the manager's residence; while the Rutland Arms was built for the workers in 1842 in a terraced row directly opposite the mill. Both the King's Head and the Rutland Arms were demolished in the 1970s to allow the A6 to be widened. Another former pub was the Red Lion half way up Cromford Hill, plus two beerhouses called the Thorn Tree and Wheatsheaf.

A pub called the Thorn Tree also existed in the mid 1800s in **Birchover**; while **Youlgrave** once had a fourth pub, the Thornhill Arms, situated opposite the church a couple of doors down from the George Hotel.

The small communities either side of Youlgrave could also once boast their own watering holes. The Bateman Arms at **Middleton by Youlgrave**, located in Square House, was named after the famous Victorian antiquarian and pioneering archaeologist Thomas Bateman who lived at nearby Lomberdale Hall.

The Bateman Arms at Middleton by Youlgrave was named after the Victorian antiquarian Thomas Bateman.

I have seen an extremely old image of a pub called the Three Rivers Inn which once stood by the road bridge across the Lathkill at **Alport**. In more recent times the Boarding House Hotel occupied a similar site (perhaps the same?) on Alport Hill, but this was demolished just before the Second World War when the road was straightened to make it safer.

Today **Monyash** has just a single pub, the Bulls Head, but records from 1579 record the Golden Lion on Church Street, which was also known as the Golden Fleece and was where the Monyash Friendly Society met until the inn closed in 1919 (it subsequently divided into Lathkill House and Lathkill Cottage). It also shows that there were two pubs on Chapel Street: The Star (now Melbourne House) and the Bay Horse, which has a vaulted cellar where the beer was stored and is now a private house called the Old Bay Horse Inn. A couple of miles away the Plough at **Flagg** has permanently closed its doors and reverted to private accommodation.

Chucking out time

It should come as no surprise today to find that **Bakewell**, popular year-round with visitors, still supports a number of pubs, bars and a hotel. But the list of former inns and taverns is even more extensive, as research by the Bakewell and District Historical Society has shown. The Flying Childers was used as a beerhouse during the construction of the railway and occupied a signalman's house close to Bakewell Station. Nearby was the Station Hotel and at the bottom of Station Road a pub called Sign of the Talbot. On Matlock Street you could once find the Nag's Head, Todd's Vaults and Vernon Arms, and on Buxton Road stood Britain's Pride (it became Skidmore's grocers) and the White Swan. Near here was the Crown (later the King's Arms) and the New Inn, the latter built by mill-owner Richard Arkwright.

On Bagshaw Hill was the Union Hotel, while on Monyash Road you could find the Staffordshire Arms and Sheldon Lane End, and at the junction with Yeld Road stood the Royal Standard. There was the Blue Bell on Stanage Road, the Devonshire Arms on Church Alley and the Black Swan by the bridge. The Anchor Inn was knocked into the present-day Wheatsheaf, and until the early 1900s the Angel Inn was located at the corner of Water Street and Water Lane. The Three Tuns was later occupied by Williams and Glyn's Bank.

Close to the historic Market Hall was the Durham Ox, presumably a favourite with traders, and which is now the Queens Arms; while the

Pineapple Inn, off Baslow Road, was a popular haunt of men working on the construction of the adjacent Midland railway line, now the Monsal Trail.

Following the Wye downstream to its junction with the Derwent at **Rowsley**, we pass the site of two former village coaching inns – the Nag's Head (now Bridge House Farm) and Red Lion (now Vernon House), both of which closed in 1828.

South from here is **Darley Dale,** or more accurately **Two Dales**, where the Blacksmith's Inn (now a private house) and the Nag's Head (demolished) once stood.

To the north we enter the grounds of Chatsworth and come to **Edensor**. Originally there were as many as eight pubs or ale outlets, including the Edensor Inn, now the Chatsworth Institute. Boswell visited it in 1775 not long after it had opened and reported that it had a "very jolly landlord".

The neighbouring estate village of **Pilsley** once boasted the Snake and Crown, which is clearly a reference to the Duke's family crest (see Chapter 4). The Duke of Rutland in **Baslow**, next to the historic bridge, closed in 2015 and is now a Co-op store. On the other side of the churchyard is the Prince of Wales, which a few years ago changed from a pub to (more or less) a restaurant called Rowleys; then in 2019 happily turned back into the Prince of Wales pub once more.

Taddington once had six inns or alehouses, including the George Hotel, first opened in the 1750s and later turned into flats. The Bull's Head is believed to have stood opposite the present-day Queen's Arms, while the Star Inn (now Star House) was located at the western end of the village next to the church, and for some time it incorporated part of the village's historic Norman font which was used to wash dirty beer mugs.

The font was finally returned to the church in 1939.

The former Miner's Arms can be dated back

The Queen's Arms in Bakewell, with the 17th-century Old Market Hall beyond – the pub was previously called the Durham Ox.

to 1736, and at one time its cellar was used as a makeshift morgue, since the local coffin-maker lived across the street. In 1887 the pub changed its name to the Queen's Arms, to mark Queen Victoria's Golden Jubilee, and in Chapter 7 we have seen what happened when the new landlord tried to change it back a century later. Elsewhere, a beerhouse called the Traveller's Rest which opened around the 1850s later became the Marlborough Temperance Hotel (see Chapter 5), and in more modern times ended up as Marlborough House, offering bed and breakfast.

A village directory of 1928 suggests that in **Litton** you could lean against the bar of the Hare and Hounds (now a building called Woodstock, in Litton Dale) and also the Anchor pub, now long gone.

At **Tideswell** the Cross Daggers Inn burned down in 1937 and the site is now occupied by the Ex-Servicemen's Club. The Three Tuns Inn (the name was from the crest of the Vintners Company) could once be found on the Market Place, but is now a private dwelling. Nearby was the Belle Vue Hotel, later renamed the First Drop Inn (and according to some sources also known as the Last Drop Inn). It had a dining room named the Drunken Butcher in honour of William Bennett, a local poet. A ballad relates the story of a Tideswell butcher who, after a having a few too many to drink at Sparrowpit, was supposedly chased all the way home over the moors by a ghost.

You could once buy a round at the Miner's Arms on Church Street; while near the church gates was the Bull's Head and King's Head (demolished in the late 1950s). The Peacock Hotel closed in the 1970s after Freddie and Connie Lomas Fletcher, tenants for 36 years, decided to retire. Interestingly, like at Matlock, there was once a pub called the Hole in the Wall. It was approached via steps from the Market Place, and apparently acquired its name from its tiny entrance. The open space behind the building was once used for cock fighting and bear baiting. Names of other Tideswell pubs long gone include the Dog Inn, Angel Inn, Gate Inn, Marquis of Granby, Black Horse and White Hart.

Out to the west, in Cheshire, you could once drown your sorrows at the Redway Tavern at **Langley**, the Setter Dog at **Walker Barn** (see Chapter 7) and the Eagle and Child near **Gradbach** (Chapter 4).

Last chance saloon

As far back as 1577 records show that **Buxton** had three inns, eight alehouses and an hotel. Later the two main coaching inns became the White Hart, in Scarsdale Place, and the Eagle, purpose-built by the 4th

Duke of Devonshire in 1760 as a grand, four-storey coaching hotel. It replaced the Eagle and Child inn, which like the former pub at Gradbach refers to the crest of the Earl of Derby (see Chapter 4).

As you would expect of a popular spa town like Buxton, a considerable number of pubs and hotels have come and gone, including the Seven Stars (later called the Dog and Partridge), Oddfellows Arms on the High Street, and the Swan with Two Necks on Windsor Road. The Fox and Hounds was once to be found on West Road, the Horseshoe was located on Fairfield Road, and the Red Lion in Holmefield. There was also the Manchester Arms and the Jug and Glass on West Road, while the Shakespeare Inn on Spring Gardens, was another coaching inn that in its time was very popular, but after its lease expired in 1926 it was knocked down to make way for shops.

In 1811 Buxton had 17 hotels and inns, including the Shoulder of Mutton which is first recorded in that year. It was here, in about 1850, that a soldier by the name of Dawson was found guilty of having a drink without paying for it. He was taken across the road, tied to a tree and flogged, much to the displeasure of the regulars who felt he had been hard done by. So they began to boycott the pub and went elsewhere, and in an effort to restore the image of his premises, the landlord decided to change the pub's name to the Swan. Other pubs from this time included the Fountain on the High Street, Hatton and Holden on Spring Gardens, and the Cheshire Cheese on Macclesfield Old Road.

Recent casualties include the Bakers Arms on West Road, which closed in 2008 and now forms two private houses; the Prince of Wales on Fairfield Road, which ceased trading in 2011 and became a funeral directors; and the Royal Foresters in Fairfield which is now an affordable housing development. The Robin

The Bakers Arms in Buxton closed in 2008.

Hood on London Road was demolished to make way for a Premier Inn in 2016 and the Devonshire Arms once stood on the Common at Fairfield, next to the golf course.

At **Dove Holes** the Railway Inn closed in 1994 and is now a joinery supplier, although you can still just about make out the name painted in large white letters on the roof tiles; and the Wheatsheaf (which also seemed to be called the Quarryman) has also closed in the last few years. The Midland Hotel at the hamlet of **Peak Dale**, which once served the railway station opposite, closed around 2000 is now a private house.

Another Railway Hotel, by the former station at **Miller's Dale**, was renamed Dale Hotel after the closure of the line and station in 1967 and is now private dwellings.

According to the official **Chapel-en-le-Frith** town trail, a house known as Black Greyhound Cottage stands on the site of the Black Greyhound Inn and, between the early 17th century and the Second World War, a large house to the east was the former Bull's Head Inn (look for the relief of a bull's head above its doorway). Another Chapel pub that has long vanished is the Swan with Two Necks. Like its Buxton counterpart, the latter's name is almost certainly a corruption of the name A Swan with Two *Nicks*. This is derived from the annual 'swan-upping' procedure whereby the birds on special rivers such as the Thames were marked by

The Railway Hotel next to Miller's Dale Station, c1955 (copyright The Francis Frith Collection).

their owners – five nicks in the case of a royal swan, and two if it was owned by the Dyers and Vintners Companies.

Still in Chapel, the Jolly Carter closed in 2009 and has now been converted into private houses; while at **Horwich End** another jolly pub has disappeared – the Jolly Roger (also the New Inn for a bit), which closed around 15 years ago and is now an antiques shop.

The Old Packhorse once served travellers on the Manchester Road through **Tunstead Milton** and is now a private cottage. To the north of Chapel-en-le-Frith, the Cross Keys Inn closed a few years ago at **Chapel Milton** and has been replaced with new houses.

According to research by Sarah Williams via the website www.closedpubs.co.uk, among the pubs that have disappeared in **Whaley Bridge** are the Bulls Head, Coach and Horses, New Inn, Quiet Woman (in 1850 known as the Lamb and Salmon), Seven Stars, and Swan Inn. And in just the last few years other local pubs that have gone include the Navigation Inn and Dog and Partridge. In 2019 planning permission was granted to build seven new homes on the site of the White Horse, which had been a pub since the 19th century; while the Jodrell Arms, once an imposing establishment next to the railway station (see Chapter 4), remains closed and its long term future uncertain.

The Ploughboy and the Crescent have both closed in **Disley** in recent years are now residential properties.

At **Chinley**, north of Chapel, the old Squirrel Inn was replaced by the much grander Princes Hotel to cater for the increased railway traffic, and this was later renamed the Chinley Lodge Hotel. At the nearby hamlet of **New Smithy**, next to the railway bridge, stands the Crown and Mitre Hotel, built in the 1840s, which a few years ago was converted into four luxury apartments.

The Jodrell Arms, next to Whaley Bridge railway station, has remained closed for some years.

Former pubs at **Buxworth** include the Bull's Head Inn, which closed in 1960 and became a private residence (the house is now called the Old Bull's Head); the Rose and Crown, which used to stand by the upper canal basin; and the Yellow Cap. When the canal's fortunes dipped in the early years of the 20th century the last pub became a farm and was later demolished. It's reported that the stones from the building were used in the restoration of the canal basin.

Taxal, a hamlet in the Goyt Valley just to the south of Whaley Bridge, once boasted a royal hunting lodge which in 1829 became the Royal Oak. In the 1950s it changed its name to the Chimes, but that in turn closed around 20 years ago. Records from 1851 and 1871 show that there was another pub here called the Cat and Fiddle.

Further along the Macclesfield Road the Bulls Head at **Kettleshulme** is no more; and research has shown that over the years **Rainow** has had numerous pubs, including the Horse and Jockey, Plough, Black Greyhound and the Patch. In more recent times the Rising Sun and Highwayman have both been converted into private residences.

As mentioned in Chapter 3, **Bollington** had as many as 27 licensed premises. The splendid history section of the Happy Valley Bollington website lists some of the pubs that have long since vanished, including the Barley Mow, Blazing Rag, Britannia, Dagger Club, Drum and Monkey, Flying Horse, Grapes, Horse Shoe, Lord Nelson, Navigation, Orange Tree, Post Office Inn, Railway Inn, Rising Sun, Robin Hood Inn, Steam Engine Inn, Waddling Duck and Weavers Arms. In addition, the website identifies pubs in and around Bollington that have recently disappeared, including the Barge Inn, Cheshire Hunt, Queens Arms, Red Lion and Wagon and Horses (which since 2006 has been the Bayleaf Lounge Indian restaurant).

A mile to the north of Bollington is the small village of **Pott Shrigley**, but the demise of its pub early in the last century is evidence, if needed, of the dire consequences of over-imbibing on the Sabbath. The Lowther Arms was named after the Lord of the Manor, and by all accounts was a pleasant village inn. But one particular Sunday morning in 1922 as Lady Constance Lowther was emerging from church, she detected alcohol on the breath of her groom, and in a fit of moral rage promptly closed the village pub for good. However, there is a far more indecent version of this story (preferred by most locals, it has to be said) that has Lady Constance catching her groom relieving himself against the wheels of her carriage.

For expert information on **New Mills** we must turn to the excellent

The Grapes Hotel on Dyehouse Lane, New Mills (photo courtesy of Steve Lewis).

website run by local historian Steve Lewis (see Bibliography). Heading down the Sett Valley to New Mills, the Old Crescent Inn on Market Street closed while this book was being written, and it is understood that the new owner intends to turn it into an Indian restaurant. The Swan Hotel on Buxton Road has closed in the last few years, as has the Pineapple Inn and White Hart on Dye House Lane.

The Torrs on Market Street is now a cafe and holiday apartments, but was once a pub called the Crown and also, at one time it seems, the Bees Knees. A house called the Old Squirrel Inn on Buxton Road, near Newtown Station (New Mills), is another indication of an ex-pub. Other former New Mills pubs are listed on Steve Lewis's local history website (with some great archive photos), including the Bridge Tavern, Bulls Head, Cock Inn, Commercial Inn, Dog and Partridge, George, Grapes, Green Man, Hare and Hounds, Jolly Carter, North Western Hotel, Printers Arms, St Albans Inn, Sycamore Inn and Vine Tavern. Also check out the separate pages on the history of the Pride of the Peaks (formerly the Railway Hotel) and the history of Rock Tavern on Wirksmoor Road.

In New Mills Heritage Centre there is a map showing the location of up to 36 past and present pubs in the New Mills area. And also take heed of the sobering story of how one local man who lived among (and often in) these once numerous pubs took the pledge and reformed his ways – see Chapter 5.

At the nearby hamlet of **Rowarth** it's recorded that former pubs included the Lime Cart and Moorfield Arms. There was also one known

Ye Old White Hart Hotel,

NEW MILLS.

LICENSED OVER 80 YEARS.

Free from Brewer and Spirit Merchant.

If it be true that good Wine needs no bush,
It is also true that good Ale and Spirits need
no push.—*Shakespeare and Brownhill.*

(" As you like it.")

Bro. GEO. HENRY BROWNHILL,

(" BRITON'S GLORY " LODGE, GLOSSOP,)

PROPRIETOR.

An advert for the Old White Hart at New Mills (courtesy of Steve Lewis).

The sign above the door of the former Childrens Inn at Rowarth.

today as the Childrens Inn that was built in the 17th century as a coaching Inn and was previously called the Hare and Hounds. It was converted into a holiday property for children in 1926 and is now run by the Girlguiding movement. From the roadside you can view a colourful plaque above the door depicting its former name and a scene from the Cat and Fiddle nursery rhyme. The building is also used as a polling station for the 100 or so inhabitants of Rowarth.

In **Hayfield**, the Bridge Inn closed in 1923 and was demolished three years later; the Commercial Inn, opposite the Railway Inn (now the Kinder Lodge)

ceased trading in 1908; and the Junction Inn called time in 1935. In 1958, two local pubs locked up for good: the Wood Inn on New Mills Road and the Toll Bar Inn on Glossop Road; and further along in **Little Hayfield** the Grapes Inn closed a year later. For more details about former pubs in the wider Hayfield area go to the page on the 'Old Inns and Alehouses of Hayfield' page on the New Mills history website (see Bibliography).

No more cakes and ale

Heading eastwards to the central Peak once more, it's said that in the early 1800s **Eyam** boasted 11 pubs and as many as 23 ale houses. Former hostelries include the Town Head Inn, which opened as far back as the 1600s for passing packhorse trains and ceased trading during the First World War. Moving down Church Street, the Royal Oak was originally called the British Oak and until it closed a few years ago was a popular venue for local functions, with the Carnival Queen being crowned on the balcony at the front. The Rose and Crown used to occupy the building opposite the post office, while a little further along is the distinctive Brick House, where a 17th-century pub called the Stag's Parlour used to stand.

Opposite the church I remember once drinking in the Bull's Head (previously the Talbot, and before that the Shrewsbury Arms), but in the late 1990s it was sold off for redevelopment as private flats. At the eastern end of the village there were once two pubs on the Square: the Foresters Arms (now Foresters House) and the Bold Rodney Inn, the latter dating from the late 18th century and named after Admiral Rodney, who trounced the French fleet in the Caribbean in 1782. It closed in 1901, and now forms part of the Eyam Tea Rooms.

The former pubs of Eyam have been well documented in an interesting booklet compiled by Eyam Village Society, available locally, and those which are now private buildings – like the Town Head Inn, Brick House and Bull's Head – have heritage plaques attached to their exterior to denote their previous role.

Along the road at **Foolow** the Bull's Head was once joined by the Three Horse Shoes, long since demolished, and the Bird in Hand. The latter was renamed the Spread Eagle and closed in 1911, but the building survives.

At **Calver** you could once find the Bull's Head next to the three-storied London Tavern (later the Co-op) as well as the Silent Woman, Miner's Arms, and Drum and Monkey.

Detailed research by Rosemary Lockie (and others) published on the Wishful Thinking website shows that **Stoney Middleton** once had numerous pubs and alehouses. There was the Barrel Inn, Boot and Shoe Inn (later the Grouse Inn), Bulls Head, Miner's Arms, Royal Oak, Stag's Head and Sun Inn (previously the Denman Arms), as well as a number of beerhouses. The Ball Inn used to stand at the junction of Eyam Dale and Stoney Middleton Dale, but this has been demolished and is now a car park for the quarry opposite.

One especially noteworthy pub was the Lovers Leap Inn, located almost under the rock of the same name and which is famous as being the scene of Hannah Baddeley's jump in 1762. According to the story, she threw herself off the top in a suicide bid, but was saved when her petticoat billowed out like a parachute and wafted her safely down. The pub subsequently became a cafe and is now a restaurant. The last pub standing in the village is the Moon Inn, which was originally called the Old Moon and sited across the road from the present location.

Moving north to the Hope Valley, there were once at least 15 pubs and beerhouses in **Castleton**. One of the most unusual was to be found at the entrance to the gaping mouth of Peak Cavern, which was also known as the Devil's Arse and reputedly the largest cave entrance in Britain. Until

The Lovers Leap Inn at Stoney Middleton in 1916
(photo courtesy of Julie Bunting).

the last century, the cave was used by rope-makers, since it offered the necessary space and ideal atmospheric conditions (ie damp). At the turn of 1800 it's recorded that the cavern's 60ft-high mouth supported several dwellings, including a beerhouse, which in 1830 became Slack's Mineral Shop selling Blue John and other local knick-knacks.

Other long-gone Castleton pubs include the Wagon and Horses and Hole in the Wall, off Market Place. There was also a pub called the Ship Inn, located near the entrance to Castle Hill and Peveril Castle. According to an article by Peter Harrison, Chairman of Castleton Historical Society, it was so-called because its roof and structural timbers were thought to have come from wooden ships that had been taken to a breaker's yard in Manchester, and indeed he remembers going up into the roof space to admire the structure. After it closed some of the building became the Peveril Hotel and is now a private residence.

Early 19th century records show that **Bradwell** once had pubs called the George and Dragon on Towngate (now Green Dragon Cottage), Rose and Crown on Smithy Hill (now Crown Cottage) and Newburgh Arms on Netherside, which closed in 1923 and is now Newburgh House. There was also the Rose Tree and Bridge Inn, the latter becoming a cafe in the 1950s and 60s and is now a private residence called Bridge House. Bradwell Historical Society records that the Bull's Head pub (now the Old Bull's Head) closed in 1938, becoming first a house, then a butcher's shop and afterwards a hairdresser's. Although the Shoulder of Mutton survives, it is in fact the new version that was built following the construction of New Road in 1937. The old Shoulder of Mutton across the road became a café and then a private dwelling called Lyndale House.

Ex-pubs at **Hope** include the Blacksmith's Arms (at one time the Horse Shoe Inn) and the Durham Ox, which ended up becoming the village post office. The Cross Daggers Inn, now Daggers House, existed until 1860, and the sign for this attractive, 400-year-old building depicted crossed daggers, a posset pot, tankard and a bunch of grapes. Cross daggers represented the shield of the Cutlers company of Sheffield, and it is believed that salesmen carrying cutlery from Sheffield stayed here en route to Manchester. In recent years the Poachers Arms on Castleton Road has also ceased trading as a pub.

Although the former Church Hotel at **Edale** was renamed the Rambler Inn, there was also once a Church Inn that is now Church Cottage.

In the 1800s, **Grindleford** sported the Bluebell Inn on the main street; while in **Bamford** the former Cheshire Cheese Inn became the post office. I have also read that in the 1950s Dutton's Brewery demolished the

350-year-old Golden Fleece in Bamford, to considerable local protests, and replaced it with a pub called the Sir Winston Churchill nearby; but this, too, has evidently disappeared. In 2011 Ye Derwent Hotel closed as a public house and now offers holiday accommodation to groups.

Hathersage has also seen its fair share of pubs coming and going. However, thanks to research by the Hathersage Millennium Group there is plenty of information about the changing fortunes of their locals. Following questionnaires and interviews with some of the older residents, the group established that the Buck Inn once stood alongside the Buck Stone, below the causeway under Stanage Edge. Gatehouse Farm used to be the Cowgate Inn; and Cliffe House on Jaggers Lane was once known as the Bull and Mouth (c1750). The story goes that funeral processions would sometimes stop at the latter, as it was on the uphill route to the graveyard from next-door Bamford (which didn't have its own burial ground), and the coffin-bearers were sometimes in need of sustenance.

High Lees Farm was the Hare and Hounds until 1917, located on the site of an earlier thatched inn; Hillfoot Farm on Castleton Road was the Hillfoot Inn, then the Rifleman's Arms until around 1880. Old Bell House in the village was formerly the Old Bell (or Blue Bell) Inn, while Hall Cottage was once frequented as the Angel and Child.

It is said that the Old Bell and Hare and Hounds both lost their licences around the time of the First World War, when the authorities decided that there were too many pubs in the village. The Ordnance Arms Hotel on the Main Road was built in 1808 by Major A. Shuttleworth, who had served in the Royal Artillery in the American War of Independence. In the 1960s it was renamed the Hathersage Inn, and only a few years ago closed down to become an outdoor equipment shop and residential flats.

In 2019 the **Snake Pass Inn** closed as a pub and now offers self-catering holiday accommodation only. In 2020 the Wanted Inn at

The Hathersage Inn began life in 1808 as the Ordnance Arms Hotel and is now given over to retail and residential use.

Sparrowpit changed its name to the Olive Tree cafe and bar and now incorporates a farm shop.

Until around 1900 you could enjoy a drink in the Cross Daggers at **High Bradfield**, which because it was located near the gates of St Nicholas Church was locally known as Heaven's Parlour or Heaven's Gate. It was a popular haunt of the navvies who built the dams on the new reservoirs in the valley, so much so that it ended up losing its licence because they kept fighting all the time. After this it was used as a vestry, a registry office, a school and then a post office, before finally becoming a private residence.

The Cross Inn once stood in the centre of **Low Bradfield**, but closed in the late 1970s. On Annet Lane you could once find the Reservoir Inn, which eventually became known by its more popular name of the Haychatter Inn. It closed in 2003 and Haychatter House is now a private residence. The George at **Dungworth** became a farmhouse after it closed in the 1950s, and there was another, short-lived pub called the Boot and Shoe. At **Langsett** there is a record of a pub called the Dog and Partridge in 1870; and the nearby Flouch Inn disappeared in 2013 (see Chapter 3).

Perhaps the most unusual – and crushingly final – end to a pub or hotel concerns the Ashopton Inn in the Upper Derwent Valley. It was built in 1824 as a halt for coaches on the Sheffield to Glossop turnpike, a chance to change horses, refresh and make preparations for the long haul over the Snake Pass, as well as a stopping point for weary travellers who had made it successfully the other way.

However, as already outlined in Chapter 6, the narrow valley was earmarked by the Derwent Valley Water Board to create the new Ladybower reservoir to meet the growing thirst of Sheffield and the East Midlands. Early in 1943, the villages of Derwent and **Ashopton**, including the Ashopton Inn and the equally elegant and historic Derwent Hall, were closed down and emptied so that building work on the massive new Ladybower dam could proceed. The Board, which had purchased the inn from the Duke of Devonshire in 1902, did look into the possibility of rebuilding Ashopton Inn on a new site, but in the end the licence was transferred to separate premises at New Mills, and Ashopton and its ruined pub were permanently submerged beneath the water. (See separate plates for a photo of this substantial and well-known inn in its heyday.)

However, in several unusually dry periods since, most notably summer 1959 and late autumn 2018, the water levels in the reservoirs dropped sufficiently for the outline of the buildings to be clearly revealed. On the occasion of the former, it's reported that a local man went on to the bed of the reservoir and was able to recover stones from the family farm he had been forced to give up 16 years before. He ended up using them as a rockery outside his new home in Ashbourne.

In his long out-of-print booklet on the pubs around Sheffield (see Bibliography), Ron Davey identifies the Surrey Arms (now Surrey Farm) and the Norfolk Arms, both off the A57 at **Hollow Meadows** near Moscar Top.

A little to the south are the three small **Redmires** reservoirs, constructed between the 1830s-50s. What looks like a memorial stone in the roadside wall between the middle and upper reservoirs is in fact the surviving sign from a beerhouse called the Grouse and Trout, which used to stand near here. The sign features a grouse and three trout, and – although it's hard to make out and I'm going on others' say so – the Latin inscription *Ich Dien Dinner* or "I serve dinner". There was another beerhouse called Ocean View nearby, both popping up in the 1840s to help quench the thirst of the navvies constructing the reservoirs. The Ocean View closed in the 1880s, but the Grouse and Trout continued

All that's left of the Grouse and Trout by Redmires Reservoir is its former stone sign, featuring a (rather battered) grouse and three trout.

172

into the early years of the 20th century and was supposedly closed after the moorland owner feared that the new influx of sightseers and tourists served by the pub would disrupt his shooting. The building was subsequently demolished in 1934.

"Don't you people have homes to go to?"

For information on some of **Glossop's** former pubs we have to thank the Glossop Victorian Architectural Heritage website, which in turn was inspired by research by the late David Field (see Bibliography). From it we learn that among the town's many former pubs are the Bush, Junction, Hanging Gate, Rose and Crown, Britannia Inn, Market Tavern, Bridge Inn, White Lion, Peartree Inn and The Newmarket. In addition, other ex-locals that have disappeared more recently include the Drovers Arms and Nags Head on Charlestown Road, Old Gloveworks at Riverside Mill and Manor Inn.

At the time of writing the George Hotel on Norfolk Street was also shut up and looking rather forlorn. The Moon and Sixpence, a distinctive redbrick building on Bernard Street in the centre of Glossop, was originally called The Fleece and has now been renamed the Victoria Lounge. The Railway Inn on Norfolk Street was built in 1838 but demolished in 1909 to be replaced by the Conservative Club. This closed in 2013 and the imposing edifice has since been occupied, quite appropriately, by Harvey Leonards Wine and Ale Shop, which sells bottled beer from around the world as well as serving a selection on tap for you to taste and enjoy.

There were once apparently a number of pubs on Chapel Street, centred on a small but lively Irish community who had come to work in the mills and on construction jobs as the Victorian town grew rapidly in the mid/late 19th century. Pubs included the Volunteer Arms, Star Inn, Stag's Head, Spinner's Arms and Shamrock Inn. The Glossop Victorian Architectural Heritage website suggests that many of these pubs and beerhouses were lost due to the Licensing Acts of 1904 and 1910 which sought to reduce and restrict the number of licensed premises. One means of doing this was to offer financial compensation to a licensee who had his or her licence renewal refused.

In **Old Glossop**, the Hare and Hounds, Ring o'Bells and the Greyhound have all disappeared, and the Quiet Shepherd Inn near **Tintwistle** is now a private house. The Prince of Wales at **Padfield** closed in 1927 and is now two houses; and at **Crowden** in Longdendale the Commercial Inn was pulled down in the 1920s. A similar fate befell the George and Dragon, which for over 300 years stood at the nearby Holmfirth turning and was closed in 1961 because Manchester Corporation deemed it too near their reservoir and likely to pollute the drinking water.

A mile up that road (by Heyden Bridge) there once stood the Tollemarche Arms, and if you head eastwards you come to the site of the Angel Inn which until the 1920s stood in the village of **Woodhead** above the station next to the tunnel entrance. Pub, village and railway are all long gone. Nearing the top of the Woodhead Pass the former hamlet of **Saltersbrook** once included the Miller's Arms (closed in 1913) and at the summit the Plough and Harrow. The latter became known as Fiddlers Green after a semi-blind violin-player that used to entertain guests in the remote pub. The story goes that one night, almost certainly after a glass too many, he wandered out on to the featureless moors and got lost, ending up at Ronksley Water where he was found minus his fiddle. Luckily for him, shepherds came across both his violin and case some time later and managed to reunite the grateful musician with his instrument. After that the pub was known as Fiddlers Green in memory of the fortunate man.

In all, there were once six inns on the Woodhead Road across the high moorland pass; but at the summit today there is nothing in particular to see, save a few stones amid the desolate moorland, to remind us of past pubs.

One of the last shepherds' gatherings at the now demolished Millers Arms at Saltersbrook, at the head of the Woodhead Pass
(photo courtesy of the Peak District National Park Authority).

Finally, there are two other remote, moorland pubs with unusual names and both long consigned to the South Pennines history books. Bill o'Jacks was located near the reservoirs on the moors above **Greenfield**, and gained notoriety and national headlines in 1832 after the double murder of landlord William Bradbury and his son. The Isle of Skye Inn, near **Holmfirth**, may have disappeared many years ago, but the pub is still remembered by the annual Four Inns challenge walk – see Chapter 5.

Double vision?

In recent years the Peak District, like the Yorkshire Dales and North York Moors, has provided the setting for numerous TV series, adaptations and films. The long-running comedy *Last of the Summer Wine* is set in and around Holmfirth on the West Yorkshire edge of the national park, and one episode was filmed inside the former Haychatters pub near Low Bradfield. The equally popular series *Peak Practice* about rural doctors was also filmed in the White Peak and around Ashover, Crich, Longnor and Wirksworth. Quite often the setting switched from the doctor's surgery to the village pub, and this meant good business for the (genuine) local, which surrendered its premises for the day. The Black Swan at Ashover featured in several programmes, under its own name, but when the cameras rolled at Longnor, the (former) Horseshoe Inn was temporarily renamed the Inn on the Square, and the Crewe and Harpur Arms became the Cardale Tearooms. And, in a very modest personal claim to fame, I was also once an 'extra' on the film set of one particular episode by pretending to be a diner at the Black Swan at Idridgehay, south of Wirksworth. However, the pub that featured regularly as the (fictitious) Manor Inn was a detached period building in South Wingfield which at one time was in fact a coaching inn called the Horse and Groom, then later the Manor Hotel.

The village of Birchover, mid-way between Bakewell and Matlock, has also had its fair share of fictitious pubs. In 1986, Uppertown Farm featured in an ITV production of a Sherlock Holmes story called *The Mystery of Priory School* when it was converted into a period pub called the Champion Jack, featuring a cockerel on the sign. According to Jim Drury's entertaining recollections of life in Birchover, the fee paid to the farmer allowed for substantial redecorations, and the timber left by the film crew was enough to repair every gate on the farm. Some years earlier, one of Birchover's two real pubs, the Druid Inn, was dressed up as an Irish tavern for a film that sadly was never shown.

In the small Staffordshire village of Alstonefield, a pub called the White Swan materialised during the filming of *The Life and Times of Henry Pratt*; while in the 1970s, passers-by at the hamlet of Gratton, between Youlgrave and Elton, were surprised to see a sign for the non-existent Black Dog inn. It was created solely for the filming of D.H. Lawrence's book *The Virgin and the Gypsy* that was shot locally.

Hayfield was the setting of the 2013-14 TV drama series *The Village*, which told the story of a rural Derbyshire community from 1914 into the 1920s. Although exterior shots of the fictitious Lamb Inn depicted the Royal Hotel, including a fetching pub sign on the side of the building, in fact the interior scenes were filmed in the King's Arms Hotel in Chapel-en-le-Frith (just as the village train station was in fact a disguised Edale Station and the parish church in fact belonged to All Saints Church in Glossop).

At Middleton by Youlgrave the former Bateman Arms is celebrated once a year by local residents who recreate it in the village hall, where the original pub sign still resides. The evening is both a community get-together and a fund-raiser for the hall, with a range of local beers on offer.

A pub – but perhaps not as we know it

At Crich Tramway Village, a popular and award-winning visitor attraction south of Matlock, an entire period street with working trams has been created. This includes various items of street furniture, a tramshed and the frontage of the original Derby Assembly Rooms, plus – most remarkably – a former working public house called the Red Lion that was once found opposite the Potteries Electric Traction Tramway Depot in the centre of Stoke-on-Trent. It closed in 1973 to make way for road widening, but before demolition the entire façade was carefully removed, brick by brick and tile by tile, then carefully rebuilt at Crich as part of the museum's recreated Victorian street scene (see colour plates for photographs.)

The Red Lion re-opened at its new home in Crich in 2002 and to give some idea of the dedication and effort involved, not to mention the £500,000 cost of re-locating an entire pub, the *Stoke Sentinel* newspaper carried the following letter on 29th December 2007 under the heading 'Restoration was a labour of love':

Madam
It was pleasing to see a photograph of the Red Lion pub in Stoke in 'All Our
Yesterdays' on December 15. This was rebuilt at Crich Tramway Museum
in Derbyshire. The pub's landlord at the time of demolition in the 1970s
was Derek North, and it was he who ceremonially cut the tape when it was
re-opened in 2002. One of the unsung heroes of this project was architect Jim
Soper. He made trips from the museum to his home in West Yorkshire with
bricks packed into his car. At home, he cleaned them and mended the broken
ones; truly a labour of love, though what it did for his car's suspension is
another matter!"
Mervyn Edwards, Potteries Pub Preservation Group

Best of all, the Red Lion is once more open for business and serving refreshments for visitors, including a selection of cask ales. It's open daily when the Tramway Museum is open, generally March to October.

Meanwhile, guests at Callow Top Holiday Park, north of Ashbourne, can enjoy a pint and a meal at a pub called the Callow Inne. This is located within the holiday park and was opened in a converted cottage in 1982 specifically to serve visiting campers and caravanners. It's claimed that it's situated on the site of a former pub, but nevertheless this is still a real, brick-and-mortar pub serving real beer – in fact, straight from the Bad Ram microbrewery that was established in 2002 at the farm next door (see Chapter 9).

But when is a pub no longer a pub? Among those that have closed in the long list above are several that have re-opened as privately-run accommodation for large groups. They include the Poachers Arms at Hope, the Mermaid Inn on the Staffordshire Moorlands above Thorncliffe and Ye Derwent Hotel at Bamford.

Another is the Crewe and Harpur Arms at Longnor, where a 17-bed building and outhouses now offers deluxe group accommodation. As the website puts it: "Hire your very own village pub and hotel! We've cleverly converted The Crewe and Harpur Arms village pub into a total unique exclusive self catering venue. Perfect for large groups needing lots of space for dining, socialising or even working together." Indeed, the interior has been well preserved and the actual bar (complete with beer pumps, bar stools, and so on) is still intact and looks like a real public house – except, of course, that it's not. Adding to the rather bizarre feel of it all, the website goes on to explain: "We can also help with putting a keg of local ale on so that you can pull your own pints."

Maybe it's just me, but I do feel that we've arrived at a slightly surreal

The Callow Inne was created to serve guests at Callow Top Holiday Park near Ashbourne.

moment when you can hire your own pub – a genuine, historic pub – but without all the fuss and bother of over-priced drinks, closing times and, of course, other customers or locals.

On the one hand this may be seen as an alarming development that drives people away from visiting and supporting real pubs, as well as hastening the demise of those establishments that are already marginal in terms of profitability, not to mention depriving communities of a core village institution. However, on the other it's tempting to conclude that this is simply the consequence of market forces calling time on too many pubs against a backdrop of changing social behaviour. And rather than these buildings disappearing altogether or changing beyond recognition then perhaps being preserved as private group accommodation is the least worst option? Still, with some resident national park communities already under pressure from large numbers of holiday and second homes, it does run the risk of turning the most sought-after Peak District villages into a chocolate box pastiche of themselves.

CHAPTER NINE

More Than Just a Pub – The Future

The decline in the number of pubs across the UK in recent years has been both staggering and relentless, with over a quarter closing in the last two decades alone. Analysis carried out in 2018 by the Campaign for Real Ale (CAMRA), which has spearheaded the fight to reverse the demise of one of our most traditional and much-loved institutions, estimated that on average 14 pubs across Britain were closing each week; and the number of small pubs, in particular, has almost halved since 2001.

However, greater protection through local planning regulations and cuts in business rates seems to have slowed the rate of closures, so much so that by the end of 2019 the Office for National Statistics (ONS) reported that there had, for the first time in many years, even been a very small rise in numbers. According to the ONS there are just over 39,000 pubs and bars in Britain, although CAMRA and the British Beer & Pub Association (BBPA) both capture pub data in a different way and show a slightly higher figure. Apparently this welcome net increase in pub numbers has been driven mainly by food sales and the emergence of bigger pubs and more urban establishments. For instance, in 2019 national chain J. D. Wetherspoon announced plans to invest £200m in opening new pubs across the country. But, as CAMRA keeps warning, pubs in small and rural communities – like those in the Peak District – are still vulnerable and still closing.

As we've already seen, underlying changes in social behaviour and escalating property prices have proved a death knell to traditional public houses. Many of the pubs in the Peak District, especially in the honeypot tourist sites, rely heavily on the spending power of the 13 million or so visitors to the national park each year; and, indeed, the viability of many pubs almost certainly depends on the extra income generated through meals, accommodation and events.

It remains to be seen what the long term impact of the Covid-19 pandemic will be on the region's pubs. On the one hand their enforced 15-week closure from 20th March to 4th July 2020 – just as the new holiday season was getting underway – lost them vital revenue; and when they re-opened the new hygiene and social distancing measures meant that footfall was inevitably restricted. And, at the time of writing, there was a fear that pubs could once again be forced to close if overall infection numbers climbed once more. On the other hand, the surge in 'staycations' caused by limitations on overseas travel meant that there were plenty of domestic holidaymakers around over the summer.

Take Eyam, for instance, an ostensibly thriving community and a popular destination for coachloads of visitors throughout the year who come to learn about the historic plague village. As recently as 25 years ago there were four pubs to choose from, but one after the other – the Rose and Crown, Royal Oak and Bull's Head – have all been closed and sold off for conversion to private residences. Now just the Miner's Arms is left to service a large, busy village in the heart of the Peak District. (Although in common with other communities the village 'club', in this case the Mechanics Institute, also provides local people with a place to drink and socialise.)

Despite all this, there are still plenty of pubs that are well-run and

Walkers and outdoor enthusiasts are important customers for most Peak District pubs, like here at Ye Olde Cheshire Cheese Inn at Castleton.

successful, providing an attractive and high quality experience and which give you confidence that the public house as we know it may not yet have had its day. Versatility and imagination seem to be important ingredients, especially when your clientele includes a fair proportion of passing visitors and holidaymakers, as it invariably does in the Peak District.

Many pubs have expanded into the entertainment and hospitality business, but the target audience can vary in age and nature. For many years the Knockerdown Inn, near Carsington Water, sported a lively menagerie of animals, including donkeys, chickens and even ostriches, which made it quite a hit with families and younger visitors. Some farm animals do remain, but a large camping and caravan site and new ecopods have broadened the appeal and are undoubtedly more lucrative. (For more on the origin of its unusual name see Chapter 7.)

A generally older audience tends to patronise the Fishpond at Matlock Bath, a low-set, 18th-century pub which once provided stabling for a nearby hotel. Located opposite the Grand Pavilion, the pub is named after the stock pond across the road that is fed by the resort's famous thermal waters, and in which a seemingly contented shoal of fish appear to thrive.

In recent years the Fishpond has become well-known as a venue for live music. The pub's grand, first-floor ballroom holds 200 and has a beautiful arched ceiling and a sprung dance floor. It's the venue for a variety of performances – everything from rock through to folk, dance and 'open mic' nights – as well as catering for wedding receptions. In addition, and almost certainly uniquely in the Peak District, the pub has its own choir which cover a range of world music (see Chapter 2). In the past the pub has hosted films and talks, and even has its own artisan bakery serving up home-made breads, pastries and pizza.

Live artistic performances are also the order of the day at the Wilkes Head in Leek, where the landlord himself is a talented musician. The pub is a venue for the town's annual Blues & Americana Festival and also holds outdoor music events known as 'Wilkestonbury'.

Music also takes centre stage at the Old Poets Corner at Ashover. Formerly the Red Lion, this high, twin-gabled building in a mock-Tudor style (sometimes called 'Brewers' Tudor'), was renamed partly in honour of Leonard Wheatcroft, a 17th-century poet, diarist, historian and long-time parish clerk who lived in the village (and whose wife was apparently a brewer). The pub has regular open acoustic sessions ("an open invitation for all acoustic musicians to plug in and play their

The Old Poets Corner at Ashover: "We quaff thy balmy juice with glee and water leave to France".

favourite songs from any genre"), as well as rock, ragtime and a whole range of other genres performed live. But, crucially, it doesn't stop there; and perhaps the pub's enduring success is because of this wider offer. There's the familiar quiz night and curry night, of course, but more ambitiously the Old Poets holds two beer festivals every year (with live music every night of the festival). This features dozens of real ales, ciders and fruit wines, and is perhaps summed up by the pub sign outside. On one side it reads: 'Bread is the staff of life but beer is life itself' and on the other, quoting from Hogarth's famous print *Beer Street* of 1751: 'We quaff thy balmy juice with glee and water leave to France'. The pub gave rise to the Ashover Brewery (more on this later) and it has a range of accommodation, promotes local walks, hosts corporate events, and so on. In other words, it's more than just a pub.

The Pub is the Hub

Elsewhere in the Peak District other publicans have also been using their ingenuity in order to maintain the pub as a focal point of local community life, while at the same time broadening their appeal. Some Peak District pubs have diversified by welcoming entirely new strands of business, so that in addition to the usual pub sign you can now find a Post Office sign, including at the Nelson Arms at Middleton-by-Wirksworth (open three days a week in the Snug bar) and at the Anglers Rest at Bamford (see later on in this chapter).

When the village shop and post office closed at Earl Sterndale the pub stepped in, and now every Wednesday afternoon you can buy your stamps and weigh your parcels in the pool room of the Quiet Woman. And for some years an outbuilding of the Barley Mow at Kirk Ireton has been used as a community-run shop called the Stable Shop.

There's a similar story at the small village of Holme, high up on the South Pennine hillside above Holmfirth. In 2011 and following several hard winters that left the community stranded, the landlady of the Fleece Inn, Shirley Amesbury, decided to open a shop at the pub. She told the local paper why: "Over the last few years we've had really heavy snows. I decided to do it because people were getting cut off and they were coming into the pub and asking for things like milk and bread. We've developed gradually with customers' requirements and everyone in the village loves it."

The shop is called The Pantry and is essentially a converted storeroom on the side of the pub. It's open every day except Monday and serves a wide range of hot and cold food, groceries, locally-produced pork pies and sausages, plus the shop's "famous breakfast butties". In 2015 The Pantry won the Best Village Shop in Yorkshire in the Countryside Alliance awards.

To help village locals in their fight back an initiative was launched in 2001 called 'Pub is the Hub'. The scheme was inspired by the Prince of Wales (His Royal Highness – not an actual pub!) and was jointly run by the Countryside Agency and the British Beer and Pub Association, but is now a not-for-profit business that is funded by a range of organisations and businesses (including many large brewing companies). Its Chief Executive is John Longden, who explains why rural pubs, in particular, need championing: "When a business fails in the high street it usually creates an opportunity for another business to thrive. In contrast, the closure of a business in a rural community adversely impacts on the community and on the viability of several other small businesses, leading to a domino-like effect on the collapse of further local services and amenities. Often a rural pub remains the only socially significant business still running in many rural communities. Pub is The Hub is not directly about saving pubs but about supporting them and encouraging them to diversify and support other local services in this rapidly changing world."

Diversification is the key, which is why the post office facilities at the Quiet Woman have been replicated at a number of other pubs across the country. In fact, this has already gone a stage further, and there are now village pubs in deepest England which variously host a bookshop, bookmakers, and an arts and crafts shop.

Peak District pubs that have benefited from funding from the project include the George at Alstonefield, Anglers Rest at Bamford, Barley Mow at Kirk Ireton and the Church House Inn at Bollington. In Parwich, near Ashbourne, the village shop closed in 2008 but with support from Pub is the Hub it soon resurfaced in a room at the Sycamore Inn. Similar assistance was given for the development of a campsite and convenience shop at the Duke of York at Pomeroy. In the early days of the project the University of Derby hired a room above the Miner's Arms in Brassington and put on computer classes for local people.

The fact that pubs in the Peak District are prepared to branch out in this way is important on a number of counts. It offers real support for small and often remote rural communities where, as described above, the loss of the sole village shop or post office is nothing short of a death knell for the social fabric of the place. It also helps to bolster the position of the public house at the heart of the community – whether it's post office facilities, a meeting place for village groups and societies, and so on; and also it might well be a lifeline for the pubs themselves.

Home brew

Over the last couple of decades one welcome development, for beer connoisseurs at least, has been the appearance and rapid growth of micro breweries. They are typically very small, independent breweries producing locally-distinctive and usually very good quality real ale.

Leatherbritches
Brewery was
established
at the Bentley
Brook Inn
as long
ago as 1993.

A few are based at actual pubs and so sell their wares direct to their customers (what were sometimes known as 'brewpubs'). There are now well-established micro and small breweries across the wider Peak District and some, like Thornbridge, Bradfield and Peak Ales, have gone to be successful businesses producing award-winning beers sold worldwide.

One of the first of the new generation of the pub-based micros in the Peak District was Leatherbritches Brewery, established in 1993 at the Bentley Brook Inn. This imposing, half-timbered hotel sits on the A515 just to the north of Ashbourne at Fenny Bentley. Leatherbritches Brewery was founded in 1995 and its name is a throwback to the Middle Ages when officials known as ale conners would go around checking the strength and suitability of new brews. Other than tasting it, a common method was to pour a little of the beer on a bench and sit in it for a while; and if the ale conner's breeches became semi-stuck to the bench then the brew was of a satisfactory strength. Not surprisingly an ale conner's outfit came to include a pair of hard-wearing leather breeches.

Leatherbritches produces a small range of traditional cask conditioned bottled beers, including the ever-popular Hairy Helmet and one or two specialist brews, such as a porter called Scoundrel, a malty bitter called Dr Johnson and a pale ale called The Bounder. The pub's former landlord, the late David Allingham, was interviewed for the first edition of this book and lovingly described the scene when brewing was taking place: "When the wart and hops are boiling it is worth being in the brewery yard just for the aroma that floats from the chimney. Truly, it is a fragrance more comforting than newly baked bread or even early morning bacon."

The Bentley Brook Inn, which until 1956 was a private residence, used to host occasional beer festivals, although weddings and other lucrative corporate events are now its staple fare. Leatherbritches Brewery subsequently moved its brewing to the back of the Green Man in Ashbourne; and when that closed it went to a new site in the National Forest near Ashby-de-la-Zouch in Leicestershire, where it continues to flourish.

Another brew-pub is located at Marsden in West Yorkshire, on the far northern edge of the Peak District. Here, in the same year that Leatherbritches was founded, the Riverhead Brewery Tap opened inside a carefully renovated, three-storey grocers' shop on Peel Street, and you can actually view the full mash brewery through an observation window at the back of the bar. West Yorkshire-based Ossett Brewery purchased the site in 2006, but the micro brewery at the pub remains, typically producing up to five different beers each week.

Each beer is named after local reservoirs, the higher their altitude the higher the respective gravity of the beer. They include Butterley Bitter (a traditional bitter at ABV 3.8%), Black Moss Stout at 4.3%, March Haigh (a malty premium English ale at 4.6%) and a powerful malty old English Ale called Redbrook Premium at 5.5%. In the past there has also been Deer Hill Porter and Cupwith Light Bitter. The Riverhead Brewery Tap holds periodic beer festivals, as well as brewing a special beer for the annual Marsden Jazz Festival.

Small-scale brewing also takes place on a farm near Hartington, where Whim Ales has produced good quality cask ale since 1993 and which are available to take away from the Village Store in Hartington or enjoyed from the pump at selected pubs in Derbyshire and Staffordshire, including its own pub – the Wilkes Head on St Edwards Street in Leek.

Bollington Brewery began in 2005 with the purchase of the Vale Inn on Adlington Road. The town has a sizeable back catalogue of pubs, in part linked to its former industrial past (see Chapter 3); but from the beginning the successful new brewery has been about looking forward and expanding, so much so that it purchased the Park Tavern in Macclesfield in 2011 and Cask Tavern in Poynton two years later. Among its award-winning beers is a pale bitter called White Nancy that's named after the prominent obelisk on the hilltop above the town.

Further south in the Cheshire Peak District is Wincle Beer Company, set up in 2008 in a former milking parlour at Dane Bridge. The brewery produces a range of mouth-watering bottled beers and cask ales, using its deeply rural location ("the brewery in the hills") as one of its selling points; and there are now brewery tours, an on-site shop and sampling room. In particular, look out for a full bodied golden ale called Wibbly Wallaby, named after the small marsupials that once used to roam the Staffordshire Moorlands after escaping from a private zoo.

On the opposite side of the Peak District in South Yorkshire is Bradfield Brewery, established in 2005, and with three pubs of its own just outside the area: the Nags Head at Loxley, King & Miller at Deepcar and Wharncliffe Arms on the edge of Sheffield. Again based on what was a working farm, some of the beers brewed here (marketed as 'Farmers Ales') are named after breeds of cattle, including Belgian Blue, Irish Dexter and the delicious Farmers Blonde (named after a French breed of beef cattle called Blonde D'Aquitaine).

Moving into Derbyshire, Peak Ales is based on the Chatsworth Estate. It was set up in 2003 and, although a shop and visitor centre remain at the original barn site, in 2014 brewing switched to nearby Ashford-in-the-Water to provide increased capacity to produce such favourites as Bakewell Best Bitter, Chatsworth Gold and Swift Nick. There's also a pale ale called Great Ridge, named after the popular and iconic hilltop path to Mam Tor above Castleton, and Peak Ale send donations from its sales to help a major footpath repair project covering this well-walked route.

The Eyam Real Ale Company also has its own shop (at Eyam Hall Craft Centre); small scale brewing has begun at Chapel-en-le-Frith; and the Intrepid Brewing Company operates out of Brough, near Bradwell.

Located inside a former joinery and garage near the centre of New Mills,

Buxton Brewery's popular tap house and cellar.

the small Rock Mill brewery opened in September 2018 and includes a 'speakeasy' style rustic bar in which the seats are located above the old inspection pits where the mechanics would examine vehicles! In Glossop, Howard Town brewery started in 2005 and its award-winning beers include Milltown ("dark and lightly hopped with hints of toffee and coffee"), Wren's Nest and Dark Peak. A blonde beer called Longdendale Lights is named after mysterious and unexplained lights that have regularly been seen along the Woodhead Pass at the top end of the Longendale valley.

Buxton Brewery began life in a family garage in 2009 but the town's first modern brewery now has its own premises and in 2013 opened its own outlet, Buxton Tap House and Cellar, in part of the mid 19th-century Old Court House, near the famous Georgian splendour of the Crescent. Here you can not only enjoy its own range of beers but also sample craft ales from around the world.

On Buxton High Street is the Cheshire Cheese, one of nine pubs run by Titanic Brewery of Burslem, Stoke (others in the Peak District are the Roebuck at Leek and, since June 2019, the Old Poets Corner at Ashover). Meanwhile, on Cavendish Circus, in the former RBS bank, you will find Redwillow Bar which is the Buxton outpost of Redwillow Brewery of Macclesfield.

Aldwark Artisan Ales is located at a remote site in the White Peak, north of Wirksworth, and they describe their journey like this: "In early 2017 A chemist, a farm girl, 2 kids, a labrador, and a few cows and sheep, set out to convert their milking parlour into a micro brewery..." Their small range of hand-crafted beers like Nostrum Gold and Pale Ale IPA are now available in their new Matlock micropub.

Ashover Brewery was established in 2007 in the former stable block of the Old Poets Corner in Ashover, although such has been its success that in 2015 it also began brewing at a site in nearby Clay Cross. Among its varied output is a ABV 5% rich and full bodied stout called Liquorice, enhanced by the addition of liquorice to the boil which is in memory of the Basset family and confectionery dynasty. Liquorice Allsorts pioneer, George Bassett, made his home just outside Ashover and his grand-daughter Elizabeth, who died in 2005 aged 103, used to feed her prize-winning Blue Albion cows on waste sweet products such as liquorice.

The Haywood Bad Ram Brewery is located on a farm adjacent to Callow Top Holiday Park, near Ashbourne, and its tasty output can be enjoyed via the on-site pub called the Callow Inne (see Chapter 8). A golden ale called, most appropriately, Dr Samuel Johnson is one of its most popular beers. Another is Fiery Fred, full bodied and copper coloured, named after park employee Fred Gregory well known for his "lovable" temperament.

In 2018, the diminutive Chickenfoot Brewery was established in a building on the far side of the pub car park of the Barley Mow at Bonsall. The pub is famous as the home of the Hen Racing World Championships (see Chapter 5) and the hen-themed beers ('Seshen', 'Great Brithen' etc), are so far only available at the pub. At the other end of the scale is Thornbridge Brewery, which began life at Thornbridge Hall at Ashord-in-the-Water in 2005, but four years later moved its brewing to a purpose-built site at nearby Bakewell. Nowadays the scale of its operations belies any notion of 'micro' or possibly even 'small'. With multiple awards for its beers like the famous IPA Jaipur, as well as Wild Swan, Kipling and Brother Rabbit, it also has its own pubs in Sheffield and Dronfield and is one of the most successful independent breweries in the region. New visitor facilities, including a tap room and shop, have been built at its Bakewell brewery, with more planned; and Thornbridge's continuing emphasis on craftsmanship and innovation still seems a winning formula and helps put Peak District beer on many people's map.

Springs and wells

Meanwhile, for a pub on the Cheshire edge of the Peak District, it's water rather than beer that is proving good for business. The Crag Inn at Wildboarclough (also see Chapter 2) has a hillside spring within its grounds which for centuries has produced naturally soft and ever so slightly carbonated drinking water. Since it's filtered through layers of rock and sand the water is incredibly pure and for several years now has been bottled at the pub in re-usable glass bottles. Indeed, Crag Spring Water claims to be the only bottled spring water company in the north

The Red Lion Inn
at Birchover.

of England that re-uses its glass bottles, delivering and collecting the bottles in order to wash, sanitise and re-fill them. You can sample the product at the pub itself (as well as its beer, of course!).

In the past, brewpubs often had their own boreholes, springs or access to a fresh water supply, but at the Red Lion at Birchover you can peer down the illuminated 30ft, glass-topped well in the floor of the main bar to see where theirs once came from. (Many years ago a skull used to stare up at you from the bottom, which I always presumed was a mock one, but never actually asked...) Today the Red Lion still brews its own beer, thanks to the enterprising Italian-born landlord Matteo Frau who, together with his wife Alyson, has owned and run the pub for the last 14 years.

When the Red Lion first began brewing its own beer it used water drawn from the well in the bar. Brewing now takes place in the pub's outbuildings and among the fine beers on offer is Bircher Best, Cork Stone (a golden ale), Nine Ladies ("a richy tawny ale with bitter toffee and roasted nut aromas") and an IPA known as Robin Hood's Stride. Given Matteo's ancestry they also brew an Italian-style lager called Bionda which is very popular.

But the Red Lion is about more than simply good quality beer, as Matteo explains. "I want this to be an authentic village pub," he told me, "where visitors and local people alike come to enjoy good quality food and drink, but also stay to chat and socialise. In the traditional trattoria back home the food is nearly always locally-sourced, the dishes often simple but very tasty and always of really good quality. This is what I want to offer at the pub." Indeed, the pub's menu is peppered with dishes from Matteo's native Italy, including Gnocchetti Sardi (Sardinian pasta with a rich wild boar ragu) and Pollo alla Romana (chicken breast in sage butter with prosciutto and fresh tomato). However, the real deal takes place with the pub's themed Sardinian Nights where, as well as enjoying the distinctive cuisine, you can also learn about the culture and traditions of Matteo's homeland. (But beware – the number of courses runs into double figures!)

As well as being head brewer and chef, Matteo also makes his own cheese called Bircher Blue, a creamy and sweet blue cheese using high quality local milk, and which is on sale at the bar and via local shops. If ever a publican led by example it's here at the Red Lion.

Changing times

As social and recreational trends alter over time, it's inevitable that this will be reflected in the changing nature and distribution of pubs and inns. We've already seen how the temperance movement sought to cut the sheer number of alehouses and pubs, with some success; and how pressures and challenges from a variety of directions have pushed some of the less efficient or well-managed public houses under.

Over the last 50 years or so, our growing affluence and leisure time has meant that more and more Peak District pubs have dedicated themselves to food and meals, which inevitably delivers a much more significant profit margin than beer sales. And if some establishments appear little more than rural restaurants, then that's perhaps simply a reflection of what we seem to want and what pubs feel they have to do to get by.

The Rambler Inn at Edale is a good example. This large Victorian house, built early in the 20th century, was for many years known as the Church Hotel, then later the Jolly Rambler, as weekend crowds alighted from the Sheffield and Manchester trains to enjoy a day's walking in the hills.

The Old Nag's Head, located just up the road at the start of the Pennine Way, is equally busy over a summer's weekend, although today there will probably be as many car-driving visitors as those pulling on walking boots.

In the 1930s, the Cyclists' Touring Club had over 4,000 inns on their books, all of which carried the club sign and offered bed and breakfast. Today there are guides to pubs that cover all manner of things: those that serve proper real ale, or have facilities for children and families;

The Old Nags Head at Edale has a so-called Hikers Bar and is the starting point for the Pennine Way.

the ones that have an absence of piped music or jukeboxes, or others that specifically welcome dogs; and of course pubs who have specialist menus.

Today the Rambler Inn at Edale styles itself a 'Country House Hotel', with its rooms named after the various booths (old shepherd's huts) around Edale. It even hosts a so-called folk train where musicians and beer drinkers join forces for an organised trip along the scenic Hope Valley line.

Another traditional rural pub that was given the modern treatment was the Stanhope Arms at Dunford Bridge. Already alluded to in previous chapters, this 19th-century former shooting lodge in the middle of the South Yorkshire moors south of Holmfirth was built by the Stanhope family who used it for just a few weeks 'recreation' each year. In 1947 it was bought by the Barnsley Brewing Company and turned into a pub. Its high-ceilinged rooms and ornate fireplaces exuded a period elegance, and there was even a snug bar of sorts to the rear of the main bar. However, a new owner stepped in and after a complete facelift in 2003 re-opened 'The Stanhope' as an entirely different concern. "It's elegant, chic, modern, bright, airy and minimalist in style," ran the description on the pub's website at the time.

The snug bar gave way to extra kitchen space, and the lounge now boasted black leather sofas and trendy furniture. In the open-plan restaurant the deliberately plain white walls featured a silver dado rail where wall vases each held a single lily, and all this contributed to what was described as "a truly contemporary dining experience". It was light, airy and extremely stylish, and by all accounts the jazz suppers were very lively; but when does a pub stop being a pub?

Despite the modern twist, the pub eventually closed and for a while was used as a lodging house. After standing empty for almost a decade, in 2018 new owners submitted plans to turn the building into a holiday centre. "We consider the Stanhope Arms to have limited to no potential to meet no discernable need," they said. "This pub has been unable to draw the kind of footfall required to sustain it as a going concern, despite efforts to expand its appeal. Alterations in the economic climate both nationally and locally have had a significant impact on the population of Dunford Bridge, reducing trade to a seasonal, unstable form." The application for permanent change of use was approved.

Talk of the town

The emergence of so-called roadhouse pubs in the mid 20th century signalled a change in the nature of many rural pubs in places like the Peak District, and it's been exacerbated by the emergence of national pub chains or 'pubcos' which have bought up the more prominent or profitable establishments.

Around the fringes of the Peak District, in particular, there are a number of large, old pubs which have been given the branded treatment. Examples from the eastern edge alone include the Peacock (Chef and Brewer) and Moorlands (Stonehouse Pizza and Carvery) at Owler Bar, the Highwayman at Eastmoor (Beefeater) and the Fox House Inn (Vintage Inns).

Everything, inevitably, is standardised – from the interior décor to the menus and even the style of the actual pub signs – which on the one hand is fine if you want an unchallenging and reassuringly familiar place to go, but on the other is largely devoid of any distinctiveness, save the shape of the building or the view out of the window.

Another well-known and enterprising player in the national pub scene is the Wetherspoon chain, which as we've seen is expanding its

The Feather Star Ale House on St John's Street, Wirksworth – nicely quirky.

portfolio by opening new pubs in predominantly towns and urban centres. In the Peak District it already owns several historic licensed premises, including Wye Bridge House in Buxton (the former Midland Hotel dating from the 1870s) and the popular Crown in Matlock town centre. Another is the Green Dragon in Leek, reputed to be the town's oldest pub and dating from 1693 (over the years it's also been known as the Angel and the Swan with Two Necks). And in 2013 Wetherspoon refurbished the Smithy Fold in Glossop, which was part of Howardtown Mill, a 19th-century spinning and weaving mill.

However, in the last few years many Peak District town centres have also witnessed an entirely new phenomenon – micropubs. Reflecting the growing popularity of artisan or craft ales, micropubs began appearing after 2003 when the Licensing Act made it easier to convert buildings to licensed premises, often from former shops, banks and retail premises. In so doing they seem to hark back a couple of centuries to when a relaxation of the licensing laws brought in by the 1830 Beer Act led to the emergence of impromptu beerhouses. Indeed, within a few years of this legislation (which was partly designed to curb the powers of the big brewers) there were tens of thousands of new beerhouses and small pubs, in direct competition to the established inns and taverns. However, because they were typically small-scale and usually lacked the skills and equipment to brew decent beer, they ended up buying their beer off the big brewers, who in many cases also loaned them money to improve their premises; and so – rather counter productively – the modern system of 'tied houses' where pubs are controlled by major breweries was born.

The Peak District's new and growing collection of micropubs includes Stanley's Ale House on Smedley Street in Matlock, which opened in 2014 and went on to win pub of the year from the local CAMRA group. It has since been renamed Farmacy, since it's now the outlet for Aldwark Artisan Ales produced nearby in the Peak District by a pharmacist-cum-farmer (see above).

On the same street in Matlock a former newsagents and off-licence called Armitts was converted into a micropub called The Newsroom in 2018; and on Dale Road look out for Twenty Ten. In Buxton there's the Ale Stop on Chapel Street; in Chapel-en-le-Frith the Old Cell Ale Bar can be found on the Market Place; the Beer Shed on Market Street in New Mills opened in 2016 and offers both a tap room and bottle shop; check out Harvey Leonards Wine & Ale Shop in the Old Conservative Club in Glossop, plus the Cask & Kitchen on Henry Street; and pop into the Feather Star Ale House on St John's Street in Wirksworth, which occupies a former antiques shop and has a second hand record shop upstairs. Then there's the cheekily-named Malt Disley on Market Street in Disley; while one of the latest additions is the Joiners Arms, which opened in Bakewell in 2019, showcasing local ales from the likes of Thornbridge (amongst others) which brews in the town.

The sense of going full circle is echoed, in particular, in Ashbourne, where just in the last few years a number of new craft and real ale

The Joiners Arms in Bakewell is one of the new breed of micropubs in the Peak District.

bars, cafes and shops have sprung up. The Artisan on St John Street in Ashbourne is a contemporary craft ale cafe bar that opened in 2016 on the premises of a former pub called the Green Dragon; while a micropub called the Queen's Vaults on the Market Place opened in 2018 in the former office of the town's newspaper. However, originally it was a pub called the Barley Mow that changed its name to the Queen's Vaults in the 1890s in honour of Queen Victoria's 50-year reign, closing permanently in 1908.

House of Beer on Church Street in Ashbourne also opened in 2018 and is a combined beer shop and craft ale taproom in a former antique shop, boasting 14 draught taps and over 600 bottled and canned beer and cider. In 2019 plans were announced to open a pub in a listed building on Church Street in Ashbourne, which had been empty for two years after the closure of a bank. The planning application stated that the building was originally a pub/hotel called The Wheatsheaf.

Bucking the trend

Despite time being called on so many Peak District pubs over the years, it's heartening that micropubs can suddenly come along and prove that there is, after all, still an appetite for a well-run public house where people come together to socialise and appreciate good quality fare. And there are even examples of village pubs which have risen from the ashes.

The peaceful village of Sheldon, two miles west of Bakewell, seems very similar to all the other traditional limestone villages of the White Peak, and at first glance the solid and unshowy, stone-built pub seems to have been around since the time of the miners who once worked nearby Magpie Mine for lead (see Chapter 3). But remarkably, the Cock & Pullet is barely 25 years old. It was originally a barn which stood next door to the former village pub, the Devonshire Arms, that closed in 1971. The barn once held village dances, and its conversion was something of a challenge for its owners and Sheldon residents David and Kath Melland.

Interviewed for the first edition of this book, Kath admitted that building a new village pub was a bold move: "It was quite a gamble in this day and age when village pubs are closing, but we had a lot of encouragement from the village." Although the Peak District National Park Authority was also supportive, it helped enormously that David Melland was a builder by trade, since there was little of the original building left – nothing at the back, no windows at the front, and a cellar that had to be dug from scratch. It took around 18 months to complete, and opened in August 1995.

The Cock & Pullet may look centuries old, but in fact it opened in 1995.

The Cock & Pullet stands half way up Sheldon's wide main street, its modest exterior disguising the fact that inside it's been converted with care and style. There's full disabled access, a sheltered patio to the rear, and three en-suite bedrooms upstairs. The dark and cosy bar is illuminated by a glowing open fire and, at virtually every quarter hour, a chiming sound somewhere or other in the bar will alert you to the fact that the landlord has on display his vast collection of clocks.

More than anything else, the Cock & Pullet has once again provided a focal point for a fairly isolated village too small for any shops or other services. "We get all-comers," said Kath, "locals as well as visitors. We're open all day every day, with no strict rules or regulations, so that we welcome walkers and car drivers, with well-behaved children and dogs."

But local people also use the pub, and despite the presence of the nearby public hall, some village meetings are held in the pub, especially in the winter when the warming fire proves quite a lure. Local gamekeepers meet and dine at the Cock & Pullet, and the pub also has pool and darts teams.

Building your own pub might have been hard work, said Kath Melland, but running it is certainly a full-time business. "You have to work hard at it, but you also have to love it – it's a way of life, really."

Another example of a pub rising from the ashes can be found in the (even smaller) hamlet of Little Hucklow, near Bradwell. Following an unsuccessful attempt to turn the Old Bulls Head into private accommodation, the pub closed in 2005 and steadily became derelict. It was eventually put up for sale and in 2017 permission was granted for the building's re-development – as a pub! Since then the building has been totally refurbished and in 2020 re-opened under the new name of the Blind Bull. (See colour plates to see photographs of the pub in its various stages of disrepair and redevelopment.)

Owner Raab McCarthy, who lives in Little Hucklow, believes that well-run rural pubs still have a bright future. "Pubs are a British institution, an important part of our heritage," he says, "and where they are both part of the community but also have a great food and drink offer then there's no reason why they shouldn't succeed."

Raab has a background in the hospitality industry and he intends the Blind Bull to be a top notch venue for diners, serving high quality, locally-sourced dishes. "We've renovated the upstairs to provide dedicated space for eating," he explains, "as it's important that you can still simply wander into the bar downstairs and enjoy a pint and a chat. This is a real pub."

The change of name from the Old Bulls Head to the Blind Bull appears to be a simple marketing decision, designed to differentiate the pub from all the other Bulls Heads in the Peak District. "And I've never run a pub before," he admits, "so it's a little bit about me going in blind – but nevertheless optimistic!"

The Blind Bull, like the Old Bull's Head before it, is going to continue to claim that it dates from the 12th century and that it is purportedly the fifth oldest pub in England. How you prove such a claim is anyone's guess, although Raab says that he has research showing a list of previous landlords stretching back to the mid 1600s; and during the recent renovations the builders came across a coin from the time of King Charles II. Indeed, before it closed in 2005, I remember the landlord telling me about the mine shaft below the pub cellar which allowed previous innkeepers to dig for lead during the day while their wives tended the animals and brewed beer. More recently, in the 1930s, landlady Mary Anne King was well-known for her generous portions of home-cooked fare. Apparently hungry steelworkers came over from Sheffield just to enjoy the 3s 6d ham and eggs.

In some ways it doesn't really matter precisely how old the pub is or what lineage it can boast. What ultimately counts is its survival and future prosperity, and for that we must be grateful that there are entrepreneurs like Raab prepared to invest in one of the cornerstones of our rural way of life.

The community pub

An ambitious local developer might be one thing, but in another village – just a few miles down the Hope Valley from Little Hucklow – the wider community came together to safeguard their 'local'. In 2012, Bamford was in danger of losing the last pub in the village, which was a little surprising on its own, given that this is a relatively large, busy village in the heart of the Peak District.

The Anglers Rest was built in 1869-70 and for over a century was at the centre of village life, regularly hosting dinner dances, weddings and village celebrations. Previously owned by a brewery, in recent years the Anglers Rest had been sold to a pubco and, following a period of under-investment and a series of short-term tenants, had fallen on hard times and was put up for sale. With the Derwent and Marquis of Granby already gone, a group of villagers were determined not to let go of Bamford's last remaining pub, so first of all they used the provisions of the new

Localism Act to declare the pub an Asset of Community Value. This bought them a little time to see if they could make a realistic community bid to buy the business. A share offer was made and eventually a total of £263,000 was raised from over 300 people, with 80% of shareholders living in a five-mile radius. A further business loan secured the deal and in 2013 Bamford Community Society took over the pub, despite the antics of the pubco which secretly tried to sell the pub to another buyer at the same time, and the antipathy of the outgoing landlord who at one point banned the local campaigners from the very pub they were trying to buy for supposedly undermining his business.

Today the Anglers is welcoming, popular and successful. The pub itself offers the usual real ales and wide-ranging food choices, as well as live music, folk sessions and a 'vinyl club'. But it's about so much more than simply just a public house. This enterprising, community-run venue now incorporates the village post office and a cafe called The Rest, popular with local people and visitors alike and home to 'Art in the Café', a changing exhibition of original work by local artists. The U3A group meets there, as does the Knit and Knatter group, the weekly 'after yoga coffee club' and a mental health group. The pub sponsors the village football team, plus it sources as much of its food as locally as possible and employs over 20 mostly local people. In 2017 it was awarded the Peak District Environmental Quality Mark for its commitment to the environment and investment in people and the community.

Meanwhile, walkers can wash their muddy boots with cleaning brushes in the troughs outside, plus maps and guide books are on sale in the cafe. Two-wheeled visitors are offered dedicated cycle parking, a tool station and bike locks for hire.

What has happened in Bamford has been replicated elsewhere in Derbyshire. The Spotted Cow at Holbrook, south of Belper, was saved in 2017 when over 200 local residents clubbed together to buy the premises that had been closed and was earmarked for redevelopment. Now the community-run social enterprise not only manages the pub but also, like the Anglers Rest, a cafe and post office on the premises.

Liz Marshall, from Bamford Community Society, was involved from the start in the Anglers' project and says it's been a huge challenge. "The pub had deteriorated badly because of neglect, so we immediately had to overhaul the kitchen," she explains, "and since then there's been a constant need to upgrade and improve the basic facilities."

Not only was the pub looking to secure its future, but around that time Bamford's post office was also about to close, so bringing it into

The Anglers Rest at Bamford is the first community-owned pub in the Peak District.

the pub was vital for the community. "Although it doesn't really make any money for us," explains Liz, "it's an important part of our all-round service for the people of Bamford."

It's been quite a journey, but definitely worth it, says Liz. "We're now in our seventh year and we're determined to keep the momentum going, but although there's a full time manager running the pub, all of the directors are volunteers and we continue to rely on the goodwill and generosity of people across the community to help out. But we're all clear that the pub is key to thriving community life in Bamford and people have responded to this."

The Anglers, like the Spotted Cow at Holbrook, received vital support from the not-for-profit Plunkett Foundation, whose More than a Pub programme provides business development support to enable communities to own and run their own pubs. It has so far helped 58 pubs open under community ownership, pushing the total of community-owned pubs across England to over 120. Against a backdrop of almost a quarter of privately-owned or brewery-run pubs shutting down since 2008, not one community pub has so far failed.

The Anglers at Bamford shows that pubs can still play a vital role in small rural communities, particularly ones where other key services like post offices, shops or meeting venues are disappearing. They can provide a hub for local activities with tangible socio-economic benefits; and they can showcase and promote distinctive and high quality local produce, most obviously food and drink. But it goes further than this. The array of community groups that use the Anglers takes the idea of the public house back to basics, in some way. They are places where people come together, interact and socialise, helping to tackle isolation and loneliness that often hides away amongst rural communities.

As we've seen, the pubs of the Peak District come in all forms and cater for a variety of tastes, and there are many excellent and well-run tenanted pubs owned by breweries, just as there are freehouses and now community pubs and micropubs. A good pub is a good pub, but very few are able (or can afford) to stand still and not respond to changing patterns of social behaviour or the demands of their customers. Covid-19 is simply the latest in a series of challenges faced by one of our best-loved institutions, but it's one that pubs will rise to – provided they have the necessary popular support.

Whether re-built or re-packaged, a new business or community venture, the humble pub is proving that it can still be at the heart of everyday life in the Peak District.

Bibliography

David Allingham, *It Could Be a Little Gold Mine,* Johnson Publishing, 2005

M. J. Arkle, *Tuppence Up, Penny Down – Old Matlock Remembered in Words and Pictures,* 1983

Graham Armitage, *Discover Stoney Middleton: The history of a forgotten village,* 2018

Ashbourne Local History Group, *Early Victorian Country Town: A Portrait of Ashbourne,* 1978

Richard Bradley, *Secret Matlock,* Amberley, 2018

Pete Brown, *Man Walks into a Pub*, Macmillan, 2003

Julie Bunting, *A Peakland Abecedary,* 2008

Campaign for Real Ale (CAMRA), *CAMRA's Good Beer Guide,* annual since 1972

David Clarke, *Ghosts and Legends of the Peak District*, Jarrold, 1991

Liam Clarke, *Castleton Through Time,* Amberley, 2011

Neil Collingwood, *Leek – A Historic Pub Crawl,* self published, 2018

Clarence Daniel, *Ghosts of Derbyshire,* Dalesman, 1973

Ron Davey, *Pubs and People around Sheffield,* 1983

Eric Delderfield, *British Inn Signs and their Stories*, E.R.D. Publications, 1965

Eric Delderfield, *Introduction to Inn Signs, David & Charles,* 1969

Jim Drury, *Fetch the Juicy Jam!,* Birchover Reading Room, 2001

Leslie Dunkling & Gordon Wright, *Pub Names of Britain,* J. M. Dent, 1993

Peter Elliott, *Dick Turpin in Derbyshire?* 2001

Eyam Village Society, *Inn Search of Eyam,* Leaflet No 5

David Field, *History in a Pint Pot: Two Hundred Years of History Told In A Pub Crawl Around Glossop,* Glossop and District Historical Society, 1999

Peter Fellows, *Bonsall at Work,* Bonsall History Project, 2003

Glynis Greenman, *Longdendale – The Travellers' Valley,* Millscapes, 1998

Vic Hallam, *Silent Valley,* Sheaf Publishing, 1989

Peter C. Harrison, *Some Castleton History and Things Remembered*, posted at www.castletonhistorical.co.uk/history-of-castleton-2

Hartington History Group, *A Village Life: Hartington 1933-55,* 2018

Hathersage Millennium Group, *Hathersage Reviewed* and *Hathersage Remembered,* 2000

Hope Historical Society, *Discover Hope*

Cadbury Lamb, *Inn Signs,* Shire, 1976

John Leach, *The Book of Buxton*, Barracuda Books, 1987

Andrew McCloy, *Peak District Pub Guide*, Johnson Publishing, 2002

Jim McIntosh, *North Derbyshire Pubs Past and Present,* Pynot Publishing, 2008

Louis McMeeken, *Peak Place Names*, Halsgrove Publishing, 2003

Rainow Women's Institute, A Village History, 1952, available via www.rainow.org

Reg Newcombe (Ed), *Derbyshire Ale: The CAMRA Guide to Derbyshire,* 1990

Gavin Repton, *The Lost Pubs of Wirksworth* (DVD)

Ron Slack, *Paupers Venture Childrens Fortune*, Scarthin Books, 1986

Roly Smith, *Murder and Mystery in the Peak*, Halsgrove Publishing, 2004

Bob Steel, CAMRA's Peak District Pub Walks, CAMRA, 2018

Bryan Veitch, *Railway Inn Signs: Derbyshire,* Meridian, 2000

Lynn Walker & Lynn Burnet, *Oddfellows at the Duke of York*, Elton Local History Group, 2005

A Walking Heritage Guide to Whaley Bridge (undated)

Websites

https://camra.org.uk/ – Campaign for Real Ale

www.closedpubs.co.uk/ – a project listing some of England's lost pubs

www.pubsgalore.co.uk – a comprehensive listing of UK pubs

www.pubisthehub.org.uk/ – a not-for-profit organisation set up to improve services in rural communities through supporting pubs

places.wishful-thinking.org.uk/DBY/StoneyMiddleton/InnsandPubs.html – 'Inns and Public Houses in Stoney Middleton 1822-1934'

https://happyvalley.org.uk/?page_id=850 – 'Old Pubs and Breweries of Bollington'

www.crichparish.co.uk/webpages/innspubs.html

www.stevelewis.me.uk/page60.php – former pubs in New Mills and Hayfield

http://www.rainbow-web-design.co.uk/glossopvah/pubs.php – the Glossop Ghost Pub Trail & Heritage Trail

Index

Some noteworthy former pubs, especially those that have closed recently, are included here, but otherwise see Chapter 8 for ex-pubs.